Zoo Culture

D1233779

Zoo Culture

SECOND EDITION

Bob Mullan and Garry Marvin

University of Illinois Press
Urbana and Chicago

© 1987, 1999 by Bob Mullan and Garry Marvin
Reprinted by arrangement with the authors
Manufactured in the United States of America
1 2 3 4 5 C P 6 5 4 3 2

This book is printed on acid-free paper.

Library of Congress Cataloging-in-Publication Data
Mullan, Bob.
Zoo culture / Bob Mullan and Garry Marvin. —2nd ed.
p. cm.
Includes bibliographical references (p.) and index.
ISBN 978-0-252-02457-3 (hardcover : alk. paper).
—ISBN 978-0-252-06762-4 (pbk. : alk. paper)
1. Zoos—Social aspects. 2. Zoos.
I. Marvin, Garry. II. Title.
QL76.M85 1998
590'.7'3—dc21
98-25075
CIP

First published in Great Britain in 1987 by
George Weidenfeld & Nicolson Ltd.

Whatever the precise relationship between man and beasts which the pleasure principle prompts us to imagine, it clearly transforms the real animal by turning it into a symbol on which human feelings and wishes may be projected and which is therefore liable to evoke those feelings whenever we encounter either the living prototype or its image in art.

(Klingender, 1971: xxvi)

An industry, cornering the market in nature, buying up life and selling it back to us as fun, with stickers to say we've had it.

(Barzdo, Berger, Rawlance and Roberts, 1982: 41)

Contents

Preface   ix

Introduction to the Second Edition · xi

Introduction to the First Edition · xvii

1 · HUMANS IN ANIMAL SKIN · 1

2 · CONTAINMENT AND CONTROL · 31

3 · ZOO ARCHITECTURE · 46

4 · EXHIBITION · 68

5 · FROM PRINCELY MENAGERIES TO PUBLIC ZOOS · 89

6 · THE CULTURAL STATUS OF THE ZOO · 116

7 · THE ANIMAL AS COMMODITY · 137

8 · THE ZOO IN EVOLUTION · 151

Bibliography · 161

Index · 169

Illustrations follow page 88

Preface

Neither of the authors of this study approached it with any specialist knowledge of zoology or natural history. Garry Marvin is a social anthropologist who became interested in zoos as an extension of his previous work on rituals and sports which feature animals, while Bob Mullan, a sociologist, became interested after taking his children to the zoo as a treat. We wanted to understand the nature of the zoo, the processes involved in devising and maintaining the display of wild animals in captivity, and the viewing and response to such displays. Our study is an exercise in social and cultural interpretation rather than a simple criticism of the institution.

Going to the zoo is a traditional and highly popular pastime in many societies, yet a detailed interpretive account of the processes involved seemed to be lacking. We hope that this study will suggest new ways of considering the nature of that visit and will act as a spur to further work in the area.

Introduction to the Second Edition

In preparing this new edition of *Zoo Culture* we were keen to discover the significant changes in the zoo world in the decade since the original research for the book was conducted. An essential premise of the first edition was that social and cultural messages had always been encoded in the nature of the presentation of wild animals in zoos. Were the ideas about the nature of zoos and the cultural messages which could be read out of their structure and the zoo experience itself still valid? Had shifts and changes in wider social and cultural patterns had an impact on the nature of the zoo at the end of the twentieth century? We thought that with the rapid increase in technologically sophisticated leisure pursuits and the growth of ever more complex images through the screens of media such as television, cinema and computers that peering through the screens and barriers of zoos might have become a banal and outmoded practice. We also surmised that zoos in many areas of the world — particularly North America, Australasia and northwestern Europe — might have succumbed to another question of image, namely that of the ethical concern about keeping wild animals in captivity for public show, itself part of a much wider concern for animal rights which has grown ever more powerful in recent years.[1] Neither of these image problems, however, seem to have forced zoos *per se* into extinction, although many of the more feeble and vulnerable members of the species have certainly disappeared, and many others, stuck in their 'primitive' niches, have no place in the evolution of modern zoos.

Internationally, zoos have obviously remained immensely popular places to visit. The World Zoo Organization estimates that there are approximately 10,000 zoos (minimally defined as establishments which exhibit captive wild and domestic animals to the public) worldwide. The same organization estimates that annually some 619 million people, 10 per cent of the world population, visit zoos. This must be a conservative number, however, for it is based on the number of visitors to only the 1,200 zoos which participate in regional, national, and international federations — the core of the zoo world.

Among the core zoos the emphasis on conservation and education has clearly come to the fore as the paramount justification for the maintenance of captive populations of wild animals (see, for example, Bostock [1993], Maple and Archibald [1993], Marvin [1994] and Tudge [1992] for good overviews of this position). The director of one major zoo admitted that ten years ago the conservation ethic was more a rhetorical device for public relations purposes than an actual key function of most zoos. In the last few years though, especially since the publication in 1991 of *Caring for the Earth* and in 1992 of the *Global Biodiversity Strategy* and the *Guide to the Convention on Biological Diversity*, which called on zoos to play an active part in conservation, there has been a major shift in zoo strategy. Of the many narratives of human/animal relations which can be told through the enclosure of wild animals this is now the only one considered justifiable by international zoo administrators. The philosophy of the core zoos is that they must behave and structure themselves in such a way that they are perceived as part of the global movement of concern for the environment and the maintenance of biodiversity. To justify their existence to an increasingly aware and concerned public, particularly in developed western countries, they must attempt to make a genuine link between creatures confined in zoos and the perceived fate of the natural world and the creatures which inhabit it. This aim is clearly set out in *The World Zoo Conservation Strategy*, which contains a blueprint for the creation of mission statements produced in 1993 by the International Union of Directors of Zoological Gardens—The World Zoo Organization and the Captive Breeding Specialist Group of the International Union for the Conservation of Nature and Natural Resources. This blueprint suggests that zoos should strive towards this objective by

1. *Actively supporting, through co-ordinated programmes, the conservation of populations of endangered species in situ and ex situ and, through these, to the conservation of natural habitats, biotopes, and eco systems.*
2. *Offering support and facilities in order to increase scientific knowledge that*

will benefit conservation, and lending support to the conservation communi-
ty by making available relevant knowledge and experience.
3. *Promoting an increase of public and political awareness of the necessity for*
   conservation, natural resource sustainability, and the creation of a new equi-
   librium between people and nature.

(1993: 10)

It emphasises that all 'responsible' zoos will play an active role in reaching the goal. The particular wording of the mission statements for individual zoos is left to those zoos, presumably so that they can take into consideration their local social and cultural context, but the above points ought to be used as starting points to justify, in a wider context, the very existence of zoos. This international mission for zoos suggests that the existence of an individual zoo can be fully justified only if it is linked with others in a network aimed at the conservation of particular species. It is argued that this linking should also expand further outwards towards an active concern with the 'natural' habitat of these species. This is a reworking of a theme that can be seen running through the entire history of zoos — a concern with the relationship between ideas of 'the wild', the savage and nature, and the ideas, and ideals, of 'the civilised', the nature of humans and the urban through the images offered by the collections of wild animals. The changing nature of these relationships and concerns, the ways they are expressed in architecture and exhibition, and their underpinning of the experience and interpretation of animals are some of the key themes explored in *Zoo Culture*.

Zoos have evolved from unsophisticated menageries exhibiting exotic creatures from distant and strange lands to zoological parks established as living museums to conservation centres in which the message is not one of separateness and separation but one of interconnection and unity within biological diversity. This new philosophy attempts to deny a hierarchical reading of nature that places humans, and their uncontested rights over all the creatures of the planet, at the pinnacle. In this new reading of nature all living things have a right to exist, although the problem for maintenance of biodiversity is that only humans can decide what those rights might be and how they might be actualised. The major zoos have decided that for them to maintain an acceptable place in modern society they must express, and literally exhibit, the growing concern by many in the western world for the unacceptable exploitative relations humans have with animals. Although physical barriers, enclosures and structures of separation must exist in the zoo there should be, at a conceptual and imaginative level, an attempt to extinguish the barrier of exclusivity and superiority humans are so often thought to hold with regard to other animals.

The public exhibition of wild animals has always presented an emotional, intellectual and imaginative challenge to humans. Zoos have offered humans the opportunity to consider their place in relation to the natural world and, more immediately through the range of creatures on display, to see and experience what they are not. Zoos have always been galleries established to engender a particular way of looking, both literally and figuratively, at animals. Now, however, the individual creatures in the cage, paddock or artful recreation of a natural setting should not be looked at in isolation — looking must be accompanied by understanding. It is no longer enough, the zoo authorities claim, to focus on and experience a creature only in terms of its immediate, individual and idiosyncratic presence in front of the visitors. Although it is out of contact with its natural habitat and isolated from others of its own and other species with which it would 'naturally' exist, the modern zoo visitor is now asked to imaginatively recontextualise it and experience concern for that environment from which it is separated. The animal should not be experienced simply in itself but as a part of a total cultural package that consists of the immediacy of the experience, the information label on the enclosure and the educational and awareness literature about it. Ideally zoo authorities want to turn the zoo experience into one which takes the visitor back emotionally, intellectually and morally to the environment in which the animals on display should, ideally, be able to exist without a threat to their existence as a species.

Until very recent times even core zoos accepted that people simply wanted wild animals enclosed for public entertainment in urban centres. The public was not concerned with where the animals originated — except that knowing that it was distant and exotic added to the experience — or with how they lived and certainly not with how they *ought* to live. The animals should simply delight and entertain. Now, however, the challenge is precisely that *ought*. The problem for zoos, or at least those which sincerely strive for their conservation ideals, is that the immediacy of the animals in the zoo *is* entertaining, but little more than that for most people. Anthropomorphism, and everthing that comes with it, still seems to be a key process through which animals in the zoo are interpreted and understood. Although supposedly separate from and different from humans, animals still seem easily suffused with some form of humanity. Perhaps the problem partly hinges on the word *zoo* itself, a name still linked to the world of popular entertainment and mass leisure rather than education. In this context it is significant that a number of zoos are dropping the terms *zoological park* or *zoological garden* from their names in favour of terms relating to the idea of a 'conservation centre.' Whether zoos can change the stories they tell about animals and the natural world is the challenge they face going into the twenty-first century.

A key element in that challenge is still the basic fact which has been with zoos from their inception: animals exhibit a wondrous power over humans. Although animals have their own existence and, in some sense, their own identity they are also, and more significantly, the product of human thinking, desires and imagination. Although supposedly separate from humans they are suffused with a pseudo-humanity projected onto them. It is, in part, this story which humans use animals to tell about themselves that remains a fundamental theme of *Zoo Culture*.

NOTE

1. There is now a vast literature on this subject, but see particularly Ryder (1989) for a good overview and Clark (1997), Garner (1996) and Noske (1997) for more recent accounts. For a completely different perspective see Scruton (1996).

REFERENCES

Bostock, S. (1993) *Zoos and Animal Rights: The Ethics of Keeping Animals*, Routledge, London.

Clark, S. (1997) *Animals and Their Moral Standing*, Routledge, London.

Garner, R. (1996) *Animal Rights: The Changing Debate*, New York University Press, New York.

International Union for the Conservation of Nature and Natural Resources (1993) *Guide to the Convention on Biological Diversity*, Gland, International Union for the Conservation of Nature and Natural Resources Environmental Center.

International Union for the Conservation of Nature and Natural Resources, United Nations Environment Programme and World-Wide Fund for Nature (1991) *Caring for the Earth: A Strategy for Sustainable Living*, Gland, Cambridge.

International Union of Directors of Zoological Gardens—The World Zoo Organization (1993) *The World Zoo Conservation Strategy*, Chicago Zoological Society, Chicago.

Maple, T. and Archibald, E. (1993) *Zoo Man: Inside the Zoo Revolution*, Longstreet Press, Atlanta.

Marvin, G. (1994) 'Review Essay Zoo Man and Zoos and Animal Rights', *Society and Animals*, vol. 2(2), pp. 191-99.

Noske, B. (1997) *Beyond Boundaries: Humans and Animals*, Blackrose Books, Buffalo, NY.

Ryder, R.D. (1989) *Animal Revolution — Changing Attitudes Towards Speciesism*, Basil Blackwell, Oxford.

Scruton, R. (1996) *Animal Rights and Wrongs*, Demos, London.

Tudge, C. (1992) *Last Animals at the Zoo*, Island Press, Washington DC.

World Resources Institute, International Union for the Conservation of Nature and Natural Resources and United Nations Environment Programme (1992) *Global Biodiversity Strategy*, Gland, Baltimore.

Introduction to the
First Edition

BEIJING ZOOLOGICAL GARDENS,
PEOPLE'S REPUBLIC OF CHINA.
15 August 1986

Close to the main zoo entrance in a shabby dark building, a large group of American tourists are making their one and only stop in the zoo. Behind thick bars and a murky glass screen are two unnamed pandas, asleep. The Chinese visitors seem more intrigued by the blustering and cooing foreigners with their cameras than by the creatures which have drawn the people in. Nobody comments on the dingy surroundings – the important thing is being in the presence of the creatures. Eventually an adventurous woman finds a side door, and bangs on it; a panda stirs. There is a burst of excited comments and flash-gun fire from the Americans before their tour guide moves them on. They are happy because they saw a panda move. There is no corresponding excitement among the Chinese, however; none of them attempts to photograph the animals.

NATIONAL ZOOLOGICAL PARK, WASHINGTON DC, USA
14 March 1986

In an attractive exhibition area, there are displays of zoological information about the animals, and boards covered with Valentine cards and letters to Ling Ling and Hsing Hsing, together with a computer print-out 'reply' from the pandas themselves. Behind a glass screen the pandas sit with their backs to the audience quietly munching on bamboo, it being too wet to go out and play on the 'panda furniture'.

UENO ZOOLOGICAL PARK, TOKYO, JAPAN
20 July 1986

Proceeding quickly past huge and obtrusive signposts the crowds flock to see the motionless pandas. Without even noticing the rare red crowned crane (*Grus japonensis*) these Japanese visitors, escaping the megalopolis of Tokyo, find themselves disappointed not by their 'cuddly friends' but by the sign that tells them that photographs are not permitted.

PARC ZOOLOGIQUE DE PARIS, FRANCE
9 October 1986

Near the main entrance, with four signposts to indicate its presence, a giant panda is sitting in a tree in the bright autumn sunlight. There is no one looking at it.

The varying human attitudes to and treatment of *Ailuropoda melanoleuca*, the giant panda, illustrate many of the key elements examined in this book which together comprise the central thesis of our work — *that the presentation of captive wild animals in the zoo reveals more about the human societies which have constructed them — and whose members roam freely through them — than about the animals which are confined within them.* Let us briefly indicate some of the elements of this thesis with illustrations from the case of the panda.

Pandas are creatures which, as most zoo directors are fully aware, have exhibition value. Whereas many animals, the many variations of deer and antelope for example, excite the attention of few, the giant panda has an exhibition value seemingly second to none. Even though fewer than fifty living specimens have been publicly viewed outside China since the first arrival of a living panda in the west in 1936, the creature has made a profound impact on the emotions and imaginations of members of diverse cultures throughout the world. Consider its physical characteristics. It has a large round head with a flat face and large well-marked eyes, it has little or no tail, it has a rounded outline, it is black and white and it appears to be very soft. Significant elements of its behavioural qualities are that it sits vertically, it can manipulate small objects, it is playful and it is clumsy (Morris and Morris, 1981: 173–7). With these characteristics the panda seems to be uniquely suited to elicit anthropomorphic responses from many human observers. The panda becomes not a distant animal but rather a human in a panda skin. It becomes an animal imbued with a human personality, with human needs, and subject to similar emotions. So closely does it resemble the soft toys which are made in its image that the toy is played back into the perception of the real animal and thus even adult pandas become juvenilized soft toys.

These physical and behavioural characteristics are part of the nature of an animal and can be seen and interpreted when it is viewed in its natural habitat. But a qualitatively different form of viewing and interpretation occurs in zoos where the animal is removed from its natural context and framed in another setting – a man-made creation. Because this construction is the result of a complex process of planned thought and action, the zoo is clearly a cultural entity and merits interpretation as such.

At the National Zoological Park in Washington DC, the only American zoo with pandas, the animals are star attractions and are nationally known as individuals. The panda enclosure not only displays zoological information about *Ailuropoda melanoleuca* but in addition contains the packing cases (their 'home in the air') in which they travelled from China; there are also letters from admirers asking about their health and welfare (which are answered by a member of staff), and other panda paraphernalia. The outdoor enclosure consists of a well-tended lawn with an oriental tree together with special panda furniture. Contrast this with Beijing, the capital of the pandas' homeland, where two adult pandas are housed in an unimaginative building. Within a heavily barred inner enclosure the panda furniture consists of four pieces of rock cemented to the floor and two wooden-topped metal trestles. The outer enclosure has a rough mound with a large branch across it. Adjoining the enclosure for the adult pandas is one for younger pandas, in the centre of which is a brightly coloured child's climbing frame and swing, both of which accentuate the juvenile image of the creature. Unlike the Washington zoo, there is no more than a simple sign which indicates the name of the species and their distribution. The two individuals are not personalized, they are not reacted to as celebrities by the Chinese visitors, nor did the zoo designers produce luxury accommodation for them.

In addition to the panda's anthropomorphic characteristics, its special reception in those western countries which have specimens indicates a central theme in zoos – the presentation of the exotic. The nature of the exotic, of course, varies from culture to culture but essentially it involves a mixture of strangeness, distance and otherness, and as such it is important to the observer's process of self-definition. Witness the most obvious level in the zoo which separates us (humans) from them (animals). The experience of viewing a wild animal in captivity is shaped by a number of human mental constructs which will elicit a variety of responses and emotions ranging from a sense of power and domination to negative feelings of guilt and disgust or positive ones of joy and aesthetic appreciation, and finally to beliefs about association with or separation from the animal world. Such responses are not simply the product of individual psychology but rather are shaped by the culture in which the individual has been moulded. In the west, for example, the panda is perceived as a strange and rare animal which has been brought out of the mysterious orient, of which it has now become a representative, to be presented to a crowd eager for the unusual. It is significant that pandas in the west keep oriental names – Chi Chi of London, and Ling Ling and Hsing Hsing in Washington – whereas the pandas in Beijing and Shanghai have no public names at all.

While the general zoo public are attracted by exotic and strange animals, zoologists attempt to reduce this strangeness, although for them too the panda has been a mystery. Their aim has always been to understand the nature of a new creature and to fix it in terms of a taxonomic scheme which relates it to other animals. The panda has been a mystery because it has been remarkably difficult to classify; the two main modern contentions have been that it is a member either of the racoon family (*Procyoninae*) or of the bear family (*Ursidae*). Clearly this labelling process itself destroys the otherness or the exoticness of the animal by placing it in a seemingly objective international scheme. The zoologist is like the explorer in a strange land who, experiencing a chaotic otherness or difference, seeks to make sense of it and thus becomes preoccupied with:

arranging the elements of the information he has gleaned till they are contained within a comprehensive pattern. An Adam-like figure, he names all that he encounters in the hitherto uncharted (uncharted by him or his countrymen) chaos of the remote. From the moment of this naming ritual, the observed elements acquire significance and begin to be.

(Kabbani, 1986: 86)

For the scientist in this instance the panda becomes *Ailuropoda melanoleuca*.

We can now move from the immediate human emotional response to a strange and attractive creature and from the zoologist's desire to classify a new specimen, to consider certain economic and political dimensions of animals in captivity, once again using the panda as a particular case. Just as individual works of art such as Michelangelo's *Pietà* or Picasso's *Guernica* are regarded as almost priceless items in a cultural heritage, so the giant panda is a unique Chinese treasure so priceless that it quite simply cannot be bought. In recent years pandas have arrived in foreign zoos only as a gesture of goodwill by the Chinese government indicating a diplomatic rapprochement. Thus, the 1972 visit of Richard Nixon to China resulted in the gift of a pair of pandas;

so did the 1973 visits by Edward Heath and Georges Pompidou. Indian elephants, Australian koalas and New Zealand kiwis are other animals which have come to be regarded as suitable gifts in celebration of international amity.

As a result of the great European voyages of discovery and exploration from the fifteenth century onwards, all continents have been tied into a close and complex trade system (see for example Wolf, 1982). The animal trade has been no exception to this pattern. The Americas, South-east Asia, India and Africa have long been suppliers of wild animals for exhibition purposes, largely in Europe, a trade which has in part – although not nearly as significantly as hunting for trophies or for commercial purposes – led to the depletion of animal stocks in the wild.

Having benefited from the plundering of wildlife as part of the imperialist process, current serious or professional zoo thinking focuses on saving this very same, and now rapidly diminishing, wildlife. Some countries, now that they have decided on the importance of preserving wild animals in their natural habitat, attempt to impose modern western attitudes towards nature and the environment on indigenous populations and encourage them to see and respond to animals differently, particularly in terms of a conservation ethic. Such is the international appeal and rarity of the panda that it has been chosen as a symbol for one of the most respected of these organizations, the World Wildlife Fund.

When we embarked on the research for this book we were astonished that so little social science or humanities work has been directed towards understanding the zoo, whether historically or sociologically. Surely an institution which draws 3,875,000 visitors a year in Bombay, 8,000,000 in Beijing, 12,540,000 in Mexico City and more visitors than attend professional baseball, football and basketball games in the United States is of considerable social significance and thus deserving of attention and analysis? The key, we believe, to this lack of interest is that people regard the zoo as an easily understood and essentially unproblematic institution, and the zoo visit as an unproblematic event. Certainly, few have considered the complexity of the cultural processes involved in the selection, gathering and presentation of wild animals for display. Clearly, and this we repeat is our central thesis, interpreting the presentation of wild animals in the zoo reveals much more about the variety of the cultural expression of human identity than it does about the zoological nuances of the animal universe.

The zoo is a reservoir of a variety of complex human faculties: the anthropomorphic desire to see ourselves in animals; the creation of the illusion of natural habitats for these animals; the desire of humans to distinguish themselves from other animals, although they are disturbed by examples of both difference and similarity Furthermore, the history of the collecting of animals and the nature of zoo collections can be tied to that complex set of interrelations of exploration, colonization, trade routes and slavery. In the latter half of the twentieth century the development of zoo philosophy, particularly in its current western-dominated form, focuses on conservation, education, the concern for animals well-being and what could be looked upon as part of the process of post-imperial gesturing. All this reveals more about ourselves than it does about *Ailuropoda melanoleura* or *Grus japonensis*. Indeed it is this potential of the zoo experience to create conditions for human self-definition that makes zoos as institutions such revealing areas of investigation. When, for heuristic reasons, we make use of examples such as Michel Foucault's comparison between Louis xiv's menagerie and early mental asylums or prisons (1979: 203), we do so because all these institutions centre on the control of other 'creatures'. Just as human relations are power relations which inevitably have control as a central element, so is the human–animal relation in the zoo.

Zoos are peculiar places because they are totally artificial worlds. Creatures are moved from their natural habitat and placed in the habitat of man – the city – where they must be separated both from man and from the captive animals which share that space with them. When the visitor enters the zoo he enters a realm constructed of gardens, walkways, roads, buildings, cages and enclosures, and populated by creatures of man's choosing and displayed for man's enjoyment. It is a realm conceived by human imagination and controlled by human effort. Zoos are places where humans change the terms of their relations with the world of nature. Our concern is to understand the varying cultural and historical manifestations of that relationship.

The following zoo directors and zoo personnel have assisted us enormously by showing us their zoos and by discussing more generally the zoo world with us: K. Shivran, Meena Raghunath, Dhum Karkaria, Reuben David, Lavkumar Kacchar, Dr Mala R. Chinoy and Kartikya Sarabhai, Ahmedabad, India; Dr B.M. Lensink, Amsterdam, the Netherlands; Tine Griede, Wim Mager and Juust van Linger, Apenheul, the Netherlands; Derek Wood, Dr David Folwell, Kelly Tarlton and Barbara Cotton, Auckland, New Zealand; Dr Jim Jensen, Craig Sholley, Gary Camponeschi, Frederick Beal and Nancy Hotchkiss, Baltimore, usa; Josep Maria Ruiz Martin, Barcelona, Spain; Julian Tong, Beekes Bergen, the Netherlands; Dr M.V. Wani, Bombay, India; Eduardo Federico Herrera, Sra Amieva and Luis Pereya, Buenos Aires, Argentina; Dr Pedro Trebau, Dr Edgar Pérez de Armas and Dr Bartolomé Marín Saez, Caracas, Venezuela; Dr George Rabb and Dr Sandy Friedman, Chicago, usa; Tony Sumampau, Cisaua, Indonesia; Bent Jørgensen, Lars Andersson and Peter Nørresø Hasse, Copenhagen, Denmark; Roger Wheater and Rob Ollaston,

Edinburgh, Scotland; Johnny P. Chin, Simon Lee and Stephen Lee Yuen Man, Hong Kong; Robert Boutwood and Harry Teyn, Howletts, England; Dr Sutarman, Jakarta, Indonesia; Jaime Portocarrero Olave and Elciario Naranjo, Lima, Peru; Idris Abdullah Malik and Mr Ganansen, Kuala Lumpur, Malaysia; Dr Angel Francisco Amieva and Juan Jose Bianchini, La Plata, Argentina; David Jones, London, England; Toby Mainan and M. Kamal Naidu, New Delhi, India; James Doherty and David Mleczko, New York, USA; Jan Hatley, Paignton, England; Professor F. Doumenge and Kornélia Kurdi, Paris, France; Rob Colley, Penscynor, Wales; William Donaldson, Janet Jackson and Arlene Kut, Philadelphia, USA; Dr Paolo Celso Martins Brandao and Carmen Lucia da Silva, Rio de Janeiro, Brazil; Dick van Dam, Rotterdam, the Netherlands; Dr Charles Schroeder, Marvin Jones, Pegi Harvey, Sydney Donahoe, Georgeanne Irvine and Jackie Hill, San Diego, USA; Dr Luis Gonzalez, Santiago, Chile; Judith Ball, David Towne and Al Johnson, Seattle, USA Dr Gu Wenyi, He Bao-qing and Lu Sui-yung, Shanghai, People's Republic of China; Bernard Harrison, Dr Siriman Roy, Sharon Chan, Dr H.M. Wong, Singapore; Hans Ove Larsson, Stockholm, Sweden; Jack Throp, Sydney, Australia; Masaur Saito, Shiro Nakagawa and Dr Shigeharu Asakura, Tokyo, Japan; Dr Michael Robinson, Dr Bob Hoage, Judith White and Kay Taub, Washington DC, USA; Jan Louwman, Wassenaar, the Netherlands.

Other individuals who have helped us include R.L. Singh, director, Project Tiger, New Delhi, India; M. Mario Campos, Jones and Jones, architects, Seattle, USA; Bill and Penny Andrews, Hexagon Farm, San Juan Bautista, California USA; Professor Clas M. Nauman, Universität Bielefeld, West Germany; Jonathan Barzdo, Wildlife Monitoring Unit, Cambridge, England; C.H. Keeling, Shalford, England; Anne Wood and Sue Julier, University of East Anglia Library, Norwich, England; Rex Banks and Angela Jackson, Natural History Library, British Museum, London; Ian Brooke; and Juliet Gardiner of Weidenfeld for constant encouragement and editing skill.

It goes without saying that all errors are ours alone.

1
Humans in Animal Skin

A tiger is a tiger and not a human in a tiger skin. It is unfair to treat animals as human beings, it is unfair to animals. But you can't push anti-anthropomorphism too hard — it's too brutal for people to accept.

(Bent Jørgensen, Director of Copenhagen Zoo, 1986)

Many people take to animals to escape from human beings — but often it turns out because they find the animals so human.

(Louis MacNiece, 1938)

That certain people use anthropomorphic devices in order to understand animals and construct animal identities is indisputable. For many visitors to the zoo, the only way to appreciate, understand or feel for the animals is to impute to them human characteristics. Monkeys and sealions are seen as amusing or comical, lions, tigers and wolves as ferocious killers, thankfully locked away. It is not only the naive zoo visitor who holds or uses anthropomorphic attitudes — so do those who professionally and commercially operate zoos. For example, Lars Andersson of Copenhagen Zoo noted that the director of a small Danish zoo describes and presents his animals to the visitor as if they were humans — 'They are human beings sitting in the enclosures, they are personalities.' This, argues Andersson, is a poor example for a professional to set, for it gives visitors a false experience of the animals.

In this Andersson is espousing a central proposition of modern zoo philosophy — that visitors should be encouraged to view animals zoologically, ecologically and ethologically. However, despite the scientific orientation and the lead given by the major world zoos in this respect, not all of those who manage zoos follow this approach when presenting their animals. Many zoos for example willingly collude with their visitors and lead them into a false world of anthropomorphism. The Irish writer Louis MacNiece aptly captures this fantasy world populated by real creatures.

The zoo is a cross between a music hall and a museum; it bristles with pathetic fallacies and false analogies. One never goes to the zoo without hearing someone say that something is almost human. Sometimes they say this amusedly, sometimes sentimentally, sometimes with a jolly matter-of-fact air to show that they feel

1

*themselves at home there – just as they feel themselves at home in the bedroom of
Loretta Young or the racing car of James Cagney or a Shanghai Express or a Garden
of Allah or a Lost Horizon. . . . The zoo then is a dream-world that comes easy to
one. Easier than the dream-world of the art galleries which needs so many keys to
it. The same key does for the zoo that we use to put the cat out in the morning. For
everyone thinks of animals as potential pets – 'Just like a great big cat! Fancy
having him round your neck!' It is a nice sort of dream-world and you can get it
for a shilling.*

(1938: 29)

Animals held in menageries and zoological gardens have traditionally been
exotic wild animals which are thought of as coming from polar wastes, deserts,
forests, jungles, mountains and savannahs – wild lands not associated with the
realm of human habitation, lands which conjure up notions of distance and of
the wondrous. Such animals of course are part of the everyday life of certain
peoples: the hunters who deliberately seek contact with them, the pastoralists
who must protect their animals from attack from certain of them and the
agriculturalists who need to restrict the invasion of wild animals into their
crops. But significantly these are not the people who establish zoos. The
evocative power of images associated with wild animals can in no sense be
overstated. Such images tell not only of the animal itself but also of the people
and the land associated with it. The wild animal is thus not a fixed entity, and
indeed conceptions of the same animal will vary both in time and from society
to society.

WILD ANIMAL

The majority of the animals which are to be found in zoos are those which
English speakers would refer to as 'wild', a term which usually stands in
opposition to 'domestic'. The category 'wild', however, is a cultural category
rather than a zoological classification (although zoological classifications are
themselves cultural in that science is a cultural product), and the only qualities
which wild animals share is that they have not been domesticated, bred for
food, for work or as pets. In a sense it is only because we have culture and
have domesticated animals that we can have wild animals at all. Of course the
definition of what is wild and what is domestic will vary from culture to
culture, and some may well not have the distinction at all. So llamas in a
European zoo would probably be regarded as wild animals from South America,
whereas in a zoo in Quito or Lima they are likely to be regarded as domestic
animals because they are used by peoples in the Andes. Such animals would

2

hardly be regarded as exotic in that culture. In an important sense animals are human constructions. This is not to suggest that they are not real physical entities living in a real physical world, but rather to emphasize they are also man-made in the sense that they are thought about by man, and it is the animal as it is thought about rather than the animal itself which is of significance. Animals quite obviously cannot and do not represent themselves either to themselves or to other animals, and they certainly do not represent themselves to human viewers. It is man who defines and represents them, and he can in no sense claim to achieve a true representation of any particular animal; it merely reflects his own concerns.

Once brought to human attention an animal is no longer simply an animal in itself – it can only be that away from human sight, experience and thought. For instance, an Indian villager living in the same region as tigers will perceive the creature through a number of cultural filters. Living in close proximity to the forest about which many local tales are told he might fear the tiger as a potential man-eater or be thrilled by it as an exciting, seldom-seen creature living in a realm where man does not often venture, and which he certainly does not command. But if he were a herdsman, he would be concerned about the threat of attacks on his cattle by a dangerous wild animal. If a practising Hindu he would believe that all animals are imbued with sacredness and therefore deserving of respect. Finally if he were aware of issues at a national level he might know that the tiger is a rare animal which his own government is trying to save from extinction. In addition to this the villager is an individual and what he sees through his cultural spectacles will be idiosyncratic. On the other hand, an Englishman with no direct experience of India will probably share few, if any, of these cultural and cognitive responses. He might know the tiger as a beautiful but ferocious cat from the distant Asian forest (although many think it is actually an African animal inhabiting the same area as the lion). His view will be shaped by childhood literature, fictional accounts of the jungle, visits to circuses and zoos, and maybe dispassionate wildlife television documentaries. Finally an animal specialist, a zoologist for example, although similarly a product of a particular culture, may well attempt to distance himself from all folk models of the tiger in order to attempt to construct the creature in terms of an interpretation deriving from a particular scientific protocol, and moreover in terms of a particular scientific discourse. The views of people of this type are particularly important for us in conceptualizing zoos, for these specialists tend to control the institutions and to organize the presentation of animals so as to impose their view and overcome all other local cultural interpretations.

The key symbolic elements of domestic animals are that they are known,

3

they live in close association with humans, they are local and they are safe. Domestic animals are involved in social relations with humans, often with complex emotional connotations. They share human living space and become part of everyday life. Most important, domestic animals have been morphologically and psychologically shaped by man to suit his needs – they are very much cultural products. Thus all domestic cattle, sheep, pigs, horses, dogs differ qualitatively from their wild counterparts. Indeed the most extreme form of domestication, involving the most extreme transformation, is that of the pet which lives within the human household and is largely stripped of its animal quality in order to make it a pseudo-human being. Such animals are totally orientated to people.

Because they are so familiar and because they have no exciting image domestic animals simply do not attract people to zoos. A zoo which exhibited such animals and nothing else might well be regarded as little more than a farm. Indeed it is significant that in most zoos domestic animals, because they are perceived to be unthreatening, are relegated to the children's corner where people can safely touch them. If goats, sheep, donkeys and ponies attract people in this context it is precisely because they can be treated as pets.

'Wild' connotes the unknown, distant from human, foreign (with the implication of exotic) and potentially unsafe. Just as domestic animals are the product of human effort, so wild animals are seen as the opposite – they are in full possession of their animalness and are not orientated to people. Because of this distance from the human, the animals in zoos are usually strange and unusual creatures which come from little-known parts of the world. Such animals do not share their lives with man, they often do not even reveal their lives to man; so, much of the thrill of the zoo experience turns on being close to what is usually hidden or distant, a thrill which is compounded if the creature is one to which the visitor would not normally dare to get close to.

The term 'wild' not only indicates a category which implies location, it also implies character. Because the animal is not closely linked to a man or subject to his control, 'wild' is often taken to mean 'dangerous'. This is particularly important in the context of the zoo because it is the danger element which attracts many people to certain animals. Part of the thrill is being close to such an animal knowing that it cannot constitute an actual danger. Once again, this is not an intrinsic quality of the animal; rather it is a characteristic attributed to it and determined largely by its relation with man. Cages containing large cats and other carnivores often carry a warning sign, 'These Animals Are Dangerous'. But in what sense are they dangerous? In the most obvious sense they are dangerous because a person entering the cage or enclosure, or putting an arm in to touch them, is liable to be attacked. But this is only a product of the animal's predicament in being forced to be in undesired and unnatural proximity to man. The animals do not seek this closeness, they do not wish to be a danger. In their natural habitat they would be able to avoid such confrontations. Of course, in the wild, lions are 'dangerous' for gazelles, and polar bears are 'dangerous' for seals. But equally the seals are 'dangerous' for fish, and hedgehogs are for grubs and insects, though seals and hedgehogs are not normally thought of as dangerous animals. Killing does not make an animal dangerous; it is the sort of killing it engages in which is important – 'dangerous' animals are those which are a potential threat to man. The term in fact describes a potential relationship with man – once more we have an anthropocentric view of the world.

The issue of killing leads to an important question – the introduction of human judgement into attitudes towards animals which kill. Human moral attitudes are used to evaluate natural animal behaviour. Paul Shepard puts this particularly well:

The extension of the human idea to the wild can only produce mischief, for it will see in the behaviour and interrelationships among animals infinite cruelties and will seek to prevent them. The sucking of the host's blood by the parasite, the competition among scavengers to eat a carcass, the exclusion of the weak and sick, predation itself, the enormous mortality which removes the majority of the new born every year from nearly every species – all these and more, humane action will try to prevent, just as it prevents dogs from eating cats and men from eating dogs.

(1978: 248)

Such moral attitudes cause a radical restructuring of certain animal behaviours in zoos. Although many zoos claim that they want to show how animals 'really' live in the wild, none of them, even those which have the required space, show the relation between predator and prey because the public would find it distasteful. In some zoos live crickets might be fed to monkeys on public exhibition, and occasionally one might see mice running around a tank containing snakes (because, as one educational officer put it, such a creature was not obviously 'food' and nobody noticed when it disappeared), but one never finds lions being fed live goats or antelope.

Sandy Friedmann of Brookfield Zoo, Chicago, expressed this in terms of his 'bite-sized theory of eating live food', which posits that if something can be eaten in one go then it is probably an acceptable spectacle to most members of the public. He adds that attitudes also vary according to the species to be consumed – insects and invertebrates are usually 'okay, but when you get to the vertebrates there are problems'. We suggest that one of the reasons for this is that the more like 'human' food it is the easier it is to empathize with the death inflicted. It seems that people cannot accept this behaviour at close quarters in a zoo, although they might be prepared to watch it on a television wildlife documentary, where they expect to see 'real' animals living normal lives. This points to the peculiar status of animals in the zoo. Although just as real as those photographed for the documentary, they are not expected to live a similar life in the zoo. Animals in a zoo are not the same as animals in the wild, and moreover there is a qualitative difference between the experience of watching a wildlife film and a zoo experience.

The more dangerous the animal the greater the public interest, and although members of the public may be too sensitive to witness a lion killing a cow, they seem to be fascinated by the spectacle of the animal eating portions of it. Many zoo directors none the less have stopped such public feeding of the big cats as they feel that the snarling, growling and generally agitated behaviour which is displayed by the animals at this time is a poor ethological representation of their true behaviour and merely panders to popular misconceptions. In Artis Zoo, Amsterdam, for example, members of the public used to be able to pay keepers to allow them to go behind the scenes to see the big cats being fed. There was space for about thirty spectators but so popular was the feeding that every day as many as a hundred would join the queue. This was finally stopped by Dr Lensink, the zoo's current director, who did not favour the atmosphere of aggression and violence and who claimed that the show gave no useful information about the animal. And yet we know from our researches that fierceness, especially the ability to perpetrate a 'big death', is a factor which makes an animal exciting to zoo visitors and attracts their attention. Once again we suggest that this is a human-orientated concern – it is the fact that the ferocity and power could be directed against the zoo visitors which interests them.

In zoos throughout the world some visitors take delight in aggravating potentially ferocious animals because they can enjoy the fearful sensation of a powerful animal made aggressive and yet know that they run no real risk to their own safety. This anthropocentrism on the part of the visitor means that he is thinking more about himself in relation to the animal than about the animal on view. Most visitors to zoos simply do not seem to be interested in thinking zoologically, ecologically or ethologically.

The fact that human beings perceive and interpret animal behaviour in culturally specific ways naturally leads to the creation of animal stereotypes, so that it is difficult to know where the man-made image ends and the real animal begins. As we have argued, once the animal becomes the focus of human attention, the notion of a 'real animal' makes no sense, for all animals as perceived by humans are the result of human interpretations. Many of the zoos which emphasize an educational function attempt to discard such man-made images or folk models and to substitute a zoological or ethological understanding. Lars Andersson of Copenhagen Zoo put it somewhat ironically when he said that the zoo should attempt to educate the public to understand that 'Lions are not beasts,' meaning of course that they do not exhibit nor are they motivated by human beastliness. Predators generally receive a bad press because people cannot accept the killing involved in the predator–prey relationship as a normal process not motivated by viciousness. Mary Midgley helpfully asserts that traditional western beliefs mask the true nature of animal behaviour. The use of words like 'brute', 'beast', 'animal', 'pig', 'rat' and 'snake' as derogatory descriptions of humans not only judges those humans but also passes moral judgements on the animals from whom the symbolism was drawn.

It is therefore always dangerous to be an entity which carries one of these loads of significance. Many human beings and also many animals quite harmless to man and even useful, such as toads, spiders, and grass-snakes, have suffered a great deal from being draped with unsuitable symbolic values. Carnivores like wolves and lions have been viewed quite unrealistically as deliberate criminals, murdering wildly for the fun of it. The devil himself is seen as half-animal.

(Midgley, 1983: 79)

In popular usage lions are often referred to as 'enemies' of gazelles and thus the notions of predator and enemy are linked. By implication the prey becomes 'friend' and sympathetic reactions are immediately aroused.

From this position it is easy to see how the predator becomes a 'bad' animal. In North America and Europe the wolf (*Canis lupus*) is an animal which has suffered particularly from this sort of association. The wolf conservation and reintroduction programme based at Skansen Zoo, Stockholm, is an attempt to change the folk image of the wolf in order to persuade those people who live in the same area as the last few wild wolves not to kill them. Not surprisingly this has proved extremely hard to do. The workers from Skansen have tried (for the most part unsuccessfully) to persuade the local population that the wolves are not dangerous, and Hans Ove Larsson, the biologist at the zoo and director of this project, has hand-reared two pups which are walked around the zoo so that people can get close to them and touch them. His hope is that this personal experience will help in the campaign to break a particular anthropomorphic attitude and positively educate people to understand the true animal nature of the wolf. The main point of course is that the animals do not automatically savage humans; this is not their chief motivation in life, and humans are not (at least not in this sense) their enemies. It is important, says Larsson, that one explains its animal nature, but it is not his intention that his two tame wolves should be seen as pets. People must understand that the wolf *is* a predator, indeed an animal which must kill to survive, but 'we tried to show that the wolf is not dangerous in itself'. It is important to note though that these tamed wolves occupy an ambiguous status for they are not wild wolves, nor even simply zoo wolves, but rather tamed zoo wolves. Those who meet these creatures on the pathways of Skansen are not having the sort of wolf–human encounter which might occur in the wild for here the wolves' desire to escape has been lost in the taming process. However valuable their contribution to the education programme these are undoubtedly transformed wolves.

Other zoos are also concerned about the effects of the prevailing stereotype of the wolf. The National Zoological Park in Washington DC has organized educational programmes such as 'Wolves in Fact and Fiction' in which documentary film accounts of the life of wolves are shown alongside fictional accounts, such as werewolf films. In a similar way a film of *King Kong* was shown with a wildlife film of real gorillas. Most zoos which are concerned to educate the public promote a detached, objective, scientific understanding of animals and how they live in their natural habitat. Such zoos hope that the public will be able to understand the animal as a creature which has evolved a particular way of life and is subject to a variety of natural processes, completely independent of human attitudes towards them. But, as we have mentioned before, this form of seeing and understanding is itself cultural and in a sense is no more a true picture of the animal than any other. Its great advantage, however, and it is an advantage for the animal too, is that by attempting to reduce the human construction and by increasing our understanding of it as an independent entity in the world, we are perhaps led to attend to its needs as a gorilla (*Gorilla gorilla*) or as a wolf rather than as a variation of King Kong or Little Red Riding Hood's 'grandmother'.

NAMES AND THINGS

In many forms of domestication humans know their animals individually and give them personal names. Such a process indicates a level of animal incorporation into the human world and an enduring relationship with man. Wild animals do not have this sort of relationship; they are distanced from man and they are not individuated – indeed individuals are rarely recognized. Wild animals are credited with what might be called a species personality, any individual of that species being supposed to have the same character as any other member. Of course each animal does have its own personality and idiosyncrasies but in the wild these are masked by distance, lack of visibility, group existence or a combination of these. On the other hand, and importantly, marking animals as individuals and treating them as individuals can exaggerate individual personality at the expense of its species nature and animalness. This process is seen most strongly in pet-keeping where, as we have previously mentioned, animals come to be treated almost as though they were humans.

The majority of zoos do not wish to domesticate their stock. Rather they wish them to remain as much as possible the same sort of animal as those found out of captivity in their natural habitat, and certainly they hope that the visitor will perceive them in this way. There is a certain ambiguity about this wildness, however, in that most animals in the zoo are now captive-bred, that is to say selectively bred. Breeding in the wild is governed by natural factors and not by factors of human choice as is breeding in the zoo. The existence of stud books (normally associated with animals of 'high' cultural status such as racehorses and show dogs) for zoo animals in which they appear listed as individuals attests to human interest in shaping the animal. Stud books are not kept for all species but the fact that they are kept at all indicates that the species in question are regarded by the international zoo community as deserving of special consideration, for they become subject to a carefully controlled international breeding programme. What marks this controlled breeding from that of pedigree animals is that the aim is not to refine a particular species but to preserve it in a form as close as possible to the same species in the wild. It is in fact a complex cultural process designed to reproduce wild animals. Not only will those in control of zoo breeding programmes decide which animal will mate with which in their zoo, they may even fly one animal thousands of miles to mate with another. Surely a peculiar mixing of wildness and cultural sophistication.

It is perhaps inevitable though that the animals brought into or raised in the human environment of the zoo will behave in radically different ways, and this fact will lead to profoundly changed perceptions of them. Zoos tend to emphasize that the animals which they exhibit are representatives of their species, but because they have been isolated, both from their habitat and from fellow species members, and because they are subject to intense interaction with humans in the form of visitors and those who care for them on a daily basis, it is hardly surprising that many come to be treated as individuals and are given personal names to mark this.

It is possible to distinguish three sets of names in zoos: scientific, popular and individual. The first two are usually printed on identification plaques attached to the cage or enclosure; the individual name may or may not be included.

Scientific names: these are the Latin-based names of zoological nomenclature which are used internationally for identification. So, on the cage of what an English speaker would call a chimpanzee, the label would read *Pan troglodytes troglodytes*. The idea that it is a 'label' is important here for this technique is reminiscent of the labelling in a museum: it is a specimen. This name is taken from a particular culture which is scientific and of western European origin and accordingly directs attention in a particular way. Non-scientists often consider that the Latin name of the animal is in fact its real name and indeed scientists themselves seem certain that it is, but in fact all that it represents is an attempt to classify and order an almost infinite number of species according to a particular cultural scheme. It is a form of classification which transcends local, vernacular classificatory schemes, and it consists of names which evoke the authority of Latin as the language of the learned.

Although this name sometimes takes priority on the identifying label, it will be known only by a few specialists and will be used for reference and identification only at their level. The visitors to the zoo are very unlikely to make use of it.

Popular names: these are the names by which the animals are popularly known. So the animal referred to by zoologists as *Ursus arctos* will be referred to by English speakers as a brown bear, grizzly bear or Kodiak bear. These are the names by which even specialists will refer to them in everyday conversation and certainly they are the names which visitors will want to know in order to identify what is in the cage or enclosure. This name is the national or perhaps local cultural name.

Individual names: these are the names by which individual animals in the particular enclosure are known; they are personal names. For example, a walrus at Brookfield Zoo, Chicago, is called Olga, while an elephant at Dusit Zoo, Bangkok, is called Jim, and a white gorilla at Barcelona Zoo is called Copito de Nieve. Sometimes these are included on the identifying label. Again they tend to be known by only a few, particularly by those who have the closest dealings with them, and even in the zoo itself the names might well not be known above the keeper or perhaps curatorial level. These names are absolutely local. The exceptions to this are the cases where individual animals become especially well known. Thus in England in the 1960s many people would have known that the giant panda in London Zoo was called Chi Chi. Perhaps the only animal whose name is internationally known (although many will not realize that it originated with a particular animal) was London Zoo's elephant of the late nineteenth century, Jumbo.

Not all animals will be named as individuals; moreover this varies from culture to culture and species to species. So even in a culture where animals are given individual names, those which do not attract attention (those with low exhibition value) and those which live in large groups in the zoo – a shoal of fish, a herd of deer or cage of mice for example – are unlikely to be named, even though they might be recognized as individuals.

We are unable to discern any general trends in the attribution of personal names to wild animals with the exception of the giant panda. Of the forty-nine pandas which have been seen outside China, only six have had non-Chinese names. The rest of the names follow a consistent pattern – Chi Chi, An An, Shao Shao, Tian Tian, Ling Ling all retain a link with their oriental origin. There do not appear to be general rules for the naming of animals in the zoo world. In Philadelphia, for example, it seems that many keepers name animals after their children; in Skansen, Stockholm, on the other hand, they give a variety of names to the animals; while in Apenheul, Netherlands, the gorillas have 'African' names – Bongo, Mwila, Mungi, Lobo. Professor Doumenge at the Jardin des Plantes, Paris, explained that his animals were never named: 'It is an animal – one, two three, four.' A similar account was given by Sandy Friedmann when at Minnesota Zoo, where to avoid the possibilities of anthropomorphism and 'humanizing' the animals were never named; each was merely given a number. Ironically these numbers themselves became names, and so 'beaver 668' was as individuated as 'beaver 667'. If he wanted to attract his attention the keeper would call '668'; '668' became his personal name.

It is only the individual wild animal kept out of context in the zoo which can be personalized for of course in the jungle or on the plains no individuals are noticed by human observers – any gorilla is simply a gorilla, any antelope is simply an antelope.

For those who need to associate with animals in their natural habitat the act of viewing is obviously a qualitatively different experience from that of seeing the same animal in captivity. Those who watch animals in such societies do so in very different ways and for very different purposes from those who go to zoos. Those referred to by anthropologists as hunter–gatherers must carefully observe and have an intricate knowledge of the animals they pursue. That is not to say that such people have only a utilitarian interest in animals, for as Lévi-Strauss and other anthropologists have shown such societies use animals cognitively as well as culinarily – or to put it another way, to them animals are also 'food for thought'. Thus in ritual practices such as totemism hunter–gatherers use images from the animal world to structure their thought about the human social world.

Even in industrialized societies where the majority of the population is hardly ever likely to confront a wild animal in its natural habitat, people make use of wild-animal images to comment on the human condition: 'bold as a lion', 'sly old fox', 'as slippery as a snake'. Such people would never have seen a lion being bold, a fox being sly, and anyway snakes are not slippery. In zoos they certainly see the animals which figure in such imagery but here they are thoroughly marginalized, they are out of context. As Shepard observes: 'The impoverished relationship among domestic and caged animals cannot evoke that speculative attention which penetrates by parallels to the human condition, unless it is equally barren' (1978: 160). Perhaps some *are* able to make use of the imagery and draw the obvious parallel between the barren and dull life of the caged animal and the equally dull and barren life of the human prisoner. Both are marginalized from their normal society, both are engaged in enforced leisure, and both have unwanted time on their hands.

Maybe it is entirely wrong to attempt to understand the nature and significance of animals out of context in the zoo. Maybe they are not out of context at all, maybe we have had zoos for so long now that for the majority of the population the zoo is where such animals live. That is their context. Perhaps there is a whole new class of animals, not wild, not domestic, but zoo animals. Lions, tigers, elephants and giraffes are animals which live in the zoo and although television might attempt to convince us that they have a *real* life in the tropical rainforests or on the African savannah this is not a reality when visiting a zoo. In terms of the immediate experience of most urban dwellers this is where wild animals naturally occur; they are born in the zoo, and they eat, sleep, breed and die there.

With the success of breeding programmes, and the decreasing amount of natural habitat that animals could be returned to, these populations are likely to be permanent zoo populations. Certainly not all visitors seem concerned to place such animals imaginatively in their natural habitat. For others this is perhaps a painful thing to do – to have their enjoyment of seeing a tiger in the flesh marred by the thought that other tigers have different lives elsewhere and that the life of this particular specimen has been reduced to that of an exhibit simply for their benefit.

ANTHROPOMORPHISM

Randall Lockwood, an American psychologist, carefully and usefully cate-
gorizes five different kinds of anthropomorphism (1983). First, there is *allegorical
anthropomorphism*, namely descriptions of animal behaviour not intended to
be interpreted as biological fact. These descriptions use animals 'to make the
point more appealing or to conceal true identities'. This would be the form of
anthropomorphism we see in most fables, Disney films and literary or political
allegories such as *Alice in Wonderland, Animal Farm* and *Watership Down*. Since
it does not claim to portray biological reality, Lockwood considers this form
to be essentially harmless.

The second form is termed *personification*. This is when humans superimpose
their desires on the animals' actual requirements. An example is the dressing-
up of pets in human clothes. This is similar to allegorical anthropomorphism
in that there is no recognition of the true biological needs and adaptations of
the animals involved, but in this case the animals that are used to 'portray
some personal symbolic message are not literary figures – they are flesh and
blood beings who may suffer in the process'.

The third variety is *superficial anthropomorphism*, where we interpret an
animal's behaviour or temperament on the basis of surface qualities that are
correlated to those that actually regulate it. We might interpret the 'kissing'
of kissing gouramis to indicate affection because it bears a superficial resem-
blance to a human pattern of behaviour, but fishes do not fall in love. Or
indeed we may even interpret the wide-eyed alert gaze of the owl as revealing
unusual intelligence. Lockwood notes a striking example of this in the movie
The Right Stuff:

*Ham, a chimpanzee, returns from his space flight and greets those who open his
capsule with a big toothy grin that adorned the cover of* Life. *The interpretation of
this 'smile' was that he had loved his flight. In truth he was giving the 'fear grimace'
that usually accompanies a threatening or unsettling chimpanzee experience. But it
looked like a nice big smile, and that's how it was portrayed.*

(1983: 6)

More careful attention to what preceded and followed this behaviour, and some
knowledge of chimpanzees, could have led to a more accurate interpretation.

A fourth model is that of *explanatory anthropomorphism* whereby we are
inclined to offer circular definitions and explanations (tautological ones in other
words) of animal behaviour, believing that by naming a behaviour we have
in fact explained its basis. If a keeper plays with one chimp and neglects
another, and following this the neglected one attempts to wreck his enclosure,

the keeper attributes the behaviour to spite or revenge on the part of the discarded chimp. How do we recognize it as spite? Because the behaviour was spiteful.

For Lockwood all four of these forms of anthropomorphism have serious explanatory shortcomings because they either make 'no attempt to understand the animal in its own world, or they make no attempt to verify that our explanation of some behaviour is correct'. However, he sees a fifth variety, *applied anthropomorphism* as being somewhat more useful for understanding the motivation of animal behaviour. With this form we use our own personal perspective on what it is like to be a living being, to suggest ideas about what it is like to be some other being of either our own or some other species (1983: 7). Mary Midgley comments on this question of empathy, quoting Humphrey who argues that 'for all I know no man other than myself has ever experienced a feeling corresponding to my own feeling of hunger; the fact remains that the concept of hunger, derived from my own experience, helps me to understand other men's eating behaviour' (Humphrey, 1976, in Midgley, 1983: 142).

In other words, we can, according to Lockwood, make hypotheses about what it might be like to be someone or something else and make predictions on the basis of these hypotheses. Through this we might begin to know what it was/is like to be Søren Kierkegaard, Mahatma Gandhi, John F. Kennedy, a wolf, a python or Chi Chi. Or even a fly on the wall. Or perhaps not.

LITERAL ANTHROPOMORPHISM:
THE CASE OF CRIMINAL ANIMALS

In earlier centuries anthropomorphism was applied almost literally. Animals were seen in certain circumstances as possessing the same degree of will and exhibiting the same personality characteristics as certain humans. Evans' 1906 *The Criminal Prosecution and Capital Punishment of Animals* cites hundreds of events in which animals in some way harmed humans, either directly in the sense of causing them bodily harm or indirectly in the sense of destroying crops or property. The human victims of such behaviour needed to make sense of it, they needed a satisfactory explanation of why such things should occur, and they needed to be able to attribute responsibility and to respond to it. It would appear that they interpreted the animal 'attacks' as though they were motivated by human thoughts and emotions. Although it might seem to us inexplicable in terms of rational understanding, these animals were tried for their behaviour as though they were malevolent, criminal creatures. In 1314, a bull belonging to a farmer in the village of Moisy, France, escaped on to the highway where it 'attacked' a man and injured him so severely that he died a few hours afterwards. 'The ferocious animal was seized and imprisoned by the officers of Charles, Count of Valois, and after being tried and convicted was sentenced to be hanged' (Evans, 1906: 160–1). Evans cites an even more unusual case:

Mathias Abele von Lilienberg, in his Metamorphosis Telae Judiciarie. . .*states that a drummer's dog bit a member of the municipal council in the right leg. The drummer was sued for damages, but refused to be responsible for the snappish cur and delivered it over to the arm of justice. Thereupon he was released, and the dog sentenced to one year's incarceration in the Narrenkötterlein, a sort of pillory or iron cage standing on the market place, in which blasphemers, evil-livers, rowdies and other peace-breakers were commonly confined. . . . Mornacius also related that several mad dogs, which attacked and tore in pieces a Franciscan novice in 1610 were 'by sentence and decree of the court put to death'. It is surely reasonable enough that mad dogs should be killed; the remarkable feature of the case is that they should be formally tried and convicted as murderers by a legal tribunal, and that no account should be taken of their rabies as an extenuating circumstance or ground of acquittal. In such a case the plea of insanity would certainly seem to be naturally suggested and perfectly valid.*

(1906: 175–6)

A selective chronological list of some of the excommunications and prosecutions of animals from the ninth to the nineteenth centuries demonstrates the degree and strength of this anthropomorphic attitude over the centuries. Evans prefaces his list by stating that a few earlier instances of excommunication and malediction, of which knowledge is chiefly derived from hagiologies and other legendary sources, are not included – for example, the cursing and burning of storks at Avignon by St Agricola in 666, and the expulsion of venomous reptiles from the island of Reichenau in 728 by St Perminus.

Dates	Animals	Places
824	Moles	Valley of Aosta
886	Locusts	Roman Campagna
9th century	Serpents	Aix-les-Bains
1120	Field-mice and caterpillars	Laon
1121	Flies	Foigny near Laon
1121	Horseflies	Mayence
1225	Eels	Lausanne

15

(Dates)	(Animals)	(Places)
1379	Three sows and a pig. Rest of the two herds pardoned	Saint-Marcel-les-Jussey
1386	Sow	Falaise
1451	Rats and blood-suckers	Berne
1452	Sixteen cows and one goat	Rouvre
1456	Pig	Bourgogne
1460–1	Weevils	Dijon
1516	Locusts	Tréguier
1519	Field-mice	Glurns (Stelvio)
1541	Grasshoppers	Lombardy
1596	Dolphins	Marseilles
16th century	Dog	Scotland
1631	Mares and cows	Greifenberg
Before 1680	Worms	Constance and Coire
1713	Termites	Piedade no Maranhão in Brazil
1733	Vermin	Buranton
1771	Dog	Chichester, England
1866	Locusts	Pozega in Slavonia
1906	Dog	Délémont in Switzerland

(Adapted from Evans, 1906: 314–34)

Evans notes that in the 1906 case of the dog, a man was killed and robbed by another man and his son, with the 'fierce and effective co-operation of their dog'. The 'three murderers' were tried and the two men sentenced to life imprisonment, but the dog, as the chief culprit, without whose complicity the crime could not have been committed, was condemned to death.

SHOWS

Showmen who presented animals in circuses or early menageries wanted and needed (in order to attract attention) to wrap their beasts in various mythologies and associate them with fabulous lives and countries; but modern zoos (at least the major ones) are institutions dedicated to demythologization, and the wonder which they attempt to arouse in their visitors is stimulated by the true lives of the animals. They attempt to reduce the human element in the construction of the animal in an attempt to allow its true animal nature to be revealed.

Many zoos incorporate various kinds of shows as part of their presentation of animals. The problem with such shows for zoos who would maintain that their primary purpose is education rather than mere entertainment is that of maintaining credibility and not allowing the shows to slip into circus-like entertainment. Some zoos are untroubled by such concerns and the whole establishment has a show-like atmosphere into which are incorporated spectacles which are unashamedly circus entertainment.

At Samustprakaran, near Bangkok, for example, there is a combined crocodile farm and zoo. The farm is engaged in breeding programmes involving thousands of crocodiles and the resulting hybrid creatures can be seen piled on one another in a great living mass. The ideology of breeding is not closely associated with that of conservation and there is a souvenir shop which sells products such as bags and shoes made of crocodile skin.

This is a citadel of entertainment. The zoo–farm is full of amusements while the animals, visitors and staff are subjected to a relentless barrage of western popular music at high volume. All of the animals can be fed by the visiting public – and fed anything. Yet there are signs encouraging people to be 'kind to the animals'. The standards of containment are low by anyone's criteria. Dogs are kept in cages less than one yard square, a fully grown tiger in one measuring two by three yards. Most appalling is the plight of a sun bear, caged in tightly, with no visible sign of food, the animal looking as though it had been left for dead.

'Entertainment' is everywhere. A dog and a tiger, both born in 1983, are caged together – a sign explains they are 'friends' – and much amusement is had by all in watching them play together, the tiger hurting the dog on occasion. There is also a very small natural-history corner – 'Here we have stuffed animals' proclaims a sign – which contains a number of small animals and what appears to be a two-headed dog. Apart from the general entertainment provided by an assortment of caged animals the real attractions are the shows featuring performing elephants and chimpanzees, and, most important, the crocodile show.

Masses of people walk along bamboo pathways and crowd around the shallow pool where the show takes place. The pool is full to the brim with what the public are told are ferocious 'man-eating killer crocodiles'. After what seems to be an eternity of lurid descriptions of these 'killers' and a profile of the man who is to 'risk his life' by entering the pool, the public is witness to a modern entry of the gladiators. The music of *Hawaii Five-O*, the popular American police television series, the 'trainer' – a man approaching seventy years old – walks a plank into the pool. He then proceeds to poke the crocodiles repeatedly with a stick and to pull them about by their tails. With every snap of the jaws the crowd gasps with excitement. The highlight of the show is when the man puts his head between a crocodile's jaws; he then poses, almost derisively, head-in-jaws for any photographer who wishes him to do so. He is finally joined by a younger colleague and they finish the show with more heads-in-jaws and a general poke of the animals. They leave the stage to the accompaniment once again of the gladiatorial sounds of *Hawaii Five-O* and much applause. There is no commentary. The audience has been invited to witness a demonstration of man's power over 'killer animals'; a particular relationship between man and the natural world has been established or reinforced. It is this sort of attitude that many zoos seek to overcome.

The majority of zoo directors emphasize that the shows, if they have them, should be educational, but the notion of what is 'educational' varies from establishment to establisment. The very best, in zoos such as San Diego, Taronga Zoo, Sydney, and to a certain extent Singapore, do not teach animals circus-like tricks but rather take examples of natural behaviour and train animals to reproduce it on cue so that the trainer can demonstrate some aspect of animal behaviour. For example, in Singapore Zoo a gibbon is trained to swing from the back of an open-air auditorium, down a series of poles and on to the stage. The audience enjoy the movement and the trainer explains to them what brachiation is. Similarly an orang-utan peels a coconut to show the power of its hands, and the elephants are trained to show how they manipulate objects with their trunk. The danger is that shows become circus-like. The directors want to push the show towards an exposition of animal behaviour but they are trapped by the nature of the location. All animals in the zoo are unwilling actors and those on stage are quickly perceived as actors exhibiting human-like qualities. Sealions which bang their flippers together are 'clapping' and the monkeys which put their mouths to that of the trainer are 'kissing'.

In Barcelona there is a sea mammal show. Here a killer whale and three dolphins perform tricks: leaping out of the water, through hoops, retrieving footballs, 'dancing' (i.e. turning around apparently in time with the music), and, in the case of the whale, allowing the trainer to ride on its back. Certain facts are given about the size, weight, food and natural habitat of these creatures, but after that the remainder of the commentary is totally anthropomorphic, a piece of showman talk punctuated by the music of John Travolta. Part of the show features the dolphins and the killer whale coming out of the water on to a rubber mat at the side of the pool to collect fish as a reward for having performed correctly. This is quickly done by the dolphins but the whale does not return to the water when ordered to do so. The commentator asks the trainer whether it wants more food, the whale nods its head and it is given some more. But still it does not return to the water, and so even more food is given. This performance is designed to give the impression that the whale is not acting its role properly, that it has decided to do something different, that it is exercising its own will. The result is that the trainer, commentator and public are able to juvenilize it and to treat it as though it were a naughty child.

Much of the commentary plays on the notion of eating/not eating. The public has seen the whale receive fish as a reward at various points in the performance, but towards the end of the show the commentator suggests that the whale needs something special to eat after all that fish — what it wants is *un bocadillo de cabeza* (literally a 'head sandwich'). There is great excitement as the whale lifts its head out of the water and the trainer slowly puts his own head between the open jaws — a sight reminiscent of the image of the daring of man and the control of ferocious beasts which has been presented by lion-tamers for centuries. In both cases the intention is similar — that is, to emphasize the great danger that the man is in but which, because of his great bravery, he is able to risk. As a piece of circus this seems perfectly acceptable and the audience certainly enjoys it as such, but if the purpose of the zoo is to be educational and to inculcate knowledge of and respect for animals, as the director had previously informed us, it is somewhat difficult to understand. Such a presentation surely adds to the popular conception (something which the zoologist, ethologist and zoo director would want to claim as a 'mis-conception') of killer whales as dangerous to man, for the only message which could be inferred from this part of the performance was that the man was in imminent danger of being eaten by the whale.

The public relations director at Sea World, San Diego, perhaps the most prestigious establishment featuring performing sea mammals, explained that shows such as that at Barcelona were staged in his establishment many years ago, but they were now unacceptable. At Sea World the killer whales show is revealing of the enormous interest in certain sea mammals in the USA that has developed in recent years. The content, style and tone of the show have mirrored or, as the official Sea World point of view has it, in part led this change in attitude. Although the conservationists who have SAVE THE WHALE bumper stickers on their cars may not be the same people who express delight and applaud through the Shamu shows in Sea World, the two can only be understood in conjunction.

The killer whale show — the present one is called 'Celebration Shamu' — is slicker, more professional, more carefully orchestrated than the Barcelona show, but this is hardly surprising considering the difference in the number of visitors and the corresponding budgets which each have. Barcelona Zoo *is* a zoo and people visit to see a wide variety of animals, whereas at Sea World, even though there are set exhibition pieces (including the Penguin Encounter, which is a state-of-the-art exhibit), the shows are the key attractions. In a tank of millions of gallons of water, in front of an auditorium which seats 3,500, the killer whales perform several times a day. On the stage a young blonde southern Californian woman gives an excitedly Hollywood-sincere commentary about Shamu the killer whale. Occasionally there is a cut from her live commentary to the voice-over of a man who is apparently one of the trainers recounting his thoughts and experiences. To enhance the mood there is a specially composed orchestral and vocal soundtrack.

The killer whales do no tricks except to leap out of the water, carry their trainers on their backs or catapult them out of the water. Much of the performance consists of the whales and the trainers in close contact swimming or floating around the pool to the accompaniment of soft sentimental music. The educational message of the show is that of understanding another creature, but this is not done in zoological or ethological terms as there is no information, apart from the weight, given about the killer whale as *Orcinus orca*; instead understanding comes from experience. The introduction by the male trainer sets the tone by explaining how the killer whales used to be perceived even at Sea World: they were thought of as 'vicious killers. . . . The potential danger was so intimidating that it made progress slow and cautious but then one trainer decided to take a daring step and once he started he knew there was no turning back. [Crescendo of dramatic music.] All of a sudden he was riding on the back of a killer whale, he could feel the animal moving beneath him and then it began to feel okay. Suddenly he realized that the trust, patience and understanding of his relationship with Shamu had now taken him further than he had ever dreamed possible. This was only the beginning because we knew we were going to stay with Shamu now no matter where he led us.' [The chorus sings sweetly, 'It's a fact and it's now, it's a revelation.']

From the beginning the emphasis is on sharing the experience of Shamu, although exactly what that experience is for most of the audience is not clear. For one person at least the experience is direct, because someone is chosen from the audience and allowed to touch Shamu. 'Back in 1971 we were looking for a way of sharing with you the special relationship we had developed with our killer whales, and what we found has become our most popular tradition.' [Chorus: 'Starting here with beauty and wonder from the sea.']

'Hi, what's your name?'

'Yvonne.'

'Have you ever *met* a killer whale before?'

'No, I haven't.'

'How do you feel about it?'

'Excited!'

'Good, come on down here. You're going to get a very special hug from Shamu.'

At this point the volunteer kneels down at the side of the pool, opens her arms wide and the killer whale's head appears between them. A Polaroid photograph records the moment, and the final remark from the commentator stresses the importance of the role this individual has played: 'Thank you very much for being a special part of our celebration.'

A comparison with Jeremy Cherfas' account of the commentary of a similar show, 'Shamu – Take a Bow', a few years earlier, demonstrates the movement in recent years towards the concern with experience. In the Cherfas account, the presenters are recorded as giving details of the weight, length and swimming speed of the whales, and then the commentary continues:

'But what of his true potential?'

'We may never really understand, but we can experience all of his strength and agility.'

'Combined with an intelligence.'

'And in it there is a beauty, like the finest gymnast or ballet dancer.'

'And there is a spectacle. Focus your attention on the centre of the pool.'

'In one fleet moment – diving, leaping, spinning.'

'Natural grace, beauty, power.'

(1984: 48)

In the 1986 show there was no drawing of attention to the abilities of the killer whales although the members of the audience were obviously thrilled by the sight of the creatures leaping from the water. The emphasis was still on experience, but now much more so in terms of a changed understanding and a concern to establish a relationship with the whales. With both trainers and whales in the pool the commentator, with a voice full of sincerity and concern warns us: 'We mustn't forget that at one time so little was known about these magnificent creatures that killer whales were hunted and shot for the sheer pleasure of it and in some parts of the world it still occurs. We like to believe that because of marine zoological parks such as Sea World the public has turned fear into fascination and is going to respect the killer whales *and even love one* like Shamu or Kandu [our emphasis].' [Chorus: 'It's what Shamu means to you and to me.']

Apparently these performances do not come about simply because the whales are trained, rather they are manifestations of the close personal relationship that the trainers and whales have. Cherfas records part of an earlier commentary which was quite explicit about this: 'How do we create a performance like this? Well, we don't. Shamu does' (1984: 48). In the 1986 show the emphasis that Shamu determines what will happen is even stronger. Now he works with the trainer because he is his 'friend'. 'I think the greatest thing about working with Shamu is being in the water with him. All of a sudden its just you and this incredible animal. At first you feel he puts up with you but soon you realize that he really seems to like you by the gentle way he welcomes you into his world.'

The notion of friendship has obviously changed subtly from 'Shamu – Take a Bow' to 'Celebration Shamu'. From the Cherfas report we see the trainers' ability to cross the species barrier in friendship which allows them to act with the animals:

'And what about our relationship?'

'Well, whales aren't people, and sometimes we have to remind ourselves of this, but through our recognition of their true magnificence we can in a very special way become close friends.'

'The ideals of friendship and Shamu seem to go hand in hand, and over the years we've made a lot of friends together, some who live in the water and some who don't. Right now we'd like you to meet some of those who do. With them they've given us a chance to live a dream, a chance to swim with and to play with and to ride. . . the dolphins.'

(1984: 48)

By the summer of 1986 we have arrived at a much more complex level of friendship which allows for the experience of mutual understanding. To the accompaniment of soft and mellow music the trainer drifts gently around the pool with the whale and a prerecording of his voice drifts with him: 'At times it's a quiet moment that Shamu and I enjoy together when we are just lying still and not doing anything at all. I'll touch him and he'll look up at me and I'll know that he's thinking just as much about me as I am about him.'

After a few more dramatic leaps and crashings into the water (these are the 'fireworks' which the commentator tells the public are part of all celebrations), enlivened with a burst of up-tempo music, the show finishes with a final sincere message from the commentator: 'As you can see we've come a long way in our celebration. Together with Shamu and Kandu we've accomplished a great deal, but as far as we're concerned it's only the tip of the iceberg. Who knows what secrets we'll share with our killer whales in the months and years to come. Ladies and gentlemen, we invite you back to our celebration because it will be going on for a very long time to come.

22

There is an important set of questions that needs to be asked about this event: what has been celebrated, what has been experienced, and what secrets have been shared with the whales during the course of the show? The only member of the public who is allowed a direct physical experience of the killer whale is the volunteer from the audience; the others have merely watched two trainers swimming with the whales. The whales have been anthropomorphized – not in the crass way of a circus animal whose behaviour is interpreted in human terms, but rather as a creature which shares and exhibits the same deep emotions, feelings and desires of the human trainers and by implication with the rest of the human observers. Such a relationship could well be understood in terms of the general concern in this society with interpersonal relationships, but it is more complex than that, for the whale has become a special symbol of being in contact with nature. We need rather to ask whether the audience at this show have understood whales any better as a result of what they have seen and heard. Have they come to know Shamu as an individual killer whale any better?

This latter question is even more intriguing when we realize that there is not just one Shamu but *three*, and the whale which is used for the main part of the show is Shamu for that performance. Any of the whales at Sea World can represent Shamu and whaleness. Shamu is supposedly an individual and thus has an individual character and set of emotions, and yet this is not really the case in the public arena. It is significant that the three killer whales currently used at Sea World are given the interchangeable stage names Shamu, Kandu and Nandu, but when they are not performing, when they are off-exhibit, they are known by different names and in fact *are* known as individuals but only by the Sea World staff. The comparison with human actors with private lives off-screen or off-stage is obvious, and yet the whales do not quite play a part in the way that human actors do – the Shamu show is designed to suggest whaleness as a state of being and the importance of a relationship.

There is a show at Sea World, 'Spooky Kooky Castle', in which animals are thoroughly anthropomorphized. Here two sealions called Clyde and Seymour play the 'humanized' nephews who come to the castle of the supposedly dead Uncle Smedley (played by a walrus) to claim their inheritance. It is significant that such an anthropomorphic circus-like show can remain side by side with the Shamu show. It would appear that sealions do not have the same status as killer whales and dolphins. Indeed, as Jackie Hill of Sea World pointed out, while zoos can do certain things with sealions in an anthropomorphic sense they cannot do the same things with whales and dolphins (at least in this culture). The 'public is accustomed to see sealions as clowns but whales and dolphins are cousins'. Furthermore it is significant that the feelings aroused by

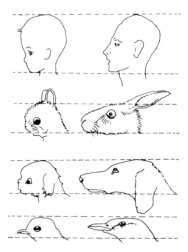

'Child schema' after Konrad Lorenz.

the round white fluffy face of the baby harp seal, an image which is used in the campaign to end the seal slaughter, does not transfer to the sealion. This can be understood in terms of neoteny, a complex set of perceptions which we will now discuss.

JUVENILIZATION: MICKEY MOUSE AND THE GIANT PANDA

In the case of the Barcelona Zoo show, a whale was shown to be like a naughty child; in other words, an attempt was made to juvenilize it. Some critics believe that in other societies there is present a belief that animals have something of significance to communicate to people. In these societies there is no suggestion that nature has a status of less than full maturity. We, on the other hand, have a tendency to turn animals into juveniles and infants. An important concept here is that of neoteny. Developed by Konrad Lorenz, neoteny describes those positive reactions to protecting the young which are released in man by those animals which correspond to the 'child schema'.

The child schema is represented by the following elements:

1 the forehead is prominent compared with the outline of the face as a whole, with the eyes positioned below the centre of the head;
2 relatively large eyes;
3 generally rounded form of head and body;
4 short extremities (in arms and legs);
5 soft elasticity of body surface.

24

In addition, the posture is pleasing if it can be maintained vertically. Even mature adult animals which retain these characteristics are likely to be treated as though they were human infants. The response to these characteristics can be seen in the case of the infant polar bear which seems to be a popular and crowd-drawing exhibit in whichever zoo it is found. In London in 1950 there was massive interest – three million visitors – in Brumus the newly born polar bear. The trouble with polar bears – unfortunately for the London Zoo administrators – is that they grow quickly, and consequently by 1951 attendance had gone down to two million. In other words there was a decrease in exhibition value.

Just as different individuals within different cultures perceive animals through unique cultural or conceptual filters, so, similarly, do perceptions vary with the age of an animal. For instance, turning to contemporary British society, Ramona and Desmond Morris alert us to two distinct types of animal symbolism practised by children. Younger children tend to see animals as parent figures, whereas older children see them more as infant figures. According to the Morris thesis, the young child, not yet rebellious, prefers animals to fit the role of the omnipotent parent. The older child, who in a sense competes with his parents, imitates them; so just as he is cared for, he in turn wishes to care for something (Morris and Morris, 1981: 170). The success of the marketing of the Care Bear doll, for example, can be attributed to these same processes.

Elizabeth Lawrence, a veterinary surgeon and anthropologist, argues that the juvenilization of fantasy animals in Disney's Magic Kingdom gives them a special capacity to bridge the gap that separates man and animal in the modern industrialized world. She argues that our sense of symbolic power over creatures deemed to be of lesser status delights us and envelops us in benign and patronizing mirth. For Lawrence to neotenize is to gain control; however, it also relieves us of the responsibility of understanding and respecting the animal in question for qualities intrinsic to their species. This indicates a lack of interest in the animal itself. What is important for the public is what they can draw out of the animal, especially in terms of affection, and in many cases such affective anthropomorphism can lead to misguided action. If we view an animal as a child the value of the animal therefore consists in its docility, playfulness and charm as a human companion, and animals that fail to meet such standards may well be written off as no use (Lawrence, 1983: 15). In Disney, the villainous animals significantly have the opposite features of neotenous ones, whereas Mickey Mouse, our lovable hero, has developed over time definite neotenous qualities.

The giant panda *(Ailuropoda melanoleuca)*, as we argued earlier, is a unique

'Though Micky tells us little about mice, he tells us a great deal about ourselves'
After Elizabeth Lawrence (1983: 19)

animal in the sense of its almost universal appeal. We say 'almost' because in some parts of the world it is treated as if it were merely another piece or item of the collection. Dr Gu of the Shanghai Zoological Gardens suggested that the popularity of the giant panda in China was in part a result of a similar process to that in the west – it was a 'funny animal', its black and white markings (incidentally, contrasting black and white coloration often seems to attract – witness the popularity of zebras, killer whales and penguins) were appealing, and it was regarded as a toy-like creature rather than as a zoological specimen. Such an image is not confined to the west for in Beijing Zoo there are two shops which sell a huge range of panda toys, models and photographs, although judging from the prices it is clear that these are aimed at foreign visitors. Chinese zoos though do exploit the juvenile and the toy-like image of pandas and may sell postcards of their pandas playing with dolls or footballs, or sitting on children's swings. Whether this is something which the zoo directors have imported, having seen how pandas have been treated in the west, is difficult to tell. What is certain is that the attention which is lavished on them has little to do with interest in the panda as a rare animal which has an existence in Chinese bamboo forests independent of human observers.

Although only forty-nine living specimens have been publicly viewed outside China, the giant panda is still in the top ten most-liked animals. Surveys show that the panda has been a particular favourite of the very young. One simple reason for this is that the giant panda appears sexless and thus harmless, as opposed for example to the essentially male gorilla, which elicits very different responses.

Morris and Morris, as we briefly noted in the Introduction, consider there to be a number of basic points in favour of an anthropomorphic appreciation of the panda:

1 It has a flat face.
   The human face is flattened, compared with most animals, and any species which resemble man in this way is at an advantage.

2 It appears to have large eyes.

Big eyes give an animal an innocent, child-like quality. Actually giant pandas do not have large eyes, but the black eye-patches nevertheless convey this impression.

3 It has little or no tail.

Human beings are tail-less and any species showing a similar condition, or having a short, inconspicuous tail, are at an advantage.

4 It sits up vertically.

Man is an upright species and any creature that regularly assumes the vertical position scores strong points, anthropomorphically. Penguins, for instance, are the most vertical of birds and are also the most popular.

5 It can manipulate small objects.

The famous sixth 'claw' of the giant panda gives it a unique anthropomorphic advantage over other species. 'To be able to sit up and carry small food objects up to its mouth gives it very human qualities indeed.'

6 It is a killer turned non-killer.

'Many carnivores are beautiful and popular animals, but they lose points because in order to survive they have to kill their prey.' The lion creates a difficult problem in this respect. It is such a beautiful and dignified creature that it gets into the 'top ten loves', yet it also attacks charming little antelopes and gazelles, with the result that it also gets into the 'top ten hates'. It is the only animal to find a place in both charts. The ambivalence it causes is not present in the case of the giant panda. Here is a species that is not only predominantly vegetarian, but has actually evolved from flesh-eating ancestors. Symbolically, it has 'seen the light and mended the wicked ways of its ancient predecessors'.

7 It is harmless and friendly towards human beings.

8 It is sexless.

9 It is playful.

'Human beings play a great deal. So do pandas, given a tyre, or a hose-pipe, or a step-ladder, a giant panda will quickly invent a whole series of gymnastics, just like a human child. Many animals never play and this works against them.'

10 It is clumsy.

This gives it all the appeal of a small child whose muscles have not yet fully matured.

11 It appears to be very soft.

Babies are soft to their mother's touch and vice-versa. Softness in animals is always appealing.

12 Its outline is rounded.

A rounded animal wins on the same principle as a soft one. Babies are rounded and the mother's breast is rounded.

13 It has an historical precursor.

'The teddy bear was already winning friends and influencing people' before the living panda came on the scene. Much of the groundwork for this particular kind of animal shape had been done. When the giant panda arrived as a kind of 'super teddy bear', it was able to build on the reputation of its plain-coloured ancestor.

14 It comes from a remote and mysterious habitat.

The almost impenetrable mountain forests where it makes its home are surrounded by mystery. 'This gives it an attractively romantic quality that a more home-grown species can never hope to acquire.' (Adapted from Morris and Morris, 1981: 712–6.)

CLASH OF MEANINGS

When we go to the zoo we take with us all our worries and our joys, our heroes and our villains, and we dole them out to the various species, casting each one in the role best equipped for it on the basis of accidental human resemblances.

(Morris and Morris, 1981: 172)

When we engage in anthropomorphic thinking we almost inevitably believe that we are somehow thinking or acting in such a way as to benefit the animal concerned. Jan Louwman of the Wassenaar Wildlife Breeding Centre in the Netherlands pointed out that this concern can often be misplaced. He noted that at one Dutch zoo a decision was taken to replace the iron bars of the orang-utan and gorilla cage with glass. This was certainly pleasing to the public because what originally gave the cage a prison image was now more aesthetically and emotionally acceptable. But what about the animals' point of view? They would hardly have thought about the prison image given by the bars, and anyway the glass still confined them in the same space. What was worse was that the animals were more restricted – a whole dimension of their space was removed because they could not climb glass as they had the bars. In many zoos it seems that there are clashes of meanings simply because humans impose their mental processes and sensibilities on animals rather than attempting to understand how an animal constructs and uses its world.

Some humans none the less do feel it proper to anthropomorphize and, within the zoo, to hand-rear and engage in interaction with the animals; others, however, suggest that the incorporation of such animals into the human world should be minimal. An important question to be considered therefore concerns the status of these captive animals. If the aim is not to turn them into domestic animals or pets, what do they become? Denied access to their natural habitat these animals become marginalized from their wild nature and begin to lose access to the mentalities and behaviours which would have been appropriate there. Such animals have a status akin to that of refugees. They are in enforced exile, but a false one at that because realistically there is no 'home' to return to.

Those animals which have their marginality reduced by being trained to interact with humans have their animality removed. An extreme case of the 'civilization' of animals by the famous zoo director Carl Hagenbeck is described who taught orang-utans and chimpanzees to behave correctly when eating:

They are not very dainty in their appetites, but like solid homely food, and devour it with great relish. At times they are given good red wine mixed with water, a beverage of which Jacob is decidedly fond, though Rosa with her more ladylike instincts cares little for it. Their manners at table are now perfectly refined and proper. Moritz acts as waiter, he has to bring in the food, which he does with great pomp and ceremony, and he has to clear away the things again after the meal is over. During the repast the apes sit patiently on chairs drawn up to the table, and await the various courses which are served to them. They eat after the manner of human beings with spoons and forks, and they are very clever at ladling up their soup with the spoon. It is true that if they thought no one was looking, they would quickly revert to more expeditious methods, dispensing with the spoon and using their lips instead; but a word from the keeper immediately recalls them to the manners of civilization and the spoon is hastily seized once more.

(1910: 282–3)

Today in Singapore Zoo, for quite a high fee, visitors can have an orang-utan to tea with them in one of the restaurants. Hagenbeck's audiences might have delighted in watching chimpanzees and orangutans eating like humans but a profound change is marked by the fact that people pay for the privilege of sharing their meal with an animal. Having an orangutan to tea is a reversal of the normal feeding pattern in the zoo in which the visitors throw food into the animal enclosure. In this case the animals are invited to leave their enclosure and join in the human condition. What this shows is an interesting mixing of the animal and human worlds — worlds which are normally sharply demarcated in the zoo.

Side by side with the development of anthropomorphism has been the equally mischievous development of zoomorphism. This is where we apply the concept of animal behaviour to human motivation and behaviour. Indeed, as Lockwood has noted, this has been followed by the more 'systematic application of principles of Darwinian fitness to human and non-human behaviour by contemporary sociobiologists who can be comfortable with freely interchanging terms drawn from studies of both human and animal behaviour' (1983: 5). Images of animalness and humanness are regularly interchanged in the contexts of violence, of madness and of institutions of human containment, the prison and asylum. It is to these that we now turn.

2
Containment and Control

The animality that rages in madness dispossesses man of what is specifically human in him.

(Michel Foucault, 1973: 74)

In crime, as in war, men revert in given circumstances to primitive conditions, often mistakenly described as animal-like.

(Heini Hediger, 1968: 3)

Human societies in different historical periods have created major social institutions in which living creatures are forcibly contained and controlled. In prisons, mental asylums and zoos, creatures are taken from their natural surroundings and, for differing reasons, held apart. All such institutions have separation as a key element in their construction even though this separation is differently managed and interpreted. They also share the characteristic that they demonstrate power relations. Prisons and mental hospitals are institutions of power in that they involve the forcible containment of those who are variously defined as problematic human beings, whereas power relations arise in zoos because in them human beings enforce the containment and display of animals in ways which unconsciously express attitudes usually of superiority and distance towards the natural world.

It is common in criticisms of the zoo as an institution to compare it, rather obviously, with the prison: in both institutions the inmates are held in captivity, often behind bars. The comparison with the mental asylum is perhaps less obvious and yet, as we will demonstrate, an analysis of the styles of containment and of the attitudes to those contained in both leads us to a better understanding of each. In general our point is that prisoners, the mentally ill and wild animals are ostensibly subject to containment for different reasons, yet a similarity of structures and themes can be discerned within the institutions that hold them.

As the sociologist Erving Goffman has pointed out, all social institutions such as hospitals, prisons, army barracks, boarding schools, ships and, we might add, zoos tend to construct and define a total enclosed world for their members. Within such institutions the members lead highly structured lives which are subject to both strict control and intensive surveillance. Such

31

institutions establish barriers against open social intercourse with the outside world – barriers which are often physical constructions such as walls, fences, gates and bars, although outsiders may enter to visit, again in a highly structured way, those on the inside.

A common-sense attitude might be that these institutions are clearly different in that prisons and mental asylums contain fellow human beings whereas zoos contain mere animals, but such a distinction is not always easy to maintain in an historical perspective.

THE HUMAN FREAK: MAN OR BEAST

Deformity in humans often leads to their being categorized not as fellow human beings but as more closely akin to animals. One of the earliest-known zoos, that of Montezuma in Mexico, consisted not only of a vast collection of animals, but also exhibited unusual human beings – for example, dwarves, albinos and hunchbacks. Prescott, in his description of the zoo as it was in 1519, observed that at the time there was a:

strange collection of human monsters, dwarves, and other unfortunate persons, in whose organization Nature had capriciously deviated from her regular laws. Such hideous anomalies were regarded by the Aztecs as a suitable appendage of state. It is even said, they were in some cases the results of artificial means, employed by unnatural parents desirous to secure a provision for their offspring by thus qualifying them for a place in the royal museum.

(1847: 320)

At the end of the eighteenth century the famous 'wild boy' of Aveyron was lodged for a while at the foremost scientific zoo of the time in Europe, the Jardin des Plantes in Paris, before Jean Itard took him into his own home. Although not there for the purpose of exhibition or public entertainment, it is perhaps significant that as an ambiguous human being it was seen as appropriate to lodge him in such a place.

Many of the menageries in England in the eighteenth and nineteenth centuries exhibited strange and unusual humans as well as rarely seen and exotic animals. Among the monkeys, elephants, bears, lions and tigers could be seen completely hairy women, giants and giantesses, bearded women, boneless children, fireproof people, humanoid animals and midgets of which the most famous was probably General Tom Thumb, who was brought to England in 1838 by Barnum the legendary showman. Among the visitors to such shows in England was the diarist Samuel Pepys. At one exhibition of giants displayed together with their normal-sized siblings, Pepys noted, 'but Lord, how strange it is to observe the difference between the same children, came out of the same woman's belly' (quoted in Altick, 1978: 36). On these visits Pepys would often have met fellow members of the Royal Society, such as Robert Hooke, whose diary jottings referring to his attendance at such shows, while more terse, further illustrate the variety of exhibitions which even men of science of the period visited:

saw India catt, Japan peacock, Porcupine, Upupa, Vultur, Great Owl, 3 Cassawaris (1672); Saw Elephant 3sh (1675); Saw tigre in Bartholomew Fair 2d (1677); Saw Elephant have colours, shoot a gun, bend and kneel, carry a castle and a man, etc. (1679); To fire[e]ater in Gracechurch Street (1675/76); saw the Dutch woman in Bartholomew Fair, very strange (1677); she was a giantess; saw boneless child (1677).

(Altick, 1978: 36)

The diary continued with a further reference to this last item, noting that the child was 'a girl, above Sixteen years of Age, born in Cheshire, and not above Eighteen inches long, having shed the Teeth several times, and not a perfect Bone in any part of her only the Head; yet she had all her senses to Admiration, and Discourses, Reads very well, Sings, Whistles, and all very pleasant to hear' (quoted in Altick, 1978: 36–7).

Just as unusual or deformed people were regarded in a similar light to exotic animals and were exhibited with them, so the mentally deranged were regarded as more animal than human, and were a source of amusement and entertainment in asylums. In his study of madness from the Middle Ages to the eighteenth century, Michel Foucault has shown both that the insane were on display to the public and how pervasive the image of animality was with regard to the interpretation of the behaviour of the insane and their treatment within the institutions which housed them. In the asylums the often cold and damp cage-like rooms had nothing more than straw and a pallet for the 'patients' to sleep on, and the more dangerous were often chained. Madmen were not treated as full human beings, because they were thought to be related to the animal world in all its strangeness. It is highly significant that what is normal behaviour in animals – their unrestrained wildness – is equated with human madness, that is abnormal behaviour. It is this, humans acting as animals, which was a source of delight for many. What matters for our study is not that the insane were denied their full humanity but rather that people came to watch them. One consequence of this was that the inmate was denied his privacy as he was thrust as an unwilling actor on to a public stage. For instance in Paris it was common for people to visit Bicêtre on a Sunday to be entertained by the mad (see Foucault, 1973: 68), and Edward O'Donoghue in his study of Bedlam finds a reference to a visit there as early as 1522 by Thomas More (O'Donoghue, 1914: 106). Ellenberger describes Bedlam in the following manner:

On each side of the gate there was a column capped by a statue of madness personified by a grimacing head, as today a carved elephant might decorate the entrance to a zoo . . . a Sunday visit to Bedlam was one of London's great amusements. It has been calculated that throughout most of the eighteenth century Bedlam received an average of three hundred visitors a day. They entered through 'penny gates', so called because the admission charge was a penny. The sums paid by the visitors constituted one of the asylum's most important sources of revenue. The visitor, after checking his sword in the vestibule, had the right to wander through all the wings, look in all the cells, speak to the patients and make fun of them. In exchange for all the rejoinders, he might give the patients something to eat, or he might give them alcohol to stimulate them further. A Hogarth print shows a degenerate terminating a career of vice in Bedlam, chained in a squalid cell while two elegant visitors look over him as if he were some curious beast. Probably the inmates of Bedlam seemed more agitated and more 'mad' than our present-day patients.

(Ellenberger, 1974: 69–70)

Robert Reed's *Bedlam on the Jacobean Stage* (1970) is more circumspect in its descriptions of Bedlam with its general culture of madness. He points out that as far as entertainment in the asylum was concerned the 'stars' were most likely those who were destined to remain longest in the hospital. They were, for example, victims of 'phrenitis that persisted until they became chronic maniacs', sufferers also from the more aggravated forms of melancholia, 'such as delusional insanity', which by Jacobean interpretation resulted from 'adjustion of the humour', and, finally, victims of extreme forms of mania who, although they had small hope of cure, had to be confined in order to prevent them from causing disturbance. Reed also notes that it is 'well to remember that the inmates of old Bethlehem, unlike inmates of a modern asylum, were constantly agitated not only by the disconcerting conditions imposed by the poor management of the hospital, but also by the visitors themselves'. Undoubtedly, 'the mad folk were often subjected to goading and, when this practice may not have sufficed, they were sometimes plied with liquor' (1970: 32). While the 'ordinary' visitor walked and talked with the inmates in their cage-like rooms, the more honoured visitors (like Pepys and his contemporary John Aubrey) would have inmates brought to the parlour where they would

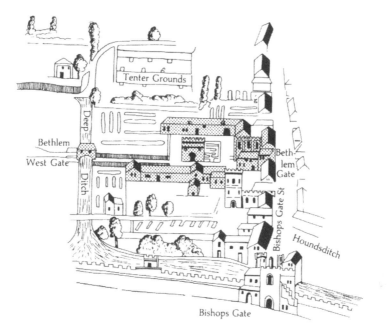

Plan of the first Bethlem Hospital (Tuke, 1882).

be entertained by the antics of some of the 'star' inmates.

Daniel Tuke's first mention *Chapters in the History of the Insane* 1882 quotes the contents of a diary kept by the London journalist Ned Ward including a visit to Bedlam in 1703, probably the best account of a visit there:

Accordingly we were admitted in thro' an iron gate, within which sat a brawny cerberus, of an Indigo-colour, leaning upon a money box; we turned in through another Iron-Barricado, where we heard such a rattling of chains, drumming of doors, ranting, hollowing, singing, and running, that I could think of nothing but Don Quevedo's Vision, where the lost souls broke loose and put Hell in an uproar. The first whimsey-headed wretch of this lunatic family that we observed, was a merry fellow in a straw cap, who was talking to himself, 'that he had an army of Eagles at this command', then clapping his hand upon his head, swore by his crown of moonshine, he would battle all the stars in the skies, but he would have some claret.... We then moved on till we found another remarkable figure worth our observing, who was peeping through his wicket, eating of bread and cheese, talking all the while like a carrier at his supper, chewing his words with his victuals, all that he spoke being in praise of bread and cheese; 'bread was good with cheese, and

cheese was good with bread, and bread and cheese was good together', and abundance
of such stuff; to which my friend and I, with others stood listening; at last he
counterfeits a sneeze, and shot such a mouthful of bread and cheese amongst us that
every spectator had some share of his kindness, which made us retreat.

(Quoted in Tuke, 1882: 76–7)

If animality made madness a thing to be seen it also, to a lesser extent, made it a thing to be heard. Elaine Showalter writes of the 'howling maniacs' of Bedlam (1981: 313), which people paid to hear. Likewise part of the excitement of the menagerie was the goading of animals, in order to experience the roar of the lion, the monkey's shriek and the growling of the bear.

Returning to Foucault's central observation of the potency of the image of animality, this profound tendency to animalize the bewildered, the chemically imbalanced or merely unhappy mental inmate redirected both the diagnostic and voyeuristic responses to madness. Quite simply madness, as Foucault shows, became a thing to look at. Madness was no longer a condition to be merely laughed at, although that of course still persisted, nor was it to be locked away and ignored, hidden or forgotten. Rather, it became a living spectacle. The madman and the madwoman exhibit the same sort of grimaces, facial tensions, gnashing of teeth and unseeing eyes that could be seen during a tantalizingly fearsome and yet secure visit to a caged wild beast. It is highly significant that the foremost menagerie in London and the most famous mental hospital seem to have been regarded as essential sights for the visitor to the city, an association which can be seen in the example of Lord Percy with Lady Penelope and her two sisters, who, taking in the sights of London, 'saw the lions (in the Tower), the show of Bethlehem (the mental hospital), the place where the prince was created and the fireworks at the Artillery Gardens' (quoted in Reed, 1970: 23).

Although the hospital inmates were human, the visitors were not coming to view fellow human beings, for their deranged behaviour robbed them of their full humanity. The equation of the beast in the menagerie and the madman in the asylum is quite understandable for, as Andrew Scull points out, if in seventeenth- and eighteenth-century practice the 'madman in confinement was treated no better than a beast, that merely reflected his ontological status. For that was precisely what, according to the prevailing paradigm of insanity, he was' (1981c: 108). It was the controlled operation of reason which separated man from animal, for as William Bynum argues:

Insanity was conceived as a derangement of those very faculties that were widely assumed to be unique to man; as a matter of fact, we sometimes find in the literature the presumed absence in animals of any condition analogous to sanity taken as proof that man's highest psychological functions result from some principle totally lacking in other animals, that is, the soul.

(1981: 39)

Such notions were indicative of the dominant world-view of the period. Indeed such notions could be viewed as confirmation of one of the period's critical organizing principles, namely the idea of the continuity and gradation of nature in what Arthur Lovejoy has termed 'the Great Chain of Being'. As Scull argues, the very idea of a chain, with no discontinuities or gaps, 'implied that no rigid barriers existed between one part of creation and another, that there always existed intermediate forms'. Scull adds:

The division between apes and men was a permeable, not an absolute one in eighteenth-century conceptions of nature — an assumption which was exemplified in a number of different ways: in the denial of the concept of common humanity to the slave; the ready identification of apes and savages (even extending to speculation on fertile copulation between blacks and apes); the portrayal of criminals in animalistic terms; and the assimilation of the mad to the ranks of brute creation.

(1981c: 109)

To the eighteenth-century mind the lunatic's apparent insensitivity to heat or cold, hunger or pain, his refusal to abide clothing, that is to say his indifference to normal human concerns, were simply taken as confirmation of the correctness of the basic explanatory schema.

If madness deprives man of his humanity it is hardly surprising that the subsequent treatment of the madman was in keeping with the containment of real animals. The techniques of force and fear are appropriate to the management of 'brutes'. Thus, when we look at the treatment of the insane prior to 'reform',* we must realize that it was considered, as Foucault points out, that 'unchained animality could be mastered only by *discipline* and *brutalizing*' (1973: 75). We may add that Foucault's use of the term 'brutalizing' is particularly apt, for both men and animals were connected by the derogatory term 'brute'.

---

*As a result of reforms in the nineteenth century, asylum inmates began to be treated as full human beings. It is not until the middle of the twentieth century that there is significant reform in the zoo when, in some cultures, people began to regard animals as having rights and humans as having a certain obligation to them.

THE PRODUCTION OF DOCILITY

One of the most visible behavioural characteristics of the inmates of both the mental asylum and the zoo is that the inmates cannot live normal lives they do not have to engage in behaviour directed to maintaining themselves in the world, and this contributes to lethargy together with an apparent lack of interest in the world about them. How is this change of character induced by captivity? A suggestive line of enquiry comes from Russell Barton's 1959 study of institutional neurosis in the asylum. Barton states that patients enter into the mental hospital with one illness and the hospital may independently give them another. Among the clinical features of this syndrome are apathy, lack of initiative, loss of interest in the outside world, submissiveness and resignation. Although obviously animals are not 'committed' to the zoo as patients are to the asylum, for they have no disease, the conditions in the institution undoubtedly cause a complex change in their character such that the animal equally suffers from apathy, lack of initiative, loss of interest in the outside world and submissiveness. Barton identifies the causes of institutional neurosis as:

1 *loss of contact with the outside world*
2 *enforced idleness;*
3 *authoritarianism of staff;*
4 *loss of personal friends, personal possessions and personal events;*
5 *effects of drugs;*
6 *ward atmosphere of poor furniture, decoration and lighting, poor diet, noise, unpleasant smells, and the appearance of other patients;*
7 *loss of prospects.*

(1959: 17)

Some of these factors are exclusively physical in nature, others more organizational and cultural.

A comparable list might well be produced for the captive animal:

1 separation from natural habitat;
2 enforced idleness;
3 direct control by humans;
4 loss of life in normal social groups;
5 drugs, and medical and fertility control;
6 caging, a totally alien environment with artificial infrastructures, lighting, artificial diet, unusual noise, strange odours and the unnatural proximity of both alien species and the human visitor.

Obvious parallels in organizational culture can be seen in the day-to-day management of both institutions. The traditional tour of inspection of the zoo by the director and higher members of his staff at the beginning of each day and the consultant's ward round symbolize power relationships especially in relation to the intermediary staff. The visits illustrate the tendency for both the animals and the insane to be looked at rather than treated as equal partners in a social and visual interaction. In the zoo the animals, of course, are also looked at by the visiting public.

Furthermore both institutions operate with strict timetables, which manage everyone's reality. One of the first daily tasks for the hospital attendants and for keepers is to release their charges from night confinement, whether this be their beds or their cages, and into the more public arena of the ward/dayroom or the outdoor enclosure. Just as patients are fed at set meal times during the day, events which give a sense of the day passing for them, so too the animals' sense of time and rhythm of existence is to a large extent determined by the ritual of feeding. At the end of each day patients and animals are given 'free time' and both are, in a sense, taken off the public stage. Animals are then free from the stress of public gaze, as are the mental inmates, who similarly are free from kind and not so kind visitors and staff. The majority of mental inmates can then bed themselves, but a few have to be assisted or even coerced into night-time submission. The animal population, in the majority of cases, have to be lured from the now empty public stage and into prepared sleeping quarters.

HUMAN CAGE

The specialized architecture of asylums, prisons and zoos emphasizes separation, such that those within it are forced to submit to the will of others; a stance of submission is seen to express both a necessary and an appropriate relationship between the keepers and the kept. This was exactly the situation in the late Victorian era in England, where, as Scull points out, the mental asylum itself was the major weapon in the 'struggle to cure the insane'. This, he adds, marks a 'profound contrast with the eighteenth century', where neither the 'private madhouses nor the charity asylums of the period can be thought of reasonably as purpose-built' in the sense in which that term becomes applicable in the nineteenth century. Scull argues:

Little connection was seen at the time between architecture and cure, the latter being held to depend (if it were possible at all) on various forms of physical treatments. Apart from its uses for decorative purposes or for show (for example, the exterior of

*the second Bethlem, built in 1676, was modelled on the Tuileries), the architecture
of these places was primarily designed to secure 'the safe confinement and
imprisonment of lunatics'. Consequently, later generations often commented on the
'prison-mindedness of eighteenth-century insane asylum designers'.*

(1981a: 9–10)

This is perhaps not surprising if one considers, for example, that George Dance
the Younger, the architect of St Luke's Hospital, probably the most influential
of the eighteenth-century English charity asylums, was also responsible for
the design of the new Newgate Prison. John Walton, in his study of the
Lancashire Asylum in England (1816–70), describes the architecture of the
asylum in such a way that the reader cannot help but draw an analogy between
it and the prison. For it had 'high windows with "strong iron bars", "massive
iron gates", gloomy rooms, chains, and leg locks', which were accepted as part
of the natural order of asylum management. He adds that in the 1830s in
Lancaster the attendants were known as 'keepers' and wore a 'police-like garb'
(1981: 171–9).

The images produced by Walton are reminiscent of the zoos of the same
period, where in an attempt to contain and control the wild animals there was
a similar exaggeration of restraint. In both institutions the structure and
technique of control were based on the strategy of attempting to cope with
unpredictability. Wildness, whether human or animal, was seen as potentially
chaotic and hence dangerous, and therefore had to be totally controlled.

Foucault is particularly instructive on the methods of control in the prison.
For example, he bases his account of discipline on the premise that it proceeds
from the 'distribution of individuals in space', and to achieve this end it
employs several techniques. First, 'discipline sometimes requires *enclosure*, the
specification of a place heterogeneous to all others and closed in upon itself.
It is the protected place of disciplinary monotony' (1979: 141). This requirement
was incorporated into the structure of asylums, prisons and indeed zoos.
Foucault proceeds with the claim that this principle of enclosure is insufficient
in itself because the disciplinary machinery 'works space' in a much more
flexible and detailed way. It does this first of all on the principle of 'elementary
location or *partitioning*. Each individual has his own place; and each place has
its individual':

*Its aim was to establish presences and absences, to know where and how to locate
individuals, to set up useful communications, to interrupt others, to be able at each
moment to supervise the conduct of each individual, to assess it, to judge it, to*

calculate its qualities or its merits. It was a procedure, therefore, aimed at knowing, mastering and using. Discipline organizes an analytical space.

(Foucault, 1979: 143)

Just as each prisoner is confined to his individual cell within which he is framed as a known individual, so in the menagerie at this time individual animals were located in individual space, an isolation which was not merely for the purposes of simple physical control but moreover represented a categorization usually in terms of local–cultural taxonomy.

A brief and selective survey of the history of prison architecture allows us to examine the changing nature and increased specialization of spaces of control. Norman Johnston's 1973 study, *The Human Cage*, emphasizes that early places of confinement were crude structures, seldom built for the use to which they were finally put. They were likely to be no more than strong cages within a fortress or castle, or subterranean portions of public buildings. Although both classical Greece and Rome are reported to have used stone quarries as prisons, and a number of large public prisons existed in Rome for different kinds of offenders, the only place of confinement about which there is much detailed information is the Mamertine Prison:

Begun about 640 BC *by Ancus Martius, and later enlarged, it appears to have been a 'vast system of dungeons' constructed, for the most part, under the* Cloaca Maxima, *the main sewer of Rome. The construction existing in the late 19th century consisted of two chambers, one below the other. The upper room measured 30 × 22 feet and received light from a hole in the ceiling 16 feet above the floor. The lower chamber, which was reached by means of an aperture in the floor of the room above, was cone-shaped with a diameter of 20 feet and was completely dark.*

(Johnston, 1973: 5)

In the medieval period all that can be said for certain is that the structures which were developed for keeping prisoners were invariably substantial and secure. Some fortresses, of course, were used primarily for prisoners of state and consequently gained sinister reputations: the Tower of London, the Bastille, Vincennes and Bicêtre in France, and Petropavlovsk in Russia are examples.

The sixteenth century's answer in some countries in Europe to the growth of social unrest, petty crime and vagrancy was the workhouse (or house of correction), an institution built around the supposed rehabilitative value of regular work together with the formation of 'habits of industry'. Workhouses were frequently constructed in the form of a hollow square, much like the hospitals and convents of the time; indeed many were located in buildings once used for such purposes.

The use of cellular confinement, in the modern sense of the term, is usually traced, according to Johnston, to the famous *casa di correzione* established in the hospice of San Michele in Rome in 1704. The architect, Carlo Fontana, was probably influenced considerably by knowledge of Dutch workhouses. He designed:

a rectangular structure with 30 outside rooms or cells arranged on three tiers with balconies or galleries on each level. Each cell contained a mattress and had a latrine, an outside window, and a solid door with a small aperture opening onto the balconies, which could be closed from without by a small covering. These sleeping rooms faced a large centre hall which was used as workroom, dining room and a chapel. The boys, with leg chains, worked in silence manufacturing articles for the Vatican state.

(Johnston, 1973: 12)

In 1772 a house of correction was established in Ghent (Austrian Flanders) by the then government. The principles governing the institution had never before been put into practice together: night isolation of prisoners, separation of the sexes and separation of prisoners of the same sex according to categories based on age, degree of criminality and length of sentence. Importantly, Ghent can be regarded as the first large-scale penal institution in which 'a conscious attempt was made to bring architecture to the aid of the treatment philosophy' (Johnston, 1973: 13). We noted earlier a similar evolutionary process with respect to the lunatic asylum, but in relation to the menagerie it would seem that cellular confinement was from the beginning the most typical form of containment.

In the eighteenth and early nineteenth centuries different characteristics developed, but most often circular, polygonal and radial layouts were conceived. The most forceful exponent of the circular forms for prisons was Jeremy Bentham, who in 1787 proposed a blueprint for a prison (based on an idea developed in Russia for a circular textile mill where all the workers could be observed easily). Described as a 'totalitarian housing project' by Aldous Huxley, Bentham's Panopticon prison was never in fact built, but it did serve as a model for others. Indeed several circular institutions were built in Spain in 1852 and in Holland in the 1880s. Johnston adds:

A large number of semi-circular prisons were built in Ireland, Scotland and England and several on the Continent in the 30 years following the Panopticon *proposal, in most cases either directly or indirectly influenced by Bentham's efforts. The* D-shaped *Edinburgh House of Correction contained 129 'sleeping closets' and 52 much larger 'working cages'. At the centre of the half circle was a 'dark apartment...from which the governor or his deputy without being themselves visible, can see at a glance what is doing in all parts of the house'. Although this institution was roofed over between inspection towers and cells, most jails were not, and in fact the original degree of surveillance intended by Bentham was usually quite impossible.*

(1973: 21)

Foucault argues that Bentham's Panopticon demonstrates that 'visibility is a trap'. It is an element of hierarchical observation. The exercise of discipline, in other words, presupposes a mechanism that coerces by means of observation. The Panopticon functions as a kind of 'laboratory of power' (Foucault, 1979: 205).

Foucault speculates that Bentham was in fact inspired by the design of the menagerie built for Louis xiv at Versailles. As we argue in greater detail in chapter 5, in terms of design this menagerie was particularly novel in that rather than have the animal enclosures or houses spread over the extent of a park, Louis decided to concentrate them in one place. Central to the menagerie was an octagonal pavilion, from seven sides of which radiated the animals' cages. These could be viewed from the pavilion's balcony (Loisel, 1912: vol. 2, 104, 108). One finds, as Foucault points out, in the programme of the Panopticon 'a similar concern with individualizing observation, with characterization and classification, with the analytical arrangement of space. The *Panopticon* is a royal menagerie; the animal is replaced by man, individual distribution by specific grouping, and the king by the machinery of a furtive power' (1979: 203).

As we will have cause to illustrate later, the designs behind European menageries were exported to other non-European nations. Similarly there was a parallel process in the exportation of prison design. For example, early Latin American prisons were almost always radial, a reflection of either direct North American or British and continental influences. Following 'prison reform' in Japan, the first of the new prisons, Miyagi (1879), was designed by an English architect, and until recently the most common plan in the Japanese prisons, as in the 1879 design for Tokyo, has been that of Pentonville in England. Johnston concludes his account of pre-twentieth-century structures by stressing the continuation of the use of gothic style and notes that by the 'second half of the nineteenth century these façades had taken on the curious Victorian "gingerbread" appearance of most city halls, schools, orphanages and hospitals of the time, so that the only thing which distinguished them as prisons was the high stone or concrete wall which was invariably attached' (1973: 41). When we examine nineteenth-century architectural styles in the zoo we find similar processes at work (fanciful reproductions of castles, mosques and temples), and the only thing which distinguished them at all as zoos was the exotic creatures they contained.

Driven by a more humanitarian spirit, the twentieth century has seen an attempt to renovate or displace the nineteenth-century prisons. However, despite the number of reforms that have been made, which have resulted in the elimination of some of the prison-like qualities of prisons, they remain prisons — closed institutions of control. Johnston concludes his journey into prison history damningly, and employs, as Foucault does of asylums, the term 'brutalize':

Prison structures have continued to be built in a way which manages by one means or another to brutalize their occupants and to deprive them of their privacy, dignity, and self-esteem, while at the same time strengthening their criminality. The nineteenth century allowed vast and dreary buildings and physical cruelty to grind down the prisoner. The contemporary prison seems to allow mechanical contrivances to dominate the prisoner.

(1973: 54)

Although, in reforming countries, many of the prison-like qualities of zoos have been removed, the animals must none the less be contained. Within the structure of the prison, reforming governors developed more social welfare concerns in order to ameliorate the conditions for the prisoners. Similarly reforming zoo directors have concerned themselves with the social welfare of the animals in an attempt to get them out of the cage and into conditions which in however restricted a manner allow them some semblance of normality.

But it is far easier to create diversions for humans than for animals, because unlike the human inmate who may devise his own keep-fit programme or exercises in mental stimulation, the animal is more limited in that capacity. Attempts at 'behavioural enrichment' (see Markowitz, 1982) may range from the removal of an animal from solitary confinement and into a social group, to the provision of equipment within the enclosure in order to stimulate the animal: climbing frames, food that has to be foraged for, and a whole collection of playthings. Thanks to man's cognitive complexity, with its powerful memory capacities and with constant reinforcement from the previous personal and social environment, the human in prison can recreate normal life in the imagination although it cannot be lived out. In the prison there is no attempt to pretend that the inmates can live a normal life, whereas in the zoo this is exactly what some directors think they can achieve for those in their care.

What we have tried to argue here is that the comparisons in terms of genesis, process, structure and development of the three institutions help advance our thesis that zoos are about humans, for zoos tell us stories of human power, the exercise of control and domination. Although we have used both prisons and mental institutions for the purpose of comparison, our concern is not with their social history, and thus we must proceed to a more specific analysis of the architecture of the zoo itself.

3
Zoo Architecture

... I received a protest that was perfectly understandable from an Indian Muslim
against animals being kept in a mosque-like building. He could have found other
buildings of this kind in many European zoos at that time. His argument was that
European Christians would probably not have appreciated it if animals in the
Orient were kept in church buildings.

(Heini Hediger, 1970: 201)

Prisons and asylums have been compared in chapter 2 with zoos in order to shed light on the complex cultural processes at work in the maintenance of a captive population of wild animals for public presentation and in the response to that presentation. As we said earlier we do not wish to claim that there is an exact equivalence between the three institutions (there are of course significant differences between prisons and asylums themselves), for it must always be borne in mind that prisons and asylums process human beings while zoos process animals. As John Berger has argued:

All sites of marginalization – ghettos, shanty towns, prisons, madhouses,
concentration camps – have something in common with zoos. But it is too easy and
too evasive to use the zoo as a symbol, the zoo is a demonstration of the relations
between man and animals: nothing else.

(1980: 24)

It is therefore necessary to focus more precisely on that relationship between man and animals in terms of the physical structures in which animals are housed in captivity.

The very notion of 'housing' and 'home' points to an interesting set of anthropomorphic attitudes because animals do not have a home in the sense that human beings do and yet one finds a Lion House, Elephant House, Monkey House and Reptile House in many zoos. Of course they construct a variety of shelters for themselves – nests, burrows, dens – but can this species-specific behaviour really be termed architecture? It is highly doubtful whether animals can reflect on the nature of the shelters they build or concern themselves with questions of style; they do not think about or plan the sort of shelter they would like, and unlike humans they do not purposely set out to build it. Animal constructions have a design in the sense that they have a particular shape but this is not an expression of meaning, it is a given; style here is utility. All natural swallows' nests are more or less similar and the same is true of polar-bear dens in the wild. However, a polar-bear den in Philadelphia Zoo is not the same as one in Singapore Zoo, and indeed one built in 1887 is unlikely to be similar to one built in 1987. Each represents a product of human thought and culture, and whether conscious or unconscious these designs are expressive. They are the result of human interpretation of how the natural world is to be presented.

Various forms of containment are shaped for animals to live in, whether these be small cages for household pets, aquaria, or stables, sheds and pens for domestic animals. The style of all of these indicates aspects of how humans perceive their relationships with animals. As A.H.N. Green-Armytage puts it, zoo architecture is a 'unique branch of the art because in the nature of things the customer, the creature that is going to live in the building, cannot be consulted.... Few if any wild animals, for instance, would choose to live in full view of human beings, yet in a zoo they must.' (1964: 71) The building of shelters for animals therefore is a further example of the attempt to bring them within the sphere of human control and to shape the human experience of them. In other words, it constitutes a framing device. The zoo, in that it is a space containing wild animals in what is predominantly an urban environment, is in itself a frame; this frame ensures that our experience of the zoo animal is qualitatively different from our experience of that very same animal in a different setting. Individual species are further framed *within* the zoo by a particular style of enclosure.

The construction of the zoo is a complex process, for not only must it be ensured that animals do not escape or mix with each other, but in addition the enclosures must be suitable for exhibiting the animals. All architecture is a process of creating and shaping space, and in the zoo the space has to be created for two sets of creatures. The animals must be housed, but the area between the cages or enclosures is highly significant for it is the zone of human movement – our space in the zoo.

In the earliest zoos the physical presence of the living animal was the only important factor. The concern was to confine the animals and yet allow for their maximum visibility. It was only later, in fact well into the twentieth century, that people began to become concerned with the quality of the presentation of the animal and the quality of life within the cage or enclosure. In early zoos in Europe for example – and this attitude can still be found in many parts of the world – there was no particular interest in seeing the natural behaviour of animals in the zoos, rather visitors simply wanted to see the unusual.

The designers of the earliest menageries or zoo buildings showed no real concern for the needs of the animals. Instead they were preoccupied with shaping that part of the building which surrounded the basic brick or iron enclosed area in which the animals lived. Menageries from the earliest times, such as that of Louis xiv at Versailles in 1662 or the imperial menagerie at Schönbrunn in 1752, were designed to please the visitors rather than to promote the welfare of the animals held in them. From a modern perspective these buildings would be totally unacceptable for habitation by animals. Of course their architects had no desire to cause suffering to the animals – it must be remembered that until well into the twentieth century very little was known about animal behaviour and zoologists themselves did not concern themselves with such matters. The architecture was not specifically designed to accommodate the animals' needs but rather was intended to create a mood in order to emphasize what was felt to be some cultural quality associated with the animal.

The zoos of the nineteenth and early twentieth centuries in many parts of the world were, as David Hancocks has argued (1971), conspicuously attractive edifices designed in whatever was the then current fashionable style. They were places for outings in pleasant surroundings. In France, for example, Parisians could stroll through the Jardin des Plantes and enjoy a combination of elegant architecture, strange animals and beautiful flowers. Hancocks himself quotes the case of Berlin Zoo, which stressed the 'exotic east', and where most of the 'houses [were] exact imitations of Chinese pagodas and Indian temples. The magnificent elephant house was built in the form of a Hindu temple, with domes painted yellow, brown and blue. Huge columns supporting the roof had carved elephants' heads for capitals, and in the centre of the house stood the skeleton of a full-grown elephant.' Hancocks notes that the:

ostrich house, based on Egyptian architecture, was decorated both inside and out with copies of Egyptian murals, and on the back wall of the public area two immense figures, painted in a sitting position, were bathed in a deep and glorious sunset. Likewise the giraffe house, which was elliptical in plan, was decorated with minarets, each pierced with a large golden sphere.

(1971: 110–11)

The practice of exhibiting exotic animals in exotic buildings was not confined to Berlin. Gordon Woodroffe, for instance, refers to Antwerp's Egyptian temple, which was a faithful reproduction of an ancient temple on the Isle of

Philae. Moorish-looking elephant houses were common (and can still be seen at Cologne and Lisbon), and Arabian-styled temples and African-type huts were designed at 'Budapest for elephants and hippos respectively; mosques and wooden Swiss-type chalets for ungulates – dark, forbidding and riddled with rats – were favourites' (Woodroffe 1981: 43). Not only does this reveal a great deal about human attitudes to animals and about how architects went about creating a sense of the exotic, but it also exposes western European attitudes to the foreign peoples that they were busy colonizing (see for example Edward Said, 1985, and V.G. Kiernan, 1969).

As we have indicated, this architecture was not in any sense for the benefit of animals but rather was designed to produce a sense of the exotic. Architectural styles and buildings of cultural significance were transposed from their indigenous setting to the rather trivial situation of the zoo where they functioned as shelter for wild animals. In other words, from the chantings of mantras and the human devotional experience we move both continents and cultures to a German public being entertained by the elephant. From the perspective of late-twentieth-century cultural awareness, we can share Hediger's earlier recognition of the derogatory manifestation of cultural imperialism. However, we must constantly bear in mind that the nineteenth-century zoo architect was operating with a set of mental constructs and moral sensibilities radically different from our post-colonial ones. In other words such architecture was not designed to be degrading.

It would be wrong to suppose that such architectural styles were confined to those societies directly involved in the colonizing process, for they are to be found in the New World. Indeed the zoo which most completely exemplifies the style of the period is that of Buenos Aires; and this style is still visible.

JARDÍN ZOOLOGICO DE LA CIUDAD DE BUENOS AIRES

At the turn of the nineteenth century there was both considerable wealth and a sense of progress in Buenos Aires, which was expressed in part in the construction of ornate parks in the city. The founding of the zoo arose out of the development of the Parque Tres de Mayo, designed specifically for the recreation of the upper classes.

The monumental buildings of the zoo reflected the sense of the wealth and prestige of the time. As Luis Pereya, one of the current architects of the zoo, remarked, they reflect a period when 'the animals were mere objects of curiosity and the impression given by the buildings was more important than how the animals were exhibited'. As well as buildings for the animals there was a range of objects designed to beautify the park and to offer services, each of which was 'artistic'. The main gate was a copy of the Titus arch in Rome, there are imitations of Byzantine ruins from Trieste, there are statues in neo-classical and Romantic styles, there is a room for nursing mothers, the Temple of Vesta, built in Corinthian style, tea rooms, a theatre, administrative buildings, fountains and wells, all of which emphasize good taste and style. Indeed on visiting the zoo the impression one still has is that the striking buildings were designed to be imposing, to be noticed and to be admired as pieces of architecture. But it is important to remember that they were none the less designed as zoo buildings, there for the specific purpose of exhibiting animals.

The architect clearly attempted to stress the exotic nature and curiosity value of the animals by his choice of design. The giraffes, for example, were housed in a way which was supposed to evoke the Arab world. The slender columns and arches and the geometric designs on bright white walls were obviously inspired by pictures of mosques. Elephants were kept in a highly ornate building called the Temple of Nimaschi decorated by Hindu statues – a replica of a temple constructed by the Rajah of Tirumal in Bombay. A brightly painted Japanese pagoda was a shelter for a group of Japanese deer; there was a small Egyptian-style house with a pavilion for monkeys; the big cats were in an elaborate Renaissance-style pavilion (a copy of that in Breslau); a vast German gothic castle housed the bears; an English cottage sheltered the European deer; and the hippos had a concrete copy of a Congo hut.

There was no attempt to recreate the natural environment of the creatures in the zoo. Indeed the buildings indicated that there was no desire to understand the context of these animals, their actual place in the natural world. There was no desire to transport visitors imaginatively to the jungle, the desert or the mountain peaks – people were simply not there for an experience of the natural world. Rather animals on display were strange creatures from distant lands and that quality was emphasized by relating them to a series of images of the strange human societies which inhabited the same far-off places. Elements of human cultural styles become indicators of distance and difference and are used therefore as markers for the animals.

THE MODERN ZOO

In the early twentieth century there was a major reform in zoo architecture and exhibition philosophy which can be attributed to the imagination of one man, the German Carl Hagenbeck. Hagenbeck was one of Europe's leading suppliers of wild animals to zoos and circuses, until he decided to create a zoo of his own. His zoo at Stellingen on the outskirts of Hamburg opened in 1907 and was to have an enormous impact on the zoo world as a whole; even now basic Hagenbeck designs are being created around the world.

Hagenbeck had seen animals in the wild and wanted to create a zoo where he could give an impression of how these animals really lived. As he wrote in his autobiography, 'I desired to refute the prevailing notion that luxurious and expensive houses with complicated heating apparatus were necessary for keeping wild animals alive and healthy.... I hoped to show that far better results could be obtained when they were kept in the fresh air and allowed to grow accustomed to the climate' (1910: 40). Animal enclosures were thus designed to be open-air panoramas with concealed moats rather than bars confining the animals to their allotted space. For the first time the public could stand in front of wild animals and see them without the intrusion of any visual obstruction. The fact that visitors could not easily see what divided them from the animals must have contributed to making the experience a strange and powerful one for audiences which had been used to animals such as lions, tigers and bears securely locked into heavily barred enclosures. A fundamental element in Hagenbeck's design was the creation of the illusion that there was no separation between certain groups of animals (something which was particularly impressive with predator–prey groups) and between animals and humans; he blurred the edges of the animal and human worlds (although of course this was no illusion for the animals, which must have known very well the physical limits of their world). Zoos were (and are) predicated on separation and enclosure, but whereas traditionally the means of achieving these were highly visible Hagenbeck contrived to make them invisible.

Clearly a key element in Hagenbeck's design was the desire to escape from barred enclosures. The obvious association of bars with prison brings us back to the question of anthropomorphism. Bars in early designs signified the presence of a dangerous beast which had to be separated from humans; once in such a cage the character of the animal could be read off from the image of the cage. Not only does such a barrier fulfil the practical purposes of physical separation but it is also a symbolic device heavily laden with significance. As Frank Beddard observes, the 'strength of the rhinoceros is attested by the thick bars which hedge it in its cage at the zoo, and its danger to human beings by the iron "refuges" for the keepers to escape into if hard pressed' (1905: 56). Here the image is played back on to the animal itself. The architect obviously saw the creature as dangerous to man and designed an enclosure to accommodate this image – a process which in fact further reinforces it. Much modern zoo design is in opposition to both the thinking (or lack of it) and the reality which led to such images. Such barred enclosures have been objected to not only on moral or animal-welfare grounds but, more importantly, because it has been felt that such frames portray the animal in an inappropriate manner. It should be emphasized once again that the bars are predominantly a problem for the human visitor because they create an unsettling prison image.

Modern zoo designers on the other hand argue that the animals must never be second in importance to the buildings themselves. People must go away from the zoo spellbound by the animals and not by the architecture. Many directors will repeat the comment attributed to Bill Conway (director of the Bronx Zoo) that 'the most dangerous animal in the zoo is the architect'. The real problem is that architects usually wish to create something to be seen; that is, they think first in terms of art and aesthetics in themselves, and sometimes forget the purpose for which the buildings are designed. As George Rabb, director of Brookfield Zoo, Chicago, argued, 'You want people to have a good experience and so forth, but you don't want them to be conscious of the same elements that they are conscious of in downtown Chicago.' Jim Jensen of Baltimore Zoo echoed these sentiments and declared that the 'animal concept' must come across in any zoo exhibit; exhibits should not be allowed to become artwork. An exhibit could well be 'a bold artistic statement but be no good in a zoo'. His view that it was difficult to tell an architect 'to go back to nature' was one that was shared by many directors of zoos which could afford to develop new exhibits.

The basic problem we are faced with is that architecture is a cultural process and architects themselves are shaped by a complex of aesthetic, technical, social, cultural and historical forces – and their view of the natural world must be similarly shaped. It is rare that architects have to design a replica of the natural world, yet that is exactly what many modern zoos want them to design. However, even when architects attempt such a replica, it is not simply a process of copying item by item the elements in a particular section of that world. Rather that world is perceived and made sense of through a set of cultural spectacles. We must not assume that because numerous zoos are attempting to recreate sections of the natural world that this is a neutral act or can be understood as something set apart from the previous history of zoo architecture. It still reveals one aspect of man's relation to wild animals.

Parks and gardens are part of a similar process in that they are an aspect of nature tailored and shaped to serve human interests, which vary historically and cross-culturally. The relationship is also clearly indicated in the full name of the zoo – the Zoological Garden or Zoological Park. In other words the fact that certain zoos, in certain parts of the world, have at certain times attempted to give an impression of naturalness in the highly artificial surroundings of the zoo is most significant. David Hancocks comments:

In our cultural history buildings provided for keeping wild animals in captivity have often been of splendid and elaborate design. They boasted of the might and wealth of their owners, and echoed not only the magnificence of the brute beasts, but also man's eventual conquest of these bizarre creatures.

(1971: 194)

Hancocks suggests that the housing of wild animals still needs splendid and elaborate architecture but that nowadays it should be for different reasons, namely the demonstration of the ethological and ecological context. We would argue, however, that whatever the designs, these are still indicative of how certain people see the proper relationship between man and beast. The attempt to recreate a section of the natural world in which to exhibit animals or birds is clearly a cultural statement of how the designers believe people ought to view the animals. It is part of their attempt to shape the experience of the visitors. A modern exhibit which is at the opposite extreme of the barred cage, which has always indicated danger and the need to subdue nature, is that of 'Jungle World' in the Bronx Zoo, New York.

A JUNGLE WORLD IN THE BRONX

The style of the Jardín Zoológico in Buenos Aires emphasizes the nature of the building which frames the animal as something which helps to shape one's preconception of it. Such buildings represent the furthest extreme from the environment in which the animals would normally be found. They are totally culturalized, there is no attempt to provide them with a natural setting, and they are marked by human cultural indicators. At the opposite extreme is the 'Jungle World' exhibit opened at the Bronx Zoo in New York in June 1985. Although the exhibit is nearly an acre in extent it is not the building which attracts attention; rather the architectural structure merely forms a neutral container, and it is significant that in none of the press photographs of 'Jungle World' does the external architecture feature. Despite its size the architects have designed a non-building, at least in the sense that the visitors do not attend to the structure around them. The real architecture, the design and construction of space, is to be found inside, and what is inside is a representation of the rainforest, the mangrove swamp and the scrub forest of Asia.

Obviously this is not an Asian forest, as Asian forests do not grow in New York. Yet in this world full of trees and dense foliage punctuated by the colour of bright tropical flowers through which birds fly and other animals move, and with the rich smell of vegetation and the sounds of a busy jungle, it is almost impossible to remember that one is in fact within a building. Yet it is a man-made forest not just in the sense that trees and plants have been put in a particular location by man, but in the more profound sense that many of the trees are actually manufactured by man. The huge tree which dominates one of the areas is actually made out of steel tubing over which there is metal cloth which is itself covered by an epoxy resin textured and painted so carefully that most people would never guess that it is fake. But the vines which climb around it are real vines. Some vines however are *not*, and those which are provided for the gibbons to swing on are fibre-glass. The mist which envelops the tree tops is real mist but it is produced not by natural conditions, but by the sort of machine used in commercial citrus groves. The rockwork (except for the small pebbles) is artificial but it is a base on which real peat moss and algae grow. Although it might seem that one is in the midst of an undivided tract of forest this is not so; the rocks help form barriers to separate species which may not mix in these conditions. Here one can see animals which actually do live in Asian forests, but what one does not see is the animals living as they would do in that forest. The sound of the cooing of the forest dove is real but it was recorded in Thailand.

It needed architects, zoologists, botanists, graphic designers, construction workers, welders, carpenters, painters, electricians, plumbers, audio specialists, gardeners, muralists, cabinet-makers and glaziers to build a jungle to human specifications in New York. All this then is man-made space, a human interpretation of a jungle world designed, constructed and managed by human effort in order to generate a particular experience of the natural world. Here it is not the building itself which has to carry the cultural message but that which it contains. This complex illusion of an Asian forest is still a zoo exhibit, a setting designed to shape our perception of animals just as much as the mosque for the giraffe or the castle for the bears. What is radically different is the sort of message intended, for here the attempt is to present the animal on its own terms rather than as a cultural artifact. Whereas the separation of human and animal is unambiguous in the traditional zoo, in 'Jungle World' the attempt is to create a sense of walking through a jungle. As William Conway, the general director of the Bronx Zoo, has written:

Could we find ways to separate visitors and Jungle World animals unobtrusively? Could we keep leaf-eating primates (capable of eating ten leaves a minute) in lush leaf environments? Could we establish uncommon animals in common Jungle World spaces in ways compatible with the requirements of other species and the need for the zoo-goer to view them? Could we convey hard information to visitors without damaging the affecting message of the habitat's naturalness and soft beauty?

Not all the answers are yet in hand, but if the power to affect visitors, to arouse concern and admiration for tropical forest is a proper criterion, the experiment has been a success.

(1984–5: 4)

At the opposite climatic extreme to 'Jungle World' and on the opposite coast of the USA there is another well-known state-of-the-art exhibit. In 1983 Sea World, in San Diego, opened its 'Penguin Encounter', an exhibit which represents a section of the Antarctic. On entering the building the visitors move from blinding sunlight into semi-darkness, past huge sets of photo-murals of Antarctic scenes rendered more vivid by a soundtrack of a powerful, chilling wind. Then they are transported by a moving walkway across a darkened room which has a 100-foot-long window through which can be seen the central feature of the exhibit – a 5,000-square-foot section of an Antarctic world inhabited by penguins. Although this, like 'Jungle World', is an attempt to recreate a part of the natural world, here there is no attempt to take the visitor into it for the conditions are simply too unpleasant for them. Once again it is a world of simulation designed to achieve a natural effect. The air temperature never rises above freezing point in the exhibit, no more than it would in the Antarctic, but of course it is produced by machines. The rockwork is artificial, as is the ice which is designed to simulate the edge of the polar ice-shelf; but over this 10,000 pounds of fresh ice is laid every day in order to provide a realistic surface for the penguins. The artificial rock edges a penguin swimming pool, seven and a half feet deep, which is kept at about 45°F. The other major artificial effect is the carefully controlled lighting in the exhibit which is kept at a level only just above the light conditions prevailing in the Antarctic at that season.

Once again one is in a building for this is the only way to create such an environment in the heat and bright sun of southern California. Although the public relations information tells us that on the exterior the 'White stucco panels represent the Antarctic landscape', the building does not hold the attention; it is the creation of a natural world in an unnatural environment *on the inside* which is important. Unlike 'Jungle World' there is no attempt to create a natural setting for the public, to give them a direct experience of the Antarctic environment; there is no attempt to subdue the sense that one is in a luxury building. Not only is there the moving walkway, but, having gone past the exhibit, visitors can go to an upper-level viewing area which has seating and is equipped with a bank of sixteen television monitors which show videos giving more information about penguins and their world. In that sense it is not an illusion as 'Jungle World' is, but it is still an attempt to replicate the natural world so authentically that the visitors are drawn into it.

Behind both these exhibits there is a desire to give the visitor a more complex and rich experience than can be obtained simply by seeing a monkey in a barred cage or a penguin outside in a concrete pool. The aim is to take people to a nature they have probably never seen by bringing nature to them and fashioning it in a form which it is hoped will both entertain and instruct.

Apart from the complex interpretation which can be given to such constructions it is important to emphasize that they rely on sophisticated technical developments. To cool several million gallons of water in southern California in order to create suitable conditions for the killer whales or to simulate the Antarctic climate requires considerable technological skill. Such a fashioning of nature is a triumph over it, a tribute to human ingenuity, for it indicates not only that humans can reshape the natural world as they find it but also that they can replicate it in totally alien climates and environments. Technical knowledge is important but this can only be supported by massive amounts of money. 'Jungle World' cost $9.5 million and 'Penguin Encounter' $7 million. Such sums are simply not available in many parts of the world. Although many directors of Third World zoos know of and have seen splendid examples of modern zoo-keeping in different parts of the world and would like to transform their zoos away from the menagerie image which many of them have, they are simply unable to do so because building for animals is a luxury and a low priority. For example the Parque de las Leyendas in Lima, Peru, is controlled by the Ministry of Housing, and much as the directorate of the zoo want their institution to be a high-quality one, it is difficult to get money for improvement projects in the zoo when the ministry has such a problem housing humans. Attractive modern buildings which are common in quite modest North American or European zoos would be unthinkable here. This particular zoo in Lima has a splendid set of framed 'artist's impressions' of a new glass and concrete lion house which an American team designed for the zoo some years ago. This building will never be constructed because, as the assistant director, Elciario Naranjo pointed out, they cannot justify such a building when there are people in Lima without roofs over their heads; apart from that it had nothing to do with their own culture – it was a stylistic imposition. In Lima they were building their zoo out of what they had to hand – wood, bamboo and adobe. Elciario Naranjo added:

This zoo is orientated to the poor. The poor have nothing to do in Lima and the park is an important recreation area. We are a poor country, we are not going to build cages of cement, glass and aluminium because it is against the people's reality.

*People cannot come from poor housing in Lima to see elegant houses for mere
animals. It is simply against Peruvian reality.*

Dr Gu, the director of Shanghai Zoo, likewise said that although some of the
zoo buildings might look somewhat shabby many of the animals were housed
far better than people. It is still the case that for probably the majority of the
zoos in the world design ideas are limited to some basic stockyard enclosures
for hoofed animals and some version of stone, brick or concrete box fronted
with glass, mesh or bars for most other animals. In some cases this lack of
concern with design is probably the result of lack of finance but in many others
it would seem that there·is little concern to go beyond it. These constitute the
simplest way to exhibit animals, and nothing else needs to be done.

The zoos of many countries are simply unable to have exhibits of the quality
of the major world zoos like San Diego, the Bronx, London and Sydney, and
yet these major zoos can influence standards of design in such countries if
they are supplying animals to them. Zoo Negara in Kuala Lumpur, for example,
was forced to build a sealion enclosure to American specifications before the
supplying zoo in California was willing to send the animals to occupy it. Idris
Abdullah Malik, the assistant director of Zoo Negara, pointed out that both
the Americans and Australians specify the conditions which must be created
for any animals which come from them. Needless to say Malaysia does not
have the same power to impose on other zoos. In a sense a reversal has
taken place. In the nineteenth and early twentieth centuries European zoos
expropriated the cultures of colonized nations in the form of zoo architecture;
nowadays western nations are able to impose a standardized western design
concept on other countries. Moreover it seems that such colonized nations
themselves do not make use of their own cultural artifacts nor those of alien
nations to frame their own exhibits. There are no Hindu temples in Indian
zoos, or pagodas in Japanese ones, and the only case known personally to the
authors of a mosque in an Islamic zoo was one in Ragunan Zoo, Jakarta, where
it was used for its proper purpose – religious devotion.

With the development of international zoo organizations, for example the
International Union of Zoo Directors, there has been a considerable sharing
of technical information. Directors travel to other zoos to meet in international
gatherings with other directors, ideas are shared and inevitably designs which
have been developed in a zoo in one country are taken up, modified and built
in other countries. Consultants design and build zoos for countries other than
their own, and of course those zoos which have money want to have the best
possible buildings. There is prestige in having state-of-the-art exhibits. This
process of uniformity among zoos is lamented by some, who regret the decline

of individuality and cultural specificity. It is interesting that many directors stress that each zoo should be unique, that it should have its own style of presentation which relates to a community it serves. Yet the trend would seem to be towards international uniformity. It was probably Hediger however who first clearly enunciated this idea of cultural uniqueness:

A zoo however should be much more than the required norm; its contribution to the city should reflect something that is of significance to the locality. Its site, historical connections and its functions in the community should have the stamp of the individuality of the particular city. In my opinion there can be no single blueprint for zoos. Each zoo must reflect the peculiarities of its city architecturally; its organization and the animals it keeps should all be considered in relation to the local situation, quite apart from the fact that climatic conditions must be taken into consideration. A zoo in central Europe must differ in several respects from one in Texas, South Africa, Pakistan or Australia. In principle even zoos that are close neighbours such as Rotterdam and Amsterdam, Basel and Zurich, or Frankfurt and Cologne, ought to show distinct differences from each other; this is because for one thing every visitor to the zoo from another city should be offered something new, something different from the zoo of his own city. Every zoo like every city should have its individual image; in practice this is not always easy to achieve.

(1970: 202)

Hediger notes that when a city such as Athens is ready to build a replacement zoo, 'and in the long run it will not be able to desist from doing so', the whole conception should take into consideration the 'unique grandeur' of the city. The site, the layout of the buildings and the organization of its animal stock should be prepared by a team of architects, zoologists, archaeologists and tourist experts working in close collaboration. The aim should be to achieve a zoo that is unique in taste and style, appropriate to the history and landscape of the city. Hediger notes that in principle this should apply to every city, but for one with such important classical associations these considerations are overriding. An industrial city needs a zoo planned and organized in a different way; 'again a city on the sea coast requires something different from a town in the hills; one should not aim at the average or standard but at uniqueness' (1970: 202).

The argument is that the zoo should be harmonized with other human architecture and with historical and cultural processes. An important question which might be asked, however, is why there should be a desire for the architectural uniqueness of the zoo, especially if the general orientation of zoos is to promote a scientific understanding of the animals they contain. One might think that the best conditions for zoo animals are the same whatever the culture in which they are presented, but it would appear that what is being allowed for are sets of unique cultural interpretations of the animal world.

The implication here is that animals are the same wherever they are exhibited; thus it is the style of the presentation that makes a particular zoo experience unique. The architecture of the place shapes the experience of viewing the animal, as we have already noted. It is this which conveys a sense of that animal to the viewing public; the animal does not convey a sense of itself on its own.

DESIGNER ARCHITECTURE

Architects have been used for centuries to design animal enclosures, but what is significant in the modern zoo world of the affluent nations, where there is economic abundance with urban populations eager to consume ever more sophisticated leisure activities, is that there are firms of architects which specialize in zoo architecture. They are very careful to reproduce authenticity and they attend to the animals and their natural environment in great detail in an attempt to attain that end.

Jones and Jones, architects of Seattle, Washington, and probably the best known of specialist zoo designers, describe themselves in their publicity handout in this way:

Jones and Jones has had the opportunity to prepare master plans and exhibit designs for some of the most innovative new zoos, aquaria, and exhibits in the country. Our work emphasizes the display of animals in social grouping, providing environments which closely replicate natural habitats in all ten of the world's major bioclimatic zones. We have personally researched the foremost zoological gardens and aquaria in the United States and Europe, gathering an in-depth understanding of natural and artificial habitat requirements, behavioral characteristics and their interrelationship with both visitors and staff. [Publicity Handout 1986]

In other words they try to replicate natural habitats. Their most famous work is that of Woodland Park, Seattle, which we examine below in greater detail.

Moving from a simple duplication of natural habitat, Jones and Jones are now interested in developing storylines for zoos. At the Blue Ridge Zoological Park, Virginia, they duplicate Livingstone's treks and also the Lewis and Clark journey. As they say in the 1985 Blue Ridge Master Plan, Livingstone's final trek took him 'the rest of his life, as he explored Lake Tanganyika and the Upper Lualabe River valley to the west'. Here, they add, he finally penetrated the great Central African forest, an environment vastly different from those he had experienced before. Moving through dense 'jungles, he traversed habitats alive with chimpanzees and colobus monkeys and resounding with the cries of colorful parrots and turacos'. This rainforest area is 'full of interesting smaller animals, some of which will be exhibited in the African Exploration Centre in naturalistically forested enclosures'. Jones and Jones assert that they will continue the theme and future exhibits could focus on Humboldt in South America, Burke and Wills in their crossing of Australia, 'perhaps even Marco Polo on the steppes of Asia'. Above all, 'visitors to the park will be encouraged to explore and discover for themselves'.

To suggest that these are the conditions for a replication of the actual experience of a Livingstone or a Lewis and Clark is nonsensical. The truth is that the visitors cannot really explore in this environment. They cannot discover anything other than that which has been prepared for them. The whole construction is theatre-like – once more they are invited to enter an illusory world. At best such exhibits are a pleasing attempt to create 'natural worlds' for those visitors who would prefer to view animals in such settings, and who would prefer at the same time to experience the jungle or desert safe in the knowledge that they are in the USA. The Disney-like creation of totally artificial but remarkably realistic worlds seems to have had a considerable influence on the thinking behind much American zoo design. At the Epcot Centre in Florida, visitors can enter a Mayan temple. The scene becomes that of a Mexican village at night; above there are stars, in the distance is a volcano and somewhere outside the village a jaguar howls. Such constructions can evoke a sense of place in the visitor and many zoos now feel the need to compete by creating such total worlds into which the visitor can escape.

Of course it is admitted that these worlds are but replicas of environments in the real world, for central to the philosophy of such zoos is the message that the real environment must be preserved. The Jones and Jones Kansas City Master Plan, for example, begins with a message of conservation:

A new approach to zoo design begins with the presentation of animals in such a way that their right to exist is self-evident. The educational message accompanying this presentation should be clear and persuasive. Whole habitats should be exhibited, with rock and soil substrates and vegetation supporting communities of species typical of the environment and logically associated. Visitors should feel they are passing through a natural environment, with a feeling of intense involvement. The point should be made that animals live in habitats, and it is the destruction of these habitats that is the principal cause of wildlife extinction today.

(1985: iv)

The theme is continued in their Belize Zoo Master Plan, Central America:

The world is losing its tropical forests at the rate of 150,000 square kilometers per year. As the forests diminish, the habitats and animals that rely on them are lost. In Belize (formerly British Honduras), only 45% of the forest remains. Less than half of the Belizean population is familiar with its own native wildlife, thus conservation education is critical to the preservation of their diminishing forest resources and wildlife. The master plan for the existing Belize Zoo will focus on a 'walk through Belize', a journey through a series of replicated natural habitats for a significant number of animal species found in Belize. The new zoo will provide expanded educational programs both for residents and for the growing number of tourists. Emphasis will be placed on local ecosystems, wildlife appreciation, the impact of human activities upon natural habitats, endangered species and conservation efforts. The zoo site, approximately 1,000 acres of pine/oak savanna, is located mid-way between Belize city, the population centre, and, Belmopan, the capital of Belize. The Belize Zoo will stand as an example of the critical role a zoo can play in wildlife conservation.

(1985: 2)

WOODLAND PARK ZOO, SEATTLE

Woodland Park Zoo is the most famous example of Jones and Jones' zoo work. As David Hancocks writes in his history of it, 'the zoo at Woodland Park can only be said with certainty to have officially existed for the past 75 years. In 1904 a menagerie of animals maintained at Leschi Park was transferred to Woodland Park, and the Zoological Gardens grew sporadically from that casual and humble beginning.' He adds, 'But animals had been maintained at the Park for several years prior to that. When Woodland Park was the private estate of Mr Guy Phinney, various species of animals, ranging from American deer to African ostrich, had been kept at the Park' (1979: 1).

It was against the background of the development of the Jardin des Plantes in Paris, and subsequently the Zoological Gardens of London (1826), that zoos developed all over the world in rapid succession. And indeed it was against this same background that Phinney set up a small private zoo in Woodland Park in the 1880s which was taken over by the city of Seattle in 1904.

Phinney had set out to develop a traditional English park. The public were admitted under strict conditions: 'positively no dogs allowed in this park. Any dog seen within its limits will be shot'; and 'Any person molesting or teasing any bird or animal or disturbing any bird's nest will be arrested and fined'.

The Seattle City Annual Report for 1904 contained the first 'catalogue of zoo animals' of Woodland Park:

8 peafowl	6 eagles
3 owls	4 ring doves
1 muscovy dove	3 brent geese
2 brown bears	3 seagulls
1 catimondi	2 coyotes
5 elk	1 racoon

In 1931 the director, Dr Gus Knudson, made some recommendations to the Board of Park Commissioners, which included 'a comprehensive plan for the development of a modern zoological garden at Woodland Park. Cardinal features of this plan should be large barless dens for carnivores, spacious paddocks for hoofed animals, pools of water with connecting streams [and] well-lighted, warm and sanitary quarters for all.... Landscaping and plantations should be carried out along the outside borders and throughout the interior of the park, to give the zoo a naturalistic setting... it is advisable that the entire area be fenced.' References to comprehensive plans, natural habitats, large barless dens, spacious paddocks and naturalistic settings were being made and attempted in only two or three other zoos in the world. They were not put into practice in Seattle.

Dr Knudson's pleas were to be repeated for a long time before any action was taken. Indeed, the zoo perimeter was not fenced until 1951, although reports of vandalism had been submitted for many years. In 1946 Dr Knudson reported that the 'usual vandalism' had occurred, 'such as throwing rocks and breaking windows, firing rifles and beebee guns, using sling shots, poking sticks at the monkeys, and even giving them lighted cigarettes and matches'.

In 1975 a Seattle Zoo Advisory Committee reported on the future direction of Woodland Park, and concluded that the principal objective was that the Woodland Park Zoological Gardens should be a 'Life Science Institution, demonstrating the value and beauty as well as behavioral and physical adaptations of animal life. As such, primary emphasis should be placed on fostering public understanding of the history of animal life and its relationship to ecological systems.' The report outlined four major policies under the headings of education, conservation, research and recreation, and specified a series of recommendations to be included in the new plan. David Hancocks, the British architect who had specialized in zoo design, was hired as design co-ordinator in 1975 to implement the comprehensive plan. The plan was developed by

Jones and Jones. In their *Woodland Park Zoo: Long-Range Plan, Development Guidelines and Exhibit Scenarios* (1976) they assert that:

Future development at the zoo will be based on the Social Biology Exhibition theme and the Bioclimatic Zone Presentation Theme. To satisfy these requirements, several specific design principles will be incorporated into the development of the comprehensive plan for the zoo. . . . All new habitat reconstructions will be designed to give as natural an appearance as possible in order to visually replicate the animals' native environment. The location of any of these habitats will be determined by reference to the bioclimatic-zone maps revealed in the long-range plan. . . . The animal collections within these exhibits will reflect an emphasis on social groupings through representing natural-sized groups as much as possible. Thus, areas given to animals will invariably be larger than in the traditional zoo concept, with fewer species represented but with a larger number of individuals.

(1976: 1)

Jones and Jones add that to benefit the public viewing of animals, all possible effort would be made to avoid visual barriers, with viewing areas chosen for the most sympathetic appreciation of the 'habitat experience'; and they would create situations where the exhibition of the animals could be achieved through a landscape solution, thereby eliminating exhibition houses, unless these proved essential. In order to emphasize the ecological aspects of the zoo site, all recreational activities which are not related to the zoo experience, or are of an energetically active nature, would be excluded. However, at the perimeter of the site, the environmental zones will all be designed to reflect local landscapes and will be 'integrated to benefit the surrounding community, by contributing to its passive recreational needs' (1976: 2).

The old menagerie and the traditional zoo had an architectural design which can best be described as a cube-like shell punctuated with bars, which ensured the continuous visibility of the animals. The opposite extreme in twentieth-century America is epitomized by Woodland Park, where the designers have reorganized space in such a way as to ensure the safety of visitors and at the same time to give the animals a freedom to be off-exhibit as they please. No longer is it a zoo for buildings and animal houses, rather it is a zoo of natural environments.

Because of Seattle's equable climate, most exhibits can be established and maintained outdoors. Therefore construction of large, complex buildings will be unnecessary. Borrowing an analogy from ecology, successful architectural design will depend on adaptation. All structures must respond in form to their surroundings. This allows an emphasis on the naturalistic orientation of the

Bioclimatic Presentation Zone Theme, making it possible to avoid essentially unnatural and incompatible juxtapositions of wild animals with self-conscious buildings. Jones and Jones assert that this approach supports a dominant, well-knit, natural landscape in which both man and animal 'exist on a nearly equal level'. In fact, man will appear the intruder, peering from 'hidden blinds' (viewing structures) or through semi-transparent screens of vegetation into enclosures the bounds of which are indiscernible. These viewing structures, which will be the most characteristic architectural elements of the proposed development, are essential to the educational experience and enjoyment of the zoo. They will be submerged below viny bowers, under sod roofs or low-canopied trees. The viewing structures will be essentially outward-looking places giving shelter and comfort 'without turning away from the world of plants and animals' (1976: 60).

Furthermore the forms and materials to be employed in their constructions emphasize the organic and the natural:

1 *All structures should appear to grow from the landscape.*
2 *All structures should appear subordinate to and compatible with the surrounding landscape.*
3 *The use of strong contrast as a means of establishing individual architectural identity is fundamentally incompatible with the Presentation Theme.*
4 *Throughout the zoo structures should present an overall unity of character, while secondary variations in color, texture and material should be carefully integrated with the various landscapes of the bioclimatic zones.*
5 *Whenever possible, materials should be of an elemental, or at least primary, industrial nature, such as stone, wood, brick, concrete, iron etc. highly finished or processed materials such as plastic, ceramic tile, aluminium, or stainless steel are not appropriate.*
6 *Structures should incorporate a minimum of materials, each specifically suitable to the visual and functional use it is designed to perform.*
7 *Materials should be self-maintaining. The use of paints and finishes requiring constant maintenance is to be discouraged.*
8 *Materials should encourage attachment by vines or covering vegetation. Textured concrete, brick and trellised wood structures are appropriate examples.*
9 *Buildings sited near existing trees must give right-of-way to the trees without damaging root or crown.*
   a) *Shallow grade beams supported by occasional posts or palings are far less damaging to roots than are continuous spread footings.*
   b) *Building walls and eaves should be notched or otherwise modified to fit around existing trees.*

'*Don't look down on animals. The proper way to view*'
(Jones and Jones, 1982)

10 *Natural lighting and ventilation are to be exploited whenever possible, allowing controlled access to the natural variations of weather and season.*

11 *Roof forms should not dominate the skyline. Low, flat sod, or vine-covered roofs or pitched roofs of cedar shakes or shingles with low eaves and irregular or broken skylines are appropriate.*

(1976: 63)

Jones and Jones in the Woodland plans delineate general viewing guidelines which indicate the move towards the centrality of the animal in its environment:

1 Ensure that the animals are seen as only a part of the surrounding landscape which they co-occupy with the viewer.

2 Provide selected views only into the exhibit.

3 Eliminate continuous viewing of exhibit areas along circulation routes.

4 Augment the sense of anticipation by sequential staging of approach views before the animals are actually seen.

5 Screen out the cross-viewing of other people and exhibits.

6 Provide at least one major new location for the interpretation of each exhibit; this must accommodate the special needs of all age groups and the handicapped.

7 Avoid looking down directly on animals; they should be at or above eye level, the only exception being animals at or below the surface of water.

8 Eliminate views of animals from outside the zoo and from parking and entry areas.

Jones and Jones summarize their arguments by stating that design exhibits should 'avoid static, set-piece views in which the entire extent of the animal area is obvious'. Preferably, they add, exhibits should be designed to unfold 'dynamically view by view, from a variety of overlooks'. In this way exhibits will appear 'continuous with their surrounding and indefinite, i.e. unlimited, in extent' (1976: 44–5).

Through architecture and landscaping Jones and Jones are attempting to transform a traditional zoo experience into a non-zoo experience. Rather than guaranteeing a close view of the animal, the Woodland experience attempts to replicate nature, to the same extent that a trip to the country may or may not result in seeing wild animals. As Al Johnson, keeper at Woodland's, put it, 'This zoo is for people who don't like zoos.' But even a carefully constructed zoo such as Woodland Park cannot easily maintain the illusion of being somewhere other than a zoo. Despite the aim of the director David Towne to enable visitors to 'fantasize that they're in Africa', that fantasy cannot be completely sustained, not least because of the climate and the presence of the visitor amenities. There is, however, one North American zoo, an example of designer architecture, which goes to the greatest lengths to create a sense of a different natural world and perhaps most successfully holds the suspension of disbelief for the duration of a visit.

SAN DIEGO WILD ANIMAL PARK

Unlike other zoos we have considered in this chapter, the Wild Animal Park does not have an urban setting. It is located in open country in the San Pasqual Valley some thirty miles north of San Diego and comprises over 1,800 acres.

Apart from the conservation aims, which need not concern us here, the exhibition aim of the park is to present animals in their natural setting; given the extent of the park and the nature of the hilly terrain and climate, they are particularly successful in creating this illusion. From its inception in 1970 it was decided that this was not to be a safari park which visitors drove around. In order to see most of the exhibits the visitor must take a guided tour in a monorail train which makes a five-mile journey around the edge of the main exhibits. The visitors are indeed taken into the countryside. In the park there is no architecture in the sense that animals are framed by buildings, although the natural environment has been landscaped and radically reordered. It is a world which has been created for both animals and visitors.

Although the setting has been made as natural as possible, there is an important attempt to set the scene for the experience with constructions representing another culture. Animals and exhibits in the park come from and represent Asia, Australia, South and Central America as well as Africa. But the prevailing theme is that of *being in Africa*. The first experience of the park for the visitor is the seventeen-acre Nairobi Village, which consists of a complex of wooden African-style buildings which serve as restaurants, gift shops and administrative offices. Once again we have an example of architects attempting

to conjure up a sense of the exotic by reproducing a set of stylized representations of another culture. The impression is strengthened by the pro-
liferation of 'African' names from the Wgasa Bush Line monorail to the
Mombasa Cooker (hamburger restaurant), the Samburu Barbecue Terrace, the
Mahala Amphitheatre and the Kilimanjaro hiking trail. Despite the somewhat
naive anthropological approach to the human environment, in which a 'Congo
River fishing village' exists within the Nairobi Village, this naivety does not
extend to the animal area. For example, in the East African section, which
consists of 125 acres, the visitors are able to see fifteen species of animals
coexisting in arid savannah conditions as similar to their natural environment
as it is possible to reproduce in a zoo. Similarly the visitor on the monorail
can see across a sixty-acre 'Asian Plain' which offers a panoramic setting for
numerous species native to Asia.

As in Woodland Park, Seattle (which is less successful because there is more
to distract attention from the animals), people are taken *into* the natural world
in the San Diego exhibit, but the structure of the setting is such that it is they,
the humans, who are controlled rather than the animals. Of course the animals
are in fenced enclosures but these are so vast that it is easy to regard them as
limitless, and with the humans contained in a train the animals hardly respond
to them.

As we have argued, architecture frames the animals and in so doing shapes
the viewing experience and indeed defines the nature of the beast – the animal
does not convey a sense of itself on its own. In an interesting essay on the
animal pictures of Gilles Alliaud, John Berger asks the reader and viewer to:

*Imagine a table elaborately laid out for a meal, before anyone had come to eat.
According to what is on the table one would be able to form some idea of the sort
of people who were awaited. In Alliaud's world it is not a meal that has been laid
out but what used to be called the Animal Kingdom. And here, in the same way,
we are obliged to form an idea of those who are anticipated.*

(1982: 270)

We can make use of this image with regard to the architectural forms designed
to hold wild animals. If we imagine the cage or enclosure to be equivalent to
that table, we are able to form some idea of how the animal that is awaited is
perceived or how the designers wish it to be perceived.

4
Exhibition

We are now always being told it is 'no longer fashionable to collect wild animals as though they were postage stamps' by people who seem blissfully unaware that the man on the top of the Clapham omnibus likes such places and will willingly pay to visit them — and they do not need to be collections of rarities either.

(Keeling, 1985: 145)

Without seeing a zebra, you can't learn the letter Z.

(M. Kamal Naidu, director, National Zoological Park, New Delhi, India)

'As soon as he enters the zoological garden the visitor's every sense is at our mercy,' claimed James Bacon and Mark Hullet, respectively curator of Herpetology and scientific illustrator at San Diego Zoo (1981: 14). In other words the exhibition is a process of power, the power to influence; the ways in which the collections are organized and presented to the public determines to a great degree how they respond to the contents. Before we consider the structure and influence of individual exhibits within the zoo, it is first necessary to look at the environment of the zoo itself. As we have said, it is significant that the modern Anglo-Saxon name is the 'zoological garden' (and indeed a direct translation of this name is found almost universally to refer to the same institution in other cultures), for a garden is an artificial and controlled reconstruction of elements from the natural world which have been chosen and then ordered for presentation in an alien context. Moreover the zoological garden is an urban phenomenon in which items from disparate parts of the world are brought together in an attempt to give a representation of the natural world. Of course this is not a natural conjunction of items from the natural world, and the designers of this zoological space must make policy decisions regarding the style of presentation and display. The exhibition of any object necessarily involves decisions about how to represent it, whose perspective of it to adopt, and for what audience the presentation is aimed. Zoos are essentially exhibitions of human versions of the animal world. The exhibition and interpretation of animals in major modern zoos tend to be zoological, ethological and ecological – the perspective is one which separates the animal and human worlds. Although many do attempt to show how man threatens the natural habitat of many animals, he is not treated zoologically or ethologically as a specimen in the zoo – indeed in many ways he is regarded as not part of the order of nature. Although man is simply a part of the animal world, those who go to the zoo 'go to see "others"' which are seen as qualitatively different. Hancocks (1971) identifies five basic patterns of zoo displays.

Systematic: this is a taxonomic pattern whereby groups of zoologically related species are presented close together. Such displays are usually associated with more traditional zoos and in this the arrangement is somewhat like a museum arrangement of specimens where the cages or enclosures are equivalent to display cases in a museum. Zoos of this sort, which were particularly common in the late nineteenth and early twentieth centuries, exhibit a concern for taxonomy as an essential aspect of zoology. Animals are not presented in terms of how they exist and interact with other animals in the real world but according to an intellectual classificatory model which creates species and relates individuals to that and to each other in terms of morphological characteristics. The advantage from an educational point of view is that such a presentation demonstrates the relationships between species. The disadvantage, however, is that most people who visit the zoo have no interest in zoology and find that this pattern easily leads to monotony.

Zoogeographic: these are collections which are ordered according to the continent of origin. Such a display breaks with the basic natural-history-museum type of exhibit where the species are separated. The zoogeograhic exhibit links different species and finds a unity in the distribution of different species.

Habitat: here animals are collected on the basis of similar habitat, for example desert, savannah, grassland, aquatic, polar. In this pattern the exhibit is even more specific than the zoogeographic in that it brings together a variety of species which have adapted to a particular environment.

Popularity: in this case the most popular animals are placed in a central location within the zoo; for example, sealions near the main entrance and elephant rides near the central lawn. Here the concern is not with scientific zoology, ecology or ethology but with culturally specific responses to particular species.

Behavioural: this is the most recent exhibit philosophy, in which collections are grouped according to ethological factors such as swimming, burrowing or flying. Once again speciation itself is not the central concern. The pattern is founded on the relationship between physical characteristics, psychological–social characteristics and adaptations to the environment.

The visitor's perception, interpretation and understanding of a particular animal is, at least in part, conditioned by these varied structures of presentation.

A lion is much more likely to be perceived as a 'dangerous wild beast' if presented in the traditional European lion house than if in a Hagenbeck panorama-type exhibit, and even less so in a natural habitat enclosure. Howard Murphy, of the Pitt-Rivers Museum, Oxford, analyses ethnographic displays in a similar way:

the purpose of display is to affect the meaning and value of objects, by placing them in context and using them to put across ideas about the producer or the producing culture (although objects can equally easily be used reflexively to make comment on the exhibiting culture). Certainly objects do not speak for themselves but that does not mean that the same message can be put across without them.

(1986: 25)

What is particularly significant about all these (with the exception of the exhibition where animals are presented in terms of popularity) is that none of the exhibition types apparently reflect different cultural responses to animals. Once again we have a situation in which we know that different cultures have particular images of animals, that animals are interpreted and responded to in culturally specific ways, and yet those responsible for exhibition philosophy adopt a perspective which, although scientific and therefore cultural, is also in another sense an attempt to be universalist or culturally neutral. We must not assume however that the visitors share the interests of the director and his staff. They bring with them to the zoo a complete set of mental perceptions, predisposed to respond in a particular way.

DISTANCE

The traditional menagerie established a rigid separation between animals and humans while allowing the humans the closest visual experience of the animals. The notion that an animal was entitled to some sort of privacy, that it could absent itself from the human gaze, was totally alien to this sort of exhibition. It was on display, the public had paid to see it and therefore it should be visible. The move to the barless exhibit reduced the sense of the separation and meant that the public had an unobstructed view, but the price was that the animals were further away from the visitors. In many zoos the problem is that the visitors find large, 'natural' enclosures morally and aesthetically pleasing, yet they still want to see the animal, which can easily hide or withdraw in such an enclosure. Some directors have decided that the animals have the right to such privacy should they desire it and many enclosures are now built so that the public cannot walk all the way around them, or with areas into which the public cannot see. It is suggested that enclosures where the animals are distant from the public and do not respond to them and yet in which they are visible make more interesting exhibits. In Taronga Park, Sydney, for example, the twenty or so chimpanzees have a large, open enclosure where they are set well back from the public and where they are able to live as a social group. The result of this exhibit, according to the director, is that the public spends much more time watching the chimpanzees interact with other chimpanzees than in the old barred cages where they were merely individual specimens.

Many progressive zoo directors and designers, in their attempt to reconcile the animals' need for space and privacy with the public desire for proximity, seek ways of giving an immediacy of experience coupled with a naturalness of setting. They seem to suggest that it is beneficial for people's understanding of wild animals to have this sort of experience. As Sandy Friedmann, of Brookfield Zoo, Chicago, put it, 'If you stand on one side of the fence and then go just one foot forward and stand inside the fence, the effect is amazing. It is a completely different experience to be inside the fence, and part of our challenge is to create that effect while keeping the public safe.' Several directors or members of zoo staffs commented that they would like to share, with members of the zoo-going public, the experiences which they had had in the wild looking at animals. They want the wonder of the natural world to come alive for the visitors, and in order to achieve that they attempt to create some of the conditions conducive to the experience. Sometimes this is technically too difficult. For example, how is it possible to lead the average aquarium visitor into the world below the sea? Kelly Tarlton certainly attempted this in his Auckland acquarium in which the visitors travel through an acrylic tube fixed at the bottom of the tanks and thus can see the fish swimming around them. There is, however, no way of hiding the fact that they are on a moving walkway in a dry tube surrounded by water. It is close but it is not a total immersion. Even in an exhibit which the visitors can enter, like 'Jungle World', the experience cannot be complete. Although one certainly sees a jungle-like combination of flora and fauna, it is a secondary experience, or rather a primary experience of a replica jungle. It is an experience of what it might be like to be in a jungle as opposed to the experience of *being* in a jungle.

The unusually organized Apenheul ape sanctuary in the Netherlands comes close to the ideal of allowing visitors a direct experience of untamed wild animals. At Apenheul, while the potentially dangerous great apes are kept separate, the public are able to wander through a wooded environment in which various species of monkeys are living freely. Although there is no attempt to replicate the natural environment of the monkey, as in the exhibit in the Bronx Zoo for example – these are ordinary Dutch trees and shrubs, the public are allowed to share the same space as the animals. The novelty of this clearly pleases the human visitors and adds a rather special dimension to a zoo visit. Although the public are told that they may not initiate direct physical contact with the animals, such contact is perfectly acceptable, and indeed frequently occurs, if initiated by the monkeys. Also the feeding times of smaller monkeys like the squirrel monkey are arranged so that members of the public may give food to the animals under the keepers' supervision. As Tine Griede of Apenheul has suggested the intensity of this experience is a positive one in shaping people's views and appreciation of the animals.

Traditionally the only form of direct contact between visitors and zoo animals has been in the children's corner where domestic animals may be patted. But a rather unusual example of the encouragement of contact can be seen in the 'petting pool' at Sea World, San Diego. Here the public are able to touch pilot whales and dolphins which are kept in a large, shallow pool. Visitors are allowed to purchase fish to feed them, and both the whales and the dolphins readily come within touching distance. A member of staff is present to supervise this and to answer questions, but most people just seem to want to touch or to be nose to nose with these creatures. What the visitor can learn about whales here is qualitatively different from the knowledge gained from the television documentary. As Jackie Hill at Sea World pointed out, there is no substitute for the thrill of actually being soaked by one of these creatures as they splash past.

Many zoo directors are fully aware of the visitors' desire to have an active involvement with the animals in the zoo. Most of this involvement, usually of a destructive nature, is the inappropriate feeding of animals. However, some directors have risen to the challenge of converting this desire into something positive. For example, Jack Throp when director of Honolulu Zoo constructed a hand-cranked wave machine in the penguin enclosure and visitors were able to turn this handle and produce waves in the exhibit. This was for the benefit not of the penguins, for whom it made absolutely no difference, but of the humans, whom he saw as wanting to play some active part in what went on in the enclosure.

A particularly innovative aspect of Throp's gorilla enclosure at Honolulu involved a thick rope being passed from inside the cage, through the safety barrier and into the visitors' area. The visitors therefore had the opportunity to engage in a tug of war should the gorilla so desire. Here there were beneficial effects for both the gorilla (distraction and play) and for the public (who had direct experience of the gorilla's strength).

The normal and appropriate relationship between humans and wild animals is, as we have suggested, one of distance. It is difficult in the context of the zoo, with the enforced closeness of the animals, to maintain truly wild animals. A further transformation of the animals occurs if humans are allowed to engage in direct physical contact with them. For if the animal is not to flee from such an encounter, it must be accustomed to human contact, that is to say, it must be tamed. The human experience of such a creature destroys its authenticity (a quality which is linked to its independence) as a wild animal.

EXHIBITION VALUE

When we first embarked on this study we hypothesized that in each culture we would find a different range of animals which excited interest or were in some way regarded as exotic. However, it has been our experience throughout the world that there is a restricted number of animals which are essential for the zoo-going public. Whether it be in South America, the Far East, India, Europe or Australia, the elephant, giraffe, lion, rhinoceros, zebra, monkey and perhaps sealion seem to be the necessary basis for any general collection. What these animals possess is exhibition value, a cultural property (though not culturally specific) over and above their inherent zoological interest. This combination of animals seems to represent zoo animalness as well as a general sense of the exotic. The appeal of these animals derives not from any natural-history interest but from popular culture, in the sense of jungle adventure films or the circus.

If we look at the negative cases first it seems to be generally true that birds do not excite much interest or hold visitors' attention for very long. People just do not seem to be able to relate to birds. Larger birds of prey do seem to attract attention more than others because of their size and because of what is known or imagined of their feeding habits, but even they do not have great exhibition value because they are unable to move very much. It is of great significance that when zoos have shows in which birds of prey are trained to fly near the audience, considerable interest is generated. Curators of birds have also suggested to us that an important factor causing lack of interest is that people cannot recognize many species of birds. A bird is simply a bird. It may be bigger or more brightly coloured than others, but few can be named. The most successful exhibits are those, such as the Jurong Bird Park in Singapore, where careful attention has been given to the setting and environment. Here, for example, visitors are able to enter a canyon which has been netted over and can walk through a luxuriously planted and wooded area where the birds fly around them.

If it is difficult for people to relate to or take more than a passing interest in birds it is even more difficult to persuade them to take an interest in fish. Fish are completely 'other', and live in a totally alien environment. Once again what does attract is the setting, and the modern aquaria which feature total seascapes are immensely popular. In Baltimore, Maryland, for example, there are usually queues to go into the Natural Aquarium. Here the main exhibits are not the usual rectangular glass boxes but huge tanks which attempt to replicate marine environments and the diversity of life found in them. Here the visitor is not simply looking at fish as particular isolated specimens but rather is drawn into the spectacle of a complete world.

Animals that have great exhibition value are mammals which are highly active and which engage either with the public or with other individuals in the enclosure. If such animals can be easily anthropomorphized so much the better. If they exhibit anger by fighting, making a lot of noise or banging against the cage, if they exhibit what is then identified as joy or pleasure, manifested by playing or romping about, these features will certainly hold people's attention. In an important sense it is not what an animal is which is important but what it does. So people want to see monkeys because they are usually entertaining and easily anthropomorphized; but, as most directors admit, the great majority of the public would be hard put to name or identify any species of monkey, although many might claim a chimpanzee or gorilla to be a monkey. Any sort of monkey will do to represent monkeyness.

The popularity or exhibition value of indigenous animals raises an interesting question. As Hans Ove Larsson at Skansen (which is both a museum and a zoological collection), Stockholm, put it, there are in his zoo Nordic and Exotic divisions, with the animals associated with Sweden – in which they specialize – kept in a special area. A 1985 survey at Skansen demonstrated that although 90 per cent of the public said they mainly came for the animals, the same proportion said they would not come for Nordic animals alone; the bears, apes, monkeys and elephants are the most popular animals. We can perhaps contrast this with the case of Taronga Park, Sydney, where because of the unusual nature of Australian fauna (witness the rarity or non-existence of Australian animals in any but Australian zoos), the director explained that it was important for him to exhibit Australian fauna as both the local and foreign visitors wanted to see these creatures. He was keen that Australia should be reflected in Taronga Park and as part of this aim he not only exhibited Australian animals but made deliberate use of Australian flora to give his park a definite Australian stamp.

It would seem that indigenous animals do not possess exhibition value unless they have particular exhibition qualities, so the giant panda is indeed popular in China as is the koala in Australia. We do not wish to argue that geography in any way influences people's interest in animals. The exotic are creatures which simply come from somewhere else. It seems significant to us that the animals we mentioned as forming the necessary core of a general public zoo come from Africa. But we would suggest that this is not the geographical entity of Africa; it is merely that 'Africa' is a sign for the image of exoticness (note the African theme at the San Diego Wild Animal Park). We found that it was quite common for people to identify certain animals as coming from the African continent when in fact they come from elsewhere – thus it is a common assumption that the tiger is an African animal and that Indian elephants are African. We found only one case of a zoo where there is a demand for an animal from a particular region for specific cultural reasons. Ragunan Zoo in Indonesia has special concerns because it exists in a Muslim society. Although the most popular animals are the giraffe, hippo, elephant, tiger and orang-utan, camels are unusually popular because they are regarded as Muslim animals. Dr Sutarman, at Ragunan, underlined the importance for the zoo of obtaining the rare Arabian oryx because of its connection with Saudi Arabia and Muslim culture.

It is interesting to note, incidentally, that Ragunan Zoo, being Muslim, has to concern itself with particular animals in order to avoid 'pollution', and this necessarily affects the presentation of certain animals. For example, special wire is erected in front of the wild-dog enclosure so that visitors cannot come into contact with the polluting saliva. Similarly the babiroussa, an animal of the pig family, has concrete gullies around the edge of its enclosure in order to drain away the polluting urine and faeces, which are then transported to a septic tank.

Drawing inferences from the popularity of the giant panda we might be led into thinking that rarity is an important contributory factor to exhibition value. However, our observations suggest that, unless an animal possesses other qualities, rarity is not in itself a significant feature. Even particularly rare animals fail to attract more than a cursory glance. For example, Dick van Dam, of Blijdorp Zoo, Rotterdam, pointed out that despite the fact that they have rare kiwis (and is the only zoo other than Frankfurt where they can be seen in Europe) these birds only attract the attention of professionals. Similarly in Jurong Bird Park, Singapore, the kiwi exhibit is passed by with scarcely a glance. Dull brown birds in a darkened enclosure, however rare, seem unlikely to arrest the attention of the average zoo visitor anywhere in the world.

To return to the point about the importance of what animals do rather than what they are, we commented earlier in our analysis of anthropomorphism that carnivores are usually regarded as bad animals, but many of the larger carnivores still have great exhibition value. This is not necessarily because of any physical attributes but is rather because of that very ability to kill. Certain other creatures such as venomous snakes, scorpions and tarantulas also attract considerable interest in the zoo for this very reason.

PRESENTATION OF THE NATURAL WORLD

The development and popularity of the wildlife documentary in many societies is an interesting factor in the zoo experience. One might think that seeing a film of a polar bear stalking a seal in an Arctic setting, or of a herd of elephants bathing at a waterhole, is much more dramatic than seeing the same creatures shuffling around a concrete enclosure in the zoo, for however natural the setting in the zoo it must be an impoverished version of the world that can be captured on film. However, many zoo directors suggested to us that such films actually brought people to the zoo. Viewers of wildlife films are able to learn far more about the normal lives of animals and see those lives in far greater detail than is ever possible in the zoo but it appears that for many this does not affect their desire for the personal experience of the animals in the zoo. The hidden camera of the wildlife documentary gives the sensation of being in the wild without actually being there whereas the zoo experience is one of being there without it being wild. The zoo and documentary both 'capture' animals for the benefit of humans and guarantee that they can be seen. The camera is a hidden observer which does not elicit a response from the animal filmed, but produces images as though there were no observer. In the zoo the observer is obvious and intrusive and yet wild animals can be seen and experienced directly because their capture is of a direct, physical kind. Such a direct experience is almost impossible in the wild where humans tend to catch little more than a fleeting glimpse of wild creatures. Humans are intrusive in this environment and are at a disadvantage in the face of the animals' ability to observe, outwit and thus absent themselves from man's gaze. Humans, however, have developed an instrument which may intrude into the life of wild animals so unobtrusively that it may capture them without their being aware of it. The camera, as John Berger rightly points out, violates the animals' normal invisibility. Moreover, it deprives the animals of their own ability to observe; the fact that they can usually observe us has lost all significance (Berger, 1980: 14).

As we have pointed out current progressive thinking in many of the more wealthy zoos suggests that what is important is the replication of the natural world within the zoo. We would suggest that there is none the less a considerable difference between naturalistic settings such as the 'Jungle World' exhibit in New York and natural settings, for in the zoo the settings are a product of human artifice – nature itself cannot be reproduced. Few zoo specialists seem to have taken notice of Hediger's warning about the illusion of naturalness:

The best guarantee of complete naturalness is assumed to be a faithful copy of a piece of natural scenery. This apparently logical conclusion is based on a false ecological estimate that may have serious results. Even an untouched section of the natural ground, enclosed within six sides (i.e. the closest possible imitation of a section of a biotype) is likely to be unnatural.... Mistakes of this kind, resulting in a pseudo-natural arrangement of space, are due to ignorance of the following elementary fact: a cross-section of nature is not an equivalent part of the whole, but merely a piece which, on being completely isolated, alters its quality. In other words: nature means more than the sum of an infinite number of containers of space (cages), however natural.

(Hediger, 1964: 71–2, emphasis added)

Similarly Gordon Woodroffe is pessimistic not only about being able to replicate natural physical conditions exactly, but also about the problem of social grouping within the zoo:

The idea of simulating African plains, savannahs and other wild places with a colourful display of different species has been the pride and grief of many zoos. Attractive as those can be, they are doomed to failure unless certain fundamental principles are taken into consideration. Even in the smallest African national parks, the Nairobi and Lake Manyora, the only associations different species have with each other are temporary, occurring at waterholes and salt licks or when one herd passes through another's territory. A mixed group of ungulates will never behave as a single herd. In the confines of the zoo, the situation is completely reversed: animals of alien species are permanently in each other's company and it is not long before their fighting, defensive and sexual instincts lead to aggressive behaviour.

(1981: 39)

Even in the best designed of modern enclosures, ones which reveal evidence of thought and concern for animal welfare, there is a credibility gap. When the Wild Animal Park in San Diego was in its early stages of construction, the designers were sent to Africa in order to see and experience that section of the natural world which they would be required to represent in the park. Similarly when establishing the 'Tropical World' exhibit at Brookfield Zoo, Chicago, the designers carefully attended to perceived animal needs. Because they attempted the realistic construction of artificial trees they measured the distance that certain tree-using animals could jump or swing in order to construct the correct distances. The problem as we see it is that the designer is attempting to produce an environment for a member of another species; however well-intentioned such designers are, they are necessarily ignorant of the animal's perception of the environment, for they can only work with their own senses.

Arguing from the success of 'Jungle World', James Doherty of the Bronx Zoo, New York, claims that his zoo is one of the brand leaders in terms of naturalistic exhibits. However, as we stressed earlier, these are man-made environments. The animals are *on exhibit* in them, it is not their natural, or even their own, habitat. Although it is probably as close as the designers can come to the replication of the natural world, it is in fact a stage-set, not a real functioning ecosystem.

We would tentatively suggest that such complex naturalistic designs, because of the subtlety and complexity of the illusion that they are equivalent to a section of the natural world, appeal to the conscience of the zoo-goer in modern industrial western society who might well feel uncomfortable with the idea that animals are locked in cages for his benefit. It is both emotionally and aesthetically satisfying to have them presented in a natural setting and it is easy to believe that this is more than a setting. The impression which directors and designers want to give is not ill-conceived. For example, 'Jungle World' was established by people who were concerned about the state of the tropical forests in the world and who felt that if they could give a sense of beauty, harmony and excitement of the jungle then others might be more willing to show concern. The important point, however, is that although such exhibits, because of their attention to animal needs, do improve the conditions of life of captive animals, the fact that a setting looks natural is something which is for human rather than animal benefit.

Again we return to the influence of wildlife documentaries and suggest that there is a close link between the development of natural and total-world exhibits and the popularity of wildlife films. Members of the public who have had experience of such films, who have some knowledge of how particular animals live, seem to find it more satisfying to see zoo animals in what is an attempt to replicate that world. But, as Berger has pointed out, the décor of an enclosure or a cage is merely a 'token' (1980: 23). It is part of the process of illusion for the benefit of the public; the décor is part of the ensemble of props needed for this theatre of illusion. For the captive animals, on the other hand, the props constitute the barest minimum environment in which they can physically exist. The animal is the actor on a decorated stage. These decorated stages can be seen in many zoos – in Rotterdam, for example, murals provide the backdrop to the interior of the elephant house, while in the Bronx a painted

African savannah scene adds colour to the indoor enclosure of zebra and giraffe. Although it might be claimed that many of the props in cages and enclosures are used by the animal and thus constitute a source of behavioural enrichment, they are there chiefly to set the scene for the public.

Taking the theatrical analogy further, backstage there is no need to perpetrate the illusion. Backstage at the zoo animals are kept in very different conditions, not because those in control wish to treat them badly but simply because there is no need to exhibit them. It is not usually thought that animals in their natural habitat are in a setting – nor are they, until one introduces the human observer, for whom such an area is as it were a stage writ large.

THE ZOO ON THE PLAINS

The foundation of the normal zoo experience is that animals are seen out of their natural habitat, represented in a humanly designed construction, usually in the urban habitat of humans. Many countries of the Third World have been suppliers of the raw material for this experience; just as other raw materials are processed, they have a setting constructed for them so that the consumers will pay to see them. With wildlife tourism, and the use of the natural habitat as a large stage for animal viewing, this process has been reversed, for in this case the customer comes to consume the product in its country of origin. We are interested here in the activity which constitutes the commercial safari together with the subsequent experience. We are not concerned with the individuals who are keen natural historians and travel on their own or with like-minded people to explore different habitats and look for particular animals, or indeed with those who take the specialist trips to look for gorillas in Rwanda, giant pandas in China, or the Sumatran rhinoceros. We are concerned rather with those who, as tourists, travel on organized trips to be shown wildlife in a highly structured way.

Many countries now have game parks. Set up as part of conservation programmes they also admit visitors, but not all of them are popular with tourists. India for example has several national parks but most tourists do not travel to India for the wildlife – they travel to see architectural and art treasures. Tourists to Africa do not usually visit the continent for its art or architecture, but rather travel there primarily for its wildlife – in Africa it is the animals which constitute the sights for the majority. In Kenya, for example, more foreign currency is earned from wildlife tourism than from any other commodity except coffee, and in some years it in fact earns more. (For further details of the economics of game parks see Eltringham, 1984.)

Wildlife tourism is concentrated in those natural habitats where the animals are likely to be seen. If one travels from the United States or Europe all the way to Africa to see the animal sights, one expects to see them. This can be related back to our earlier point about the problem of natural-habitat exhibits which are appreciated for the quality of the presentation of animals but which often cause dissatisfaction because the animals can hide. The humans demand that the animals be available for their inspection. If one is interested in seeing animals which live in the tropical rainforest, one cannot be sure of seeing particular animals, and the effort is far greater than that needed for the package-tour comfort of a trip to Tsavo, Serengeti or Amboseli.

We suggest that the step from the zoological garden to the safari trip is not a great one: the latter is a managed experience of wildlife, and as we will suggest nature here is also arranged for human consumption. Of course those who take part in such trips do not necessarily represent it in that way to themselves, and certainly the safari companies do not present it that way. The latter tread a fine line between the romance and excitement of being out in the wild in untamed Africa and the reassurance that all your creature comforts will be taken care of:

To live in harmony with nature, to listen to the night sounds while watching the glowing sunset over the enormous expanse that is Lake Kariba. To spin stories about the day's 'one that got away' while sitting around a camp fire and awake the next morning to the haunting sound of the fish eagle.

Sanyati Safaris offer you all this from the luxury of their camp.... In this, the most exclusive of Kariba's camps, the emphasis is on living closely with nature, while enjoying the comfort of luxury chalets with bathrooms ensuite and excellent food.... There is no generator to disturb night sounds as lighting is by lamp. The central point is the dining area/bar which has a breathtaking view of the whole of Kariba's Eastern Basin.

Another company puts it like this:

A 'Wild Experience' that only few will ever experience. With a knowledgeable and experienced guide, in powerful four-wheel-drive vehicles, staying in insect-proof tents, camping out in the true wilderness area of Hwange National Park where the normal tourist never goes, adventure awaits those who love Africa.

It would seem that zoo visitors are not concerned to see animals living or reacting naturally, but that is exactly what people go on safaris for, and they believe that is what they are seeing.

Although not on a par with the management of a jungle environment in New York City, the safari-park experience none the less has to be managed. The parks might well give the appearance of untouched wilderness, but they are in fact carefully controlled environments. There must be wildlife husbandry to ensure the correct balance in the parks, and roads, lodges and other forms of accommodation have to be constructed. Daily bus loads and Land Rover loads of tourists drive into the parks to see the animals; the parks are often devoid of the hunters and herders who once lived there and formed part of the ecosystem; the distribution of the animals themselves has often been affected by the disturbing presence of tourists (see Turnbull, 1981: 34); water-holes are often established, as are salt licks, to encourage game to come within view of the tourists in the lodges; the well-watered lawns of the lodges encourage grazing animals, and finally carcasses are often put out as bait for the carnivores (see Eltringham, 1984: 256). In fact the safari event is an organization of wildlife. It involves an imposition of human will on the natural world, to fashion it for human purposes, and thus in an important sense it is a culturally created experience of nature.

Of course the animals are living quite differently from the way they would in a zoo for they are still in their natural habitat even if that is managed by man. The visitors are able to see species in numbers and combinations which would be impossible in a zoo, and they are also able to see natural processes such as hunting and killing, which they would not in a zoo. The crucial point is that they are seeing it all happen in the animals' natural habitat and it is this which makes the experience qualitatively different from a zoo experience. It is not simply that they are able to see animals which they could not at home, for in Amboseli National Park, for example, visitors spend approximately 45 per cent of their actual viewing time looking at lion and cheetah, the two species of which the park contains the fewest (see Henry, 1977, quoted in Eltringham, 1984: 253), and which can easily be seen (lions especially) in almost any zoo.

It is therefore not only that people want to see a lion – a lion in London Zoo or Longleat is not that different from a lion in Tsavo or Amboseli – rather it is the context which makes it significant. Many of the game lodges advertise that they are within viewing distance of waterholes (which as we mentioned are often established or topped up by the lodge staff), and this is regarded as an attraction because it means that many sorts of animals will come to drink. But would the average visitor to any zoo spend much time watching an animal drink water? Obviously not, but absolutely normal behaviour which is not attention-holding in a zoo becomes interesting in a game park. Drinking is exactly the same kind of biologically necessary behaviour in both locations and is hardly very exciting, but what differs is the context and how that relates to or creates the experience for the visitor. Such behaviour is interesting in the game park because the underlying feeling is that one is seeing real behaviour and that one is lucky to see it; one has had the privilege of a special experience.

On safari, visitors are guaranteed that they will see certain animals and in this the activity and experience is very different from that of the naturalist who goes into the countryside, usually on his own, and who may spend hours locating the creatures he is interested in. The key element is that such a person is not a visitor who can make demands, but one who accepts the natural world on its terms and has to blend into rather than intrude into that world. Like the camera in the wildlife documentary he does not want to be seen or reacted to. In the game park the tourist experiences the animals with other visitors. In a study carried out in Amboseli by Henry in 1977 it is reported that at 'the height of the tourist season convoys of twenty or more minibuses can be seen leaving the lodge area together and double parking around a pride of lions. . . . Nearly 80% of the vehicles use only 10% of the park's area of 300 square kilometres. The obsession with lions is responsible and sometimes 80% of all the vehicles in the park are viewing the same lion pride at the same time' (quoted in Eltringham, 1984: 257). The naturalist must employ various skills and a great deal of patience in order to be rewarded with the sight of the animals he pursues. For the tourists on the other hand the wildlife is a mere spectacle which is paraded before them or before which they are paraded.

The fact that the animals are visible is essential, for the visitors have paid large sums of money to see certain animals. It is highly significant that, as with zoos, the most important animals for the majority of visitors are lion, elephant, giraffe, rhino and hippo. This is understandable given their popularity in the zoo – having seen them in one context the visitors now want to see 'real' versions of them. They have become the sights and, as with other forms of tourism, only key items are worth noting – it is important to be able to say that one has seen certain essential sights. One hears tourists advising each other, 'If you are in Florence you mustn't miss the . . .' or 'When you get to Paris you must see . . .'. If one has seen a pride of lions in Tsavo or watched a cheetah hunt in Amboseli one immediately has a set of images, and in addition the authority to talk about how wonderful it is to see these creatures in the wild (and incidentally how sad they look in captivity).

As with zoos, it would appear that visitors to game parks are interested in seeing a very restricted number of animals. Several analysts of visitor behaviour in such parks comment that many species only warrant a few seconds' notice in most of the parks and, more significantly, the average tourist cannot correctly identify even the most common antelope. With regard to animals they *are* interested in, the lion for example, we doubt that the majority of those who have seen them on safari return knowing any more about them than those who have seen them in zoos. And yet somehow there is a sense in which they feel they have see real lions – and they will have photos to prove it.

It is in fact similar to any form of tourism. A person may have read everything about St Peter's and the Vatican, or about the architecture of the Sydney Opera House, without having the chance to see them (except in illustrations) or without having been inside them, but they can *know* more about these places at a distance than those who visit them. Of course what a person with library knowledge does not have is the experience, the pleasure and satisfaction of having been there. But what does the personal experience tell us about the significance of the building? What it does tell us is the visitor's reactions and feelings, his subjective experience. The experience does not imply knowledge of the object, but knowledge of the self. To return to lions, one does not have to see lions in the flesh or in their natural habitat to know something about them as lions, and yet part of the experience of the safari is that one has truly seen lions and therefore knows about them.

SPACE: QUANTITY AND QUALITY

It is probably the simple question of the amount of space allocated to the animals in the zoo which more than any other factor gives cause for concern among visitors. If we were genuinely concerned about the issue, we would attempt to understand the animals' needs rather than projecting on to them the dissatisfaction we would have if similarly caged. Heini Hediger in his seminal *Wild Animals in Captivity* (1964) argues that merely to expand the space around an animal will not bring us close to a 'total environment'. His general ethological point is that members of a species do not, as a rule, occupy the whole of its possible range, but confine themselves to those districts within the range within which they can fulfil their particular needs. For instance:

Among butterflies we sometimes find [similar] minute ranges. Nearly 200 varieties of the genus Zygaena *are known, all very similar ... [and] nearly all inhabit the Mediterranean, often in restricted localities. For instance, the flying area (i.e. the range) of* Zygaena seriziata *near Philippeville is only eight to ten yards wide in places.*

(1964: 6)

Robert Bendiner, for example, discusses the Busch Gardens in the USA where there was a long track specially constructed for cheetahs, which were assumed to need great space; but they hardly used it, and Bendiner wryly points to this human folly for 'unlike Jogging Man, they saw no point in needlessly expending all that energy' (1981: 67). This desire for space, in other words, is the public's desire, not the animals. As Dick van Dam, of Blijdorp Zoo, Rotterdam, puts it, 'The animals don't need the space but the public of course wants to see them roam on the big plain – they think all animals are bison.' It is difficult to convince people that birds do not fly great distances for the pleasure of it – they do so out of necessity. Similarly tigers travel many miles because they need to hunt, not because they enjoy going for a walk. What is important about space is not simply the quantity of it, but also the quality, and different animals need different qualities of space. Hancocks gives a particularly apt illustration from the human condition:

If you had to spend a weekend in a superdome without contact with other people,
you would be going up the wall with boredom by Monday morning. But if I locked
you in this office (a small one) for the weekend, and gave you a radio, books, pencils
and so forth, you would keep yourself occupied.

(Hancocks, quoted in Bendiner, 1981: 96)

As we have mentioned earlier, the problem for the progressive zoo designer is that the public both want to see the animal and apparently want to see it in an attractive naturalistic setting. The difficulty is that in the latter style of exhibit the animal is often able to hide itself from the public gaze. This problem did not seem to disturb the early menagerie designers nor those in many modern societies where the public do not anthropomorphize and willingly accept the display of wild animals in what are often little more than barred cubes or small stockyards. For them it is important to have the experience of seeing the animals themselves. As many people in the Third World who visit zoos live in conditions far inferior to those in western industrialized nations, it is hardly surprising that they are not disturbed by this sort of presentation. Western industrialized nations with vast amounts of money to spend on attempts to satisfy leisure requirements are in a position to present animals in what to an outsider must appear almost luxurious conditions. In the United States, for example, the simple act of viewing the animal has to all intents and purposes disappeared. Wild animals are made familiar by television and film – they are no longer unknown and wondrous creatures – so now the animals must be set within increasingly sophisticated environments which become greater objects of attention and admiration than the animals themselves.

But the question and challenge is how to combine the most realistic of settings with the guarantee of seeing the animals, how to have a rich and lush jungle environment where the animals are more than the occasional flash of colour or shadow in the undergrowth. Given the technology and wealth of certain nations and the demand for sophisticated leisure activities it is hardly surprising that we find naturalistic environments populated by robot animals which are so well-constructed that they can easily be mistaken for the real thing. For here the visitor can be satisfied by both a complex and rich setting and by a guaranteed sight of the 'animals' within it. On the 'Jungle Boat Ride' in Disneyland the visitor is once more transported into the wild but all is predictable, the crocodiles always snap at the moment when the visitors are close enough to see them and the hippo always surfaces to be seen. Along the banks of the river animals, now reduced to the status of animated statuary, forever repeat a piece of typical behaviour. The boat ride, with its armed guide, becomes an exciting journey into a savage land (and human savages are added for good measure) where the visitors are potentially threatened, but in the jungle world of Disney the animals act in a predictable manner. The lions might roar and the crocodiles might snap, but there is no danger that the jungle world will turn against the human visitor. A most disturbing consequence of this kind of experience is that people are often disappointed when the living animals in the zoo do not respond like clockwork.

HUMANS WITH EXHIBITION VALUE

In zoos, as we have explained earlier, humans construct settings for the display of animals. In the late nineteenth century, however, there was a period in which humans also constructed settings for the display of fellow human beings. As we will show in our historical survey it was not a new phenomenon to augment one's collection of exotic beasts with exotic peoples, but in earlier times these were not for public consumption. In the late nineteenth century Carl Hagenbeck, the leading supplier of wild animals to zoological gardens and circuses, decided to expand his business by bringing 'nature peoples' to Europe. In so doing he was capitalizing on the interest in the peoples who were being colonized at the time, an interest which was also revealed in the popularity of travel books and the rise of anthropology.

In his autobiography *Beasts and Men* (1910) Hagenbeck explains how he came to do this:

The transference of the menagerie to Neur Pferdemarkt [Hamburg] brings us to the end of the first period in the history of the business. Hitherto we have been merely animal dealers; henceforth we were to initiate and develop other, though related, branches of the trade. About the middle of the seventies the supply of wild beasts began to exceed the demand, and the profits on my business somewhat decreased.

Some remedy for this state of affairs had to be found, and the said remedy eventually came through the chance suggestion of a friend. In 1874 I happened to be importing some reindeer, and my friend, Heinrich Leuteman, the animal painter, remarked that it would be most picturesque if I could import a family of Lapps along with them. This seemed to me a brilliant idea, and therefore at once gave orders that my reindeer were to be accompanied by their native masters.

(1910: 15–16)

He describes how he felt on meeting his imported Lapps for the first time:

The first glance sufficed to convince me that the experiment would prove a success. Here was a truly interesting sight. On the deck three little men dressed in skins were walking among the deer, and down below we found to our great delight a mother with a tiny infant in her arms and a dainty little maiden about four years old, standing shyly by her side. Our guests, it is true, would not have shone in a beauty show, but they were so wholly unsophisticated and so totally unspoiled by civilization that they seemed like beings from another world. I felt sure that the little strangers would arouse great interest in Germany.

(1910: 16)

Incidentally Hagenbeck not only brought people to be exhibited alongside the animals with which they were associated, but also on occasions used native people to care for the animals — not simply in the technical sense that modern keepers are sent to accompany animals from one zoo to another, but because there seemed to be a natural affinity between the two:

Lieutenant Heinicke, who had brought [the] young gorilla to Europe in the society of two negro boys, hoped to be able to keep this rare animal alive for a long time. Over in the Kamerun he had kept it for more than a year, during which time it had enjoyed unbroken health and become a general pet of the station. He hoped to be able to overcome the difficulty of lack of society by providing the two negroes as constant associated for the animal. When the ape first arrived at my animal park he was much weakened by his long sea voyage and took little interest in anything that was going on round about, but he soon picked up, and after a time would sit and walk about on the lawn in company with his two play-fellows, apparently in the best of health and spirits. He had a strong predilection for the petals of roses, and would consume large quantities of them. When he had to be taken from one place to another one of the negroes used to carry him on his back, presenting a very droll appearance.

(1910: 291)

Hagenbeck's first ethnographic exhibition was a huge success, mainly, he claims, because of the simplicity of it, and because there was nothing in the way of a performance. The Lapplanders themselves, according to Hagenbeck, merely paid a short visit to the 'bustling civilization which they saw around them, and it never occurred to them to alter their own primitive habits of life. The result was that they behaved just as though they were in their native land, and the interest and value of the exhibition were therefore greatly enhanced' (1910: 19). From Hagenbeck's report the Lapplanders were not treated like the freaks or the mental patients we have previously referred to.

Hagenbeck soon followed up his Lapplander success with 'other wild men' from Sudan, and then with Eskimos, for he was 'desirous of carrying on my new anthropological enterprise all the year round'. In 1877 Hagenbeck exhibited his Eskimos – a man called Ukubak, 'his obedient spouse and his two little daughters' – and their dogs, sledges, tents, weapons, household implements and canoes, in Hamburg, and then took the show to Paris, Berlin and Dresden:

In Berlin the Emperor William I came to see them and was greatly interested in Ukubak's aquatic tricks. On that occasion Ukubak remained so long under the water that the Emperor became quite alarmed for his safety, until I told His Majesty the facility with which the Eskimo could recover himself when he so desired. In April of the following year, 1878, the Eskimos returned to their native land, greatly enriched by their travel.

(1910: 25)

The Lapps, Nubians and Eskimos were followed by Somalis, Indians, Kalmucks, Cingalese, Patagonians, Hottentots and others. The Cingalese exhibition of 1884 was a huge commercial success, and for the next sixty years Hagenbeck and his successors exhibited exotic peoples in both Europe and the United States.

It was not only in individual zoos that the European public were offered a sight of such peoples, because such exhibits were also integral parts of major colonial exhibitions. In the late nineteenth and early twentieth centuries Britain, for example, had virtually all her colonies intact and had developed elaborate structures for administering them. In order to consolidate consciousness of them, nations like England, France and Germany displayed their colonies to their home populations, to their rivals and to the world at large. At the British Empire Exhibition of 1924 at Wembley:

The British mounted an enormous historical pageant with a cast of 15,000 humans, 300 horses, 500 donkeys, 730 camels, 72 monkeys, 1,000 doves, 7 elephants, 3 bears and a macaw. It was called 'The Pageant of Empire: An Historical Epic' and was largely written by Rudyard Kipling with poetry by Alfred Noyes set to music by Sir Edward Elgar. It took three days to see the complete performance.

(Benedict, 1986: 5)

At the early exhibitions, as in the modern zoo, amusement vied with education. Indeed, as Benedict notes, the amusement element was not confined to the amusement zone, as exhibitions in the 'serious fair' use all sorts of entertainment to attract the public. Nowhere was this more in evidence than in the colonial exhibits. 'An ivory throne drew greater crowds than a pile of plumbago [graphite], though the latter had by far the greater commercial potentialities.' Benedict adds that 'from exotic products to exotic peoples was not a large step and one taken with more and more elaboration particularly in the French fairs. A war dance or theatrical performance drew a greater crowd than a demonstration showing natives at work on an industrial process, though, again, the latter had the greater economic potential' (1986: 6).

Living colonial peoples were shown at the Colonial and Indian Exhibition in London in 1886, at which ninety-seven natives from India, Ceylon, British Guiana, Cyprus, Cape of Good Hope, Straits Settlements and Hong Kong took part. Most were there to demonstrate their crafts, but there were also workers (notably blacks from South Africa demonstrating diamond-washing), interpreters and servants. In France ethnographic exhibitions had been held in the Jardin d'Acclimentation since 1877, showing Nubians, Eskimos, Lapps, Gauchos, Tierra del Fuegans and Guianese dressed in their native costumes in some semblance of their native habitat. This tradition was adopted at the Paris Exposition of 1889 which featured villages of natives. Such villages were also prominent features of the Paris Expositions of 1900, 1931 and 1937. The Paris Exposition of 1889 boasted not only a separate colonial palace, but also pavilions in 'indigenous' styles for Cochin-China, Cambodia, Annam-Tonkin and Algeria. In addition there were 'villages' for Senegal, Gabon-Congo, New Caledonia and Tonkin. Natives of these colonies had been imported to build the villages and then inhabit them, putting on displays of their arts and crafts. In addition they performed religious ceremonies, dances and theatrical presentations.

The exhibition of exotic peoples and exotic animals both in the zoo world and in colonial exhibitions had a commercial purpose but it also enhanced the exhibiting nations' prestige. As we will see in the historical survey that follows, attempts at such enhancement were not solely to be found at the national level.

The circus element within the zoo; human domination of the wild beast. Although not all zoos present this as an explicit theme, the very fact that zoos are collections of wild animals established for human benefit is an expression of power and domination. Samustprakaran, Crocodile Farm and Zoo, Thailand. (Authors' collection)

Captive breeding in its most basic form; a successful demonstration of human intervention in the animal world. Visitors are impressed by the sheer quantity of these dangerous wild animals. Is this successful breeding for human or animal benefit? Samustprakaran, Crocodile Farm and Zoo, Thailand. (Authors' collection)

Celebrating the latest Californian conception of 'whaleness' and how humans can relate to it and share it. 'Celebration Shamu' show featuring Shamu the killer whale at Sea World, San Diego, California, USA. (Authors' collection)

The apparent desire to make physical contact with wild creatures which normally live their lives at a distance from human beings is permitted and encouraged under supervision at the Petting Pool, Sea World, San Diego, California, USA. (Authors' collection)

Exotic architecture and exotic animals. Here a Western architect has designed a stylized version of an Indian temple which as it were 'frames' the animal and enhances the sense of oriental mystery. Taronga Zoo, Sydney, Australia. (Authors' collection)

This late nineteenth-century elephant house, a replica of a temple in Bombay, is complete with Hindu statues and complex designs. Jardin Zoológico, Buenos Aires, Argentina. (Authors' collection)

Images of distant worlds and distant cultures are brought together to create a popular animal identity. The particular theme here is Egyptian. Early twentieth-century ostrich house, Berlin Zoo, Germany. (Authors' collection)

In this castle for bears the animals sleep in dungeon-like cages below ground and during the day are on display in the cell-like structures between the arches. The image of a strong, fortress structure and high security for containing dangerous, perhaps even 'criminal', animals is a powerful one. Jardín Zoológico, Buenos Aires, Argentina. (Authors' collection)

The original entrance to the famous Hagenbeck zoo at Stellingen near Hamburg. Carl Hagenbeck was the pioneer in the development of naturalistic settings for wild animals in zoos. An example of one of his artificial mountains, copied since in zoos around the world, can be seen in the background. Carl Hagenbeck Tierpark, Hamburg, West Germany. (Authors' collection)

A humanized and juvenilized view of how animals live. A 'toy' village, complete with a church and Danish-style houses, for rabbits. Jylands Mini-Zoo, Haunstrup, Denmark. (Authors' collection)

An image of the mysterious and exotic east. Here a Japanese-style pagoda is used to house Japanese deer and sheep. Jardin Zoológico, Buenos Aires, Argentina. (Authors' collection)

The natural world does not exist in the zoo — whatever aspects of the natural world are needed must be created by man. Here high technology building is in progress on a new, highly naturalistic snow leopard enclosure. New York Zoological Park (Bronx Zoo), New York, USA. (Authors' collection)

An early Hagenbeck representation of nature. Parc Zoológique de Paris, Paris, France. (Authors' collection)

Revealing the foundations of the zoo's natural world. Even rocks can lack a certain solidity in zoos, and here, repairs to the rock-work reveal the artificial structure of a Hagenbeck-style representation of nature. Parc Zoológique de Paris, Paris, France. (Authors' collection)

The real world or a zoo enclosure? Beyond the traditional zoo, but still within the zoo, this is a human representation of an African environment. The water hole at the Eastern Africa exhibition area, San Diego Wild Animal Park, Escondido, California, USA. (Authors' collection)

An artificial world for artificial animals. These animals can always be guaranteed to be in the best place for viewing. They do not destroy the vegetation and they do not need feeding. Robotic animals on the banks of the jungle ride, Disneyland, California, USA. (Authors' collection)

Here no attempt has been made to replicate the natural world, but this thoughtfully designed climbing frame set in a Dutch parkland allows gibbons to behave as they might do in their natural environment. An unnatural construction is used to elicit natural behaviour. Apenheul Sanctuary, Apeldoorn, Netherlands. (Authors' collection)

Some visitors might oppose the prison-like structures in this enclosure, but here the bars give a creature which climbs, in this case gorillas, an added dimension for play, exploration and exercise. Howlett's Zoo Park, Bekesbourne, England. (Authors' collection)

An attractive, colorful mural depicting the African plain is the backdrop for this zebra's winter quarters. Visitors may find it appealing but how does the zebra appreciate it or interact with it? New York Zoological Park (Bronx Zoo), New York, USA. (Authors' collection)

The zoo and its association with natural history. Here the reptile cases in the Jardin des Plantes are reminiscent of display cases in a traditional natural history museum. The creatures contained in them have the status of zoological specimens. Ménagerie du Jardin de Plantes, Paris, France. (Authors' collection)

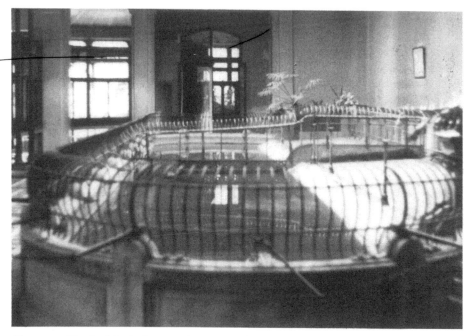

The crocodiles in this shallow pool appear to be nothing but museum exhibits. The fact that they barely move and scarcely seem alive accentuates this image. Ménagerie du Jardin de Plantes, Paris, France. (Authors' collection)

Despite the obviously barren existence forced on the chimpanzee in this enclosure, the authorities do hope to provoke a compassionate response, for one of the signs asks the visitor not to make too much noise because it disturbs the animals. Jardin Zoológico, Buenos Aires, Argentina. (Authors' collection)

This carefully designed sign on a giant panda enclosure gives information which covers the most obvious of visitors' queries. National Zoological Park, Washington, USA. (Authors' collection)

Basic instruction to the visitors. In most zoos humans demand some form of interaction with the animals. This usually takes the form of attracting the animals' attention by feeding them despite the 'Do not feed' signs. Jeermata Jijabai Bhosle Udyan, Bombay, India. (Authors' collection)

A basic, museum-like identification plaque. Hong Kong Zoological and Botanical Gardens, Hong Kong. (Authors' collection)

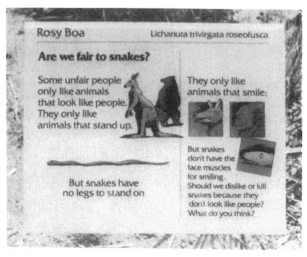

A new style of educational signs which attempt to get the visitor to think a little more about the animal in the enclosure by giving one or two interesting pieces of information. Here the aim is to help stop the stereotyping of snakes as nasty creatures. San Diego Wild Animal Park, Escondido, California, USA. (Authors' collection)

'Inferior' humans associated with an almost human animal. These young African boys were sent from Cameroon to Germany with the gorilla to provide company, the implication being that there was a natural affinity between the boys and the animal. Carl Hagenbeck Tierpark, Hamburg, Germany. (Hagenbeck 1910)

Encouraging an anthropomorphic response to animals; the incorporation of a pseudo-human into the human world. In this way the chimpanzee loses its true animal identity but without, of course, gaining a full human identity. Bellevue Zoo, Manchester, England. (Peel, 1903: 110)

The human animal in the zoo; the view from the other side of the bars. Stichting Koninlijke Rotterdamse Diergaade (Blijdorp Zoo), Rotterdam, Netherlands. (Authors' collection)

5
From Princely Menageries to Public Zoos

Madam

I wrote to your highness last year by the ships in which Guaspar Anriquez went as captain-major, and I gave you an account of how I had two civet-cats which I desired to send your highness by him; and I said that, because Alfonso Gonçalez de Botafoguo, the Superintendent, would not give me permission to do this, on account of those which he had sent your highness, I was not allowed to do so. I am now sending them by Adão Ferreira, who is clerk on board the ship on which Francisquo de São goes as Captain. Also he is carrying besides a cage with a few birds with tails (probably parakeets). I pray your highness to accept this tribute as from a poor man, who if he desires anything, it is to be able to serve your highness better.
(A letter from Simao Roiz, factor in São Jorge de Mina, written on 12 April 1557 to his Queen Catherine – quoted in Lloyd, 1971: 54)

A collection of living animals such as never yet existed in ancient or modern times . . . animals to be brought from every part of the globe to be applied either to some useful purpose, or as objects of scientific research, not of vulgar admiration.
(From the prospectus for the Establishment of the Zoological Society of London)

Our central concern in this chapter is not to document a complete history of the change in varieties of the displays of wild animals but rather to indicate key themes in this history, particularly that of the gradual shift from private collections for the pleasure and entertainment of the rich and powerful to collections designed and displayed for the pleasure of the paying public.

SACRED MENAGERIES

If we look for the origins of the interest in the display of captive wild animals we should, according to Gustave Loisel, the French historian of the zoo, take the sacred menageries associated with places of worship in ancient Egypt as the first documented examples of this process (1912: vol. 1, 14–16). The

Egyptians kept certain wild animals, which were important for their place in the religious life, in courtyards or even in the sacred buildings themselves where they were tended and fed by priests. It is recorded that members of the public were able to visit such places; for example, many went to see the lions being fed live prey, at the Temple of the Sun in Metropolis. They also visited the sacred crocodiles of Lake Moeris and fed them cakes and pieces of meat.

Although such collections of animals were displayed, or were treated as though they were on display, they were probably not collected for this purpose; the primary reason for their being where they were was their religious significance. Collections of wild animals for the purposes of displaying them have been organized according to a variety of principles however it is difficult to find cases of collections based on the sacred quality of the animals. From the archaeological records of Babylonia there is a suggestion of the existence of sacred menageries but it is difficult to be precise about this, particularly because one cannot be certain about the purpose behind any such collection of wild animals. There is little comprehensive information about menageries of the ancient civilizations of the Near East, but, as was the case in Egypt, there were religious processes which featured animals such as the bull, cow, serpent and elephant, and it is possible that the first menageries consisted of animals which had some sacred quality. In ancient Greece there is evidence to show that animals were associated with the temples and it has been suggested that such collections of (both wild and domestic) temple animals formed the majority of Greek menageries. A much later example of a menagerie where the collection of animals served at least some religious purpose was that of Montezuma, the Aztec ruler, which was first seen by a European when Hernando Cortés went there in 1519. It is reported that at least one of the purposes of the collection was to supply sacrificial victims.

The tradition of wild animals associated with places of worship survived into modern times. Towards the end of his three-volume encyclopaedic work Loisel returns to the theme of sacred menageries with which he began his history and records the example of the largest menagerie of this type in the nineteenth century, that of the Buddhist monastery of Theyboo on the banks of the River Mhyet-Nghy near Mandalay in Burma. A French traveller, Thomas Anquetil, visited in 1859 and reported that there was an acclimatization garden, large aviaries, and enclosures for sixty or so species of mammals. These included elephant, rhinoceros, panther, cheetah, lynx, horse, buffalo, bear, many species of deer, otter, hedgehog, pig, wild boar, babiroussa, cat, dog, monkey, civet-cat, pangolin, mongoose, tapir, squirrel, zibeth, and many animals from the Indian sub-continent. In Thailand, also largely Buddhist, travellers reported on the number of animals kept in or at least associated with temples. As one missionary wrote, 'the pagodas are really nothing but a place of refuge for animals' (quoted in Loisel, 1912: vol. 3, 13).

ENTHUSIASM FOR WILD ANIMALS: EARLY EXAMPLES

In the modern zoo world it is difficult to think of any example of a collection established with a religious orientation. Perhaps the closest is the Jerusalem Biblical Zoological Garden in Israel whose collection is based on animals mentioned in the Bible. But although the cages and enclosures have plaques which include biblical references to the animals the underlying philosophy of presentation is certainly secular rather than sacred.

If we return for a moment to ancient Egypt we find that not only were wild animals kept for religious purposes but in addition members of the nobility kept animals such as wild dogs and cats, particularly hyenas, leopards and cheetahs, for hunting. It has even been suggested that the pharaohs took lions to war with them. Apart from the animals for hunting, the richer members of ancient Egyptian society from the time of Memphis kept large enclosed parks which were stocked with both domestic and wild animals. There are examples of such parks illustrated on the tombs from the 4th and 5th dynasties in which can be seen herds of various kinds of antelope, gazelle and ancloryx and flocks of cranes kept under the watchful eye of the keepers. These are some of the earliest recorded examples of a theme which has been of key significance in the history of the menageries – the enthusiasm for wild things which cultured people have displayed. From this time we can also identify a significant element in the keeping of wild animals – the ability of certain individuals to command the resources to obtain animals from different parts of the world. This is important for it has always been rare, unusual and exotic animals rather than familiar local ones which have attracted and fascinated.

The animals were important not just in themselves, but also for the contacts and the power that they represented. Tuthmosis III, for example, had a variety of animals brought for him from Syria and his sister Hatasou sent an expedition of five ships to Somalia in order to obtain precious goods such as spices, myrrh, incense, ebony, gold and ivory. The expedition was very successful and when it returned to Thebes it also brought a whole variety of animals, including leopards, greyhounds, various kinds of monkeys, cattle and birds. It is further recorded that it brought aromatic trees which had been carefully dug up and transported with earth packed around the roots to keep them alive. It is important to note here that the wild animals are associated with perfumes, ebony, ivory and gold. Like the perfumes, rare materials and stones, the animals seem to have been considered exotic and therefore luxurious.

Still in the ancient world, the archaeological record and the writings of Herodotus and Ptolemy show that the kings of Babylonia kept monkeys, rhinoceros, elephants, camels, dromedaries and antelopes in captivity, and that close to their summer palaces they kept wild bulls, gazelles, deer and ibex which were hunted with dogs, lions and panthers. Most of these animals were captured in their country of origin and were transported to these menageries and parks. In order to obtain them the king either sent out expeditions or received them as tribute from the rulers of conquered nations.

In ancient China there is documentation which refers to the collections of wild animals of the politically powerful. Referred to in almost every account which deals with the history of the zoo is that of the park built about 1100 or 1000 BC for the Emperor Wen Wang in the province of Ho Nan, which lies between Beijing and Nanking. In this walled park of some 900 acres there were various kinds of deer, goats, antelope, birds and an enormous quantity of fish. Meng Tseu, the Chinese author, who writes of this park, also tells of the Emperor Chi Hang-ti who had a great park built, within which there was not only an enormous collection of mammals, birds and fish, but also 3,000 types of trees and plants which were brought from all parts of his empire. Not content with a botanical representation of his empire in miniature he had built replicas of all the palaces and castles he had destroyed during his campaigns (Loisel, 1912: vol. 1, 37). Although we do not have definite information it is probable that such collections of animals in parks were used primarily for hunting.

It is not until the thirteenth century that we get more detailed information about a Chinese menagerie – that of Kublai Khan in Shang-tu, which was described in detail by Marco Polo. At Shang-tu there was a huge marble and stone palace adjacent to a wall which surrounded some sixteen miles of parkland where game animals of all sorts were kept for hunting (see Marco Polo, 1982: 108). Not only did the Khan keep game animals but Marco Polo also reports that he saw a menagerie with tigers, panthers, leopards, lynx, rhinoceros, elephants, as well as the falcons used for hunting.

As we mentioned earlier the collection of exotic species of animals must be understood in the context of political and economic power, and in fifteenth-century China we find a case of trade, diplomacy and an exotic animal coming together. Emily Hahn reports (1968) that in 1417 Yung-lo, a Ming dynasty Chinese emperor, organized an expedition to Africa simply because of a giraffe. But it was the voyage of a statesman not of a wealthy collector in search of something special. In 1414 a group of Chinese ships had put in at Bengal at a time when there was great activity to celebrate a coronation. Chinese officers were invited to take part in the celebrations, during the course of which they saw several giraffes which had been sent from Melinda on the East African coast. The local king realized from the obvious interest displayed by the Chinese that these creatures were not known in China and insisted on sending one for the emperor. To make sure that the emperor saw at least one such creature he asked the Melindan ambassador if he could send another. As it happened, both giraffes arrived, the one from Bengal in 1414 and the one from Melinda in 1417. So pleased was Yung-lo to receive this latter gift that in 1417 the expedition sailed to inaugurate trade with Melinda, now possible by virtue of the gift. Although at the time of the arrival of the first giraffe no Chinese had sailed to Africa, the emperor is reported to have had African animals in his collection. Indeed when he went to the port to receive the second giraffe, he did so accompanied by his 'celestial horse', which Hahn identifies as a zebra (1968: 30), a fact which suggests that animals passed from ruler to ruler.

We have already mentioned that animals associated with particular cults were kept close to temples in Greece. However, Jennison in his study of animals in the Greek and Roman worlds suggests that despite the far-flung trading connections and the lively curiosity of the Greeks, which might have been thought favourable for the growth of collections of exotic animals, this did not in fact happen. The cities did not have the wealth to support such collections, the imperial power over other lands was not great enough to demand the supply of animals to form a collection and, unlike the Romans, the Greeks showed no interest in wild-animal shows (although see Jennison, 1937: 25–7 for details of shows in which tamed wild animals were used).

There was luxury to be found not only in Rome but also in the country estates or villas. Here were animal parks (particularly for hunting), huge aviaries and fish ponds kept by wealthy individuals or emperors. Such collections were maintained largely for show purposes rather than for economic profit. Jennison refers to Varro's distinction between the fish ponds of the ordinary people (*apud plebum*) and the seawater ponds which were playthings of the nobility (1937: 122). Toynbee quotes the example of Quintus Hotensius who had the dining room of his villa at Laurentum constructed in such a way as to overlook his park 'in order that his guests might see his animals converging on a servant got up as Orpheus when he blew a horn to summon them' (1973: 16).

With the development of the games and spectacles based on animal combats, for which the Romans are so notorious, there was a growth in menageries to provide beasts for use in the amphitheatres. The earliest recorded shows in Rome featuring wild animals were the *venationes* using lions and leopards given by Marcus Fulvius Nobilitor in 186 BC. The menageries in question received gifts of animals from the governors of Roman colonies and other foreign dignitaries. It is recorded that hippopotami came from the Nile, lions from Mesopotamia, tigers from Persia, large quantities of bears and onagers from Central Asia and panthers from Mauritania.

There is little information about how the Romans actually went about the organizing of supplies of wild animals to Rome, but both Loisel and Jennison make use of a case in the correspondence of Cicero as an illustration of the relation between those who wanted wild animals and those who were in the position to obtain them. In 51 BC Cicero left Italy to take up the governorship of Cilicia in southern Asia Minor. His friend Caelius Rufus hoped to be elected magistrate in Rome and would thus be obliged to hold some official games. He soon wrote to Cicero: 'As soon as you hear that I am elected, please attend to that business of the leopards.' He wrote again to remind him 'about the leopards – to set the people of Cibrya to work to see about their transport to me' (Jennison, 1937: 137). Cicero obviously did little about it because soon after Caelius Rufus' election he received another letter in which his friend complained: 'In nearly all my letters to you I have mentioned the subject of leopards. It will be a disgrace to you if, when Patiscus has sent ten to Curio, you don't get many more. Curio has made me a present of those ten, and another ten from Africa.' Later, after emphasizing once more Curio's generosity, he tells Cicero that he must put on a show and that: 'I should like you to attend to my having some beasts from your province.' Finally in yet another letter he warns him that 'it will be a disgrace to you if I don't have any Greek leopards'. Jennison comments that Cicero was being a good governor and was not interested in bothering people to collect leopards for his friend. He was diplomatic though, and replied:

About the leopards, the professional hunters are busy, acting on my commission. But there is an extraordinary scarcity of the beasts, and it is said that those that there are complain bitterly that they are the only living creatures in my province against whom any harm is mediated. So they are said to have decided to leave my province and move into Caria. Still, the business is being carefully attended to, and particularly by Patiscus. Whatever is got will be for you, but what there is to get, we do not know.

(Jennison, 1937: 140)

We never do discover whether Caelius was able to enhance his status in Rome by providing a good show featuring Greek leopards.

In Rome there were large menageries, known as *vivaria*, which were open to the public. It would seem that the dangerous wild animals were kept away from the centre of the city for fear of what would happen should they escape.

The most notable of these was just outside the Praenestine Gate; another was on the Caelian Hill, which was used as a training school for the animal fighters. Little seems to be known about the structure of the *vivaria* but Jennison (1937: 175–6) suggests that the records indicate a large enclosure some 70 yards wide and 440 yards long formed by a wall adjoining the city wall. It seems to have been nothing more than this basic rectangle and although visited by the public there was apparently no attempt to make it in any way a show place, and was perhaps little more than the sort of exhibition yard attached to present-day Spanish bull-rings where the public are able to see the bulls exhibited before the fight. Archaeologists have found remains of animal quarters on the present Vatican site. Members of the public could also see exotic animals at the port where they were being brought into the country, and in many towns *vivaria* were associated with their amphitheatres.

As well as dangerous wild animals, the emperors had, both in Rome and in the surrounding countryside, zoological parks where 'peaceful', that is docile, animals were kept. For example, on the wooded plains of Ardea emperors kept herds of elephants. These parks, to the south of Rome, were only about three miles from the sea and were at the edge of a river, so it was an easy matter to transport them from the ships which brought them from Africa straight into the parks.

It seemed to be one of the requirements of being an emperor that he should have a menagerie, and indeed all of them kept large numbers of wild animals. One of the largest seems to be that of the Emperor Trajan (AD 98–117), who had 11,000 wild and domestic animals in his collection. Another large collection was that of Octavio Augustus (29–14 BC) who had some 3,500 animals, among which are reported:

420 tigers
260 lions
600 African animals (incuding panthers, cheetahs and other carnivores)
1 rhinoceros which was exhibited to the public in the Clos des Septa
1 hippopotamus
Seals
Bears
Elephants
Eagles
36 crocodiles
A snake of 25 yards which was on display in the Comitium near the Forum.

Animals from the menageries were used for display, in triumphal processions or for official celebrations. The menageries were often open to the public and even travellers passing through Rome would call in to see unusual creatures. It was, however, for the games that the largest menageries were established and stocked. It has been estimated that in total the range of animals held in captivity by the Romans consisted of: seventeen species of dangerous wild beasts, fifty-two species of non-ferocious wild beasts, eleven species which lived within the house, five species which were kept in ponds, six species of birds of prey, twelve species of talking or singing cage birds, and twenty-one other types of birds.

PRINCELY POWER AND PRINCELY COLLECTIONS

The ownership of rare or exotic wild animals seems to have fulfilled several functions for the rich and powerful who had the resources to build such collections. The animals undoubtedly gave pleasure and stimulated curiosity in the animal world but they also indicated prestige, luxury and love of display. Various combinations of these elements can be found in the historical records of European societies.

An early example is that of Charlemagne, who it would appear shared some of the Roman emperors' love of the luxury of owning rare wild animals. In 797 there is a record of his receiving various animals including an elephant and monkeys along with perfumes and spices from Abasside Haroun-Rashid, the Caliph of Baghdad. Once again we have an example of the association of rare wild animals with other luxury items, regarded as valuable enough to be given as gifts to important rulers. Soon after these gifts Charlemagne received another visit from an ambassador, this time from the Emir of Cairo who sent him, among other animals, a lion and several bears.

It is in the court of Frederick II, King of the Two Sicilies, that we find the first large menageries in western Europe. In Palermo he created a fixed zoological garden and when he travelled he was always accompanied by a menagerie of lions, camels, elephants, panthers, dromedaries and cheetahs, taken from his collection. It was such a menagerie that it allowed him to put on what was considered to be a splendid show in Worms in 1235 on the occasion of his wedding to Elizabeth, sister of Henry III of England. It is in England that the first great menagerie of the Middle Ages was established. This was the menagerie of Henry I at Woodstock where he kept, among other creatures, lions, leopards, lynx, camels and a rare owl. Henry III used the Woodstock menagerie as a basis for the menagerie at the Tower of London. In addition he also received gifts of animals from the three collections of Frederick II, the Holy Roman Emperor. In 1251 Henry received a polar bear which was kept at the Tower of London and whose food was paid for by the people of the City of London. To reduce the costs its keeper used to take it on a leash to the Thames where it was able to search for fish. In 1254 Henry received a splendid addition to his collection when he was given an elephant – the first to be seen in England – by his brother-in-law Louis IX of France, who had acquired it during the Crusades and had brought it back as a souvenir. The animal was on show to the public in a building paid for out of their money. This obligation of the City to maintain the king's collection of animals in London seems to have been the practice until at least the fourteenth century.

Although there are references throughout the early Middle Ages to the animal collections of kings, princes and nobles, there is really very little detailed information and it would appear that exotic wild animals were not coming into Europe in any great numbers. What changed this was the increase in trade between certain European centres and other parts of the world. For example, during the early Renaissance in Italy there was a renewed interest in animal-keeping, an interest which was fuelled at least in part by new overseas discoveries and by successful commerce, which brought about prosperity and a great desire for luxury goods. Certain cities were particularly important in this regard – Genoa, Pisa and Venice for example, because of their connections with the Turkish empire, with Asia and with Africa. Naturally Venice, as the intermediary between the occident and the orient, was the most important because it controlled so much trade and had warehouses for goods from all parts of the colonies. It was Venice which was the principal supplier of wild animals to the Italian menageries. In the sixteenth century all the great cities and other Italian courts had their menageries and many were owned privately. Men such as the Duke of Calabria at his park in Poggia Reale had collections of animals such as cheetahs, red deer, roe deer, fallow deer, giraffes, ostriches, swans and other varieties of birds.

The popes also kept large collections for the chase or for the simple pleasure of owning exotic animals. Pope Leo X had a menagerie at the Vatican, but he was not the first pope to collect wild animals. Pope Benedict XII had two ostriches in Avignon which came from 'the kingdom of Robert' (Lloyd, 1971: 47), which Lloyd suggests was Sicily, and she records that Varino, the Florentine who brought them, was given a reward of ten florins. Pope Leo kept many sorts of exotic birds as well as lions, leopards, panthers and other animals in the Vatican. His particular favourite was an elephant which once more was a diplomatic gift. It came as a part of a package of wild animals from King Emmanuel of Portugal in 1514 when he requested the Church to ratify the Portuguese possessions in Africa and the Far East. Incidentally, Emmanuel also intended that the pope should receive a rhinoceros but the ship carrying it was struck by a storm off the coast near Genoa and the beast perished.

The Medicis developed a large menagerie in the Vatican. Once again they were able to draw on the resources of those in other parts of the world who wished to send expensive presents to the pope. Cardinal Hippolytus Medici had a collection of *people* of different races as well as exotic animals. He is reported as having a troup of 'Barbarians', speaking over twenty different languages, and there were also Moors, Tartars, Indians, Turks and Africans. A case concerning the Medicis vividly demonstrates how exotic animals were regarded as luxury items, so highly prized that they could be used as suitable gifts to ease diplomatic negotiations. Lloyd tells of the Sultan of Eygpt who, in 1487, sent an embassy to Lorenzo de' Medici to request diplomatic aid to secure the release of his brother who at the time was being held at the French court. The ambassador came with many presents of which the most impressive was a giraffe. The creature delighted Lorenzo and was immediately popular with the local citizens as well. In order to put diplomatic pressure on France it would seem that Lorenzo had agreed to pass the giraffe to the Regent of France, Anne of Beaujeu, in order to secure her goodwill, for part of a letter from her to Lorenzo in 1489 reads:

You know that formerly you advised me in writing that you would send me the giraffe, and although I am sure that you will keep your promise, I beg you, nevertheless, to deliver the animal to me and send it this way, so that you may understand the affection I have for it; for this is the beast of the world that I have the greatest desire to see. And if there is anything on this side that I can do for you, I shall apply myself with all my heart.

(Quoted in Lloyd, 1971: 52)

Unfortunately the beast died before it reached her.

Without doubt the largest menageries of the fifteenth century were those of René, Count of Anjou and Provence, King of the Two Sicilies and Duke of Lorraine. He had travelled extensively and had collected large numbers of animals about him. Loisel suggests that the menagerie at his château at Angers was perhaps the most complete prior to the collection of Louis xiv. When completed in 1450 it consisted of a lion house, accommodation for small mammals, an enclosure for ungulates and ostriches, a large aviary, cages for song birds, a garden with a pond for water birds. All these sections were not grouped together in a distinct whole unit as with menageries nowadays; they were scattered about the waterways and gardens of the château and each had its own keeper and a special budget (Loisel 1912: vol 1, 248).

As an example of payments to keepers it is known that King René paid 112 sous and 6 deniers per month to Jean Bidet to look after a civet-cat and to keep the cage heated. (This was obviously not a highly prestigious job considering that artisans earned some 20 sous a day at this time.) Not only did René send men to North Africa and the Levant to purchase animals for him, but in addition various important rulers sent him animals as gifts. The Florentines sent him lions and leopards, his brother-in-law, Count Vaudemont, sent him a lioness, and his friend King Alfonso v of Portugal sent, among other animals, an elephant, two dromedaries and two civet-cats.

The documentary sources give us little idea of what menageries there were on the Iberian peninsula during the Middle Ages, and there is only limited information available for the fifteenth and sixteenth centuries. There are the occasional references to lions — for example in 1411 the young Juan II of Castille sent a lion as a gift to King Charles VI of France, and we know that in the sixteenth century Don Hurtado de Mendoza had, in his castle or house, lions, tigers and bears, which were used to fight bulls.

There seem to have been few menageries in Portugal at this time, although Loisel does mention certain royal menageries particularly those at Cintra and at Ribeira. These belonged to Alfonso v, who because of his campaigns in Africa was known as 'Alfonso the African', and it would appear that his collection, which was almost exclusively of animals from that continent, reflected his territorial and trade interests. What seems particularly important in the history of noble and royal menageries is the number of times that Portugal as a supplier of animals is mentioned. In 1475 Alfonso sent a collection of animals from Guinea to Louis XI of France, and in 1477 an elephant, marmosets and monkeys to René of Anjou. It was in the next reign, that of Juan II (1481–95), that one first hears of natives from Africa arriving in Lisbon, as well as birds with beautiful plumage and monkeys which were due to be sent as gifts to various lords. With Emmanuel I, Portuguese colonization and Portuguese commerce were brought to their highest point by Vasco da Gama who, in 1498, found a route to the East Indies, and by Pedro Álvarez Cabral who discovered Brazil two years later. From then on an observer could see all manner of strange animals arriving from Africa and Asia in Lisbon, in particular the first elephants and rhinos to be brought to Europe since the destruction of the Roman empire. During the second half of the sixteenth century monkeys and birds came from Africa, destined for the royal menageries and for those of great noblemen. Officials in the colonies vied with each other to send acceptable presents to kings and queens at home.

THE INFLUENCE OF EXPLORATION AND TRADE

Despite the connections of Spain and Portugal with the Americas, animals discovered there (with the exception of some of the colourful birds) do not seem to have entered collections. Wilma George points out that all the early visitors to the West Indies and to South and Central America reported as especially impressive the coloured parrots (live specimens of which reached Cádiz in 1494; see George, 1980: 82), but they also reported other creatures. She suggests that one can see from examining the decorated maps how South American fauna were becoming known in Europe during the sixteenth century through the writings of explorers and chroniclers, and that certainly by 1550 a fair representation of this fauna could be obtained by combining the information on all the maps (George, 1969). Such creatures might well have been of interest to specialists in natural history (although as George points out the discovery of South American fauna did not supplant the native and traditional animals in the important animal encyclopaedias of the time – 1980: 87), but they do not seem to have captured the popular imagination. Renaissance artists were not interested in painting such creatures, nor were they collected as living specimens. These animals just did not seem to relate to the ideal of beauty at the time, 'an ideal favouring large noble forms rather than the picturesque. The princes of the Renaissance were not particularly interested in the spiny, scaly, little creatures brought by the sailors from South America' (Lewinsohn, 1954: 168). It seems that Africa and the Far East were the places from which the truly exotic animals came – an attitude which has not changed today among the general public.

The development of trading connections played an important role in the history of menageries in the seventeenth century when there seems to have been a resurgence of interest in keeping animals. In Holland this was facilitated by the country's key position in terms of foreign trade routes. For instance, at the end of the sixteenth century the East India and West India Companies had been formed, and the first of these soon gave the Dutch a substantial colonial empire, taken largely from the Portuguese. Amsterdam replaced Antwerp and Lisbon as a port of importance in the seventeenth and eighteenth centuries, and apart from the commercial products from the east and the Americas which were unloaded there, many exotic animals also came into the port and were then sent to the various menageries.

The Prince of Orange, for example, had many menageries. One which attracted the greatest interest was that at Loo, a royal residence. The park had for years been stocked with animals but it was not until the seventeenth century that it was decided to put a menagerie there. The collection was increased during the eighteenth century because of the number of animals sent through the colonial network. Allamand, the naturalist, writing in the Dutch edition of Buffon, argued that this menagerie was 'the most interesting in Europe from the point of view of a naturalist' (Loisel, 1912: vol. 2, 36).

The general prosperity created by the flourishing commerce in the Netherlands, the spirit of curiosity, the growth of interest in natural history, the means of communicating with the Indies, Africa and Brazil, all encouraged a climate in which affluent citizens established cabinets of curiosities and natural-history specimens, and stocked their gardens with unusual creatures. Hendrik Engel, in his list of zoological collections, mentions that many merchants kept menageries at their country residences; he adds that the East India Company had its own stables for the animals brought in by their ships, and that at the ports the captains would often show the creatures to members of the public. Engel also records a collection of animals in an inn: 'in the tavern "De Witte Olifant" on the Botermarkt (now Rembrantplein) were shown many of the animals which were destined for the menagerie of the Austrian emperor at Schönbrunn', a most important menagerie to which we will refer in the next section (quoted in Pieter Smit, 1986: 7). At the same time some of these animals were taken by travelling showmen who took menageries from town to town for the entertainmentof thr general public.

SPECIAL CASES: VERSAILLES AND SCHÖNBRUNN

Without doubt the most impressive menagerie in France, and probably in the world, in the seventeenth century was that which Louis xiv had constructed at Versailles. In terms of design what was particularly novel about the menagerie and what, with hindsight, makes it such a landmark in the thinking of how to present animals in captivity, was that rather than having the animal enclosures or houses in different parts of a large park which was what normally happened, Louis decided to have a combination of animals, plants and trees all in one place. He thus, according to some historians, created the first zoological garden. There were originally only nine or ten acres which were so arranged as to receive the greatest number of animals possible in so small a space. The notion of 'arranged' is especially important here for not only was the menagerie part of a park and garden where the natural world was rearranged to suit man's purpose but this was now selectively populated by animals selected by man. As we mentioned earlier this is a prefiguration of panopticanism in that here the guiding principle is that nature is reorganized into a pattern which converges on the house at the centre of the system and from where it can be seen at a glance.

The central feature of the menagerie was a small pleasure house, a luxurious miniature in the style of aristocratic residences of the seventeenth century, where the king and his guests could rest and survey the collection. Projecting from the house into the central courtyard was an octagonal pavilion, from the balcony of which one could see the seven animal enclosures radiating out beyond the central courtyard. On the first floor of this pavilion there was an octagonal room; of the eight walls, one was for the doorway and the other seven had large windows which opened on to the balcony from which the visitor could see all the courtyards one after the other. On the inside the walls of the house were covered with paintings of animal tableaux as though to prepare the visitor for what he was going to see. The central courtyard of the menagerie was an octagon. On one side was the house and the other seven were closed off by iron grills through which the visitors could see into the interiors of the animal courtyards which were separated from one another by large walls (see Belin 1985: 12–25 for details of this architecture).

Because of his great power and influence, Louis was constantly offered animals as gifts by many foreign leaders. In 1668 an elephant came from the King of Portugal, while in 1687 three crocodiles arrived from the King of Siam. Louis also informed the governors of his colonies (for example, the one in Madagascar) and his consuls (particularly the one in Cairo) that they must send animals to him. The shipping fleets of both Indies Companies sent creatures from America, Asia and Africa. A specialist animal buyer, Mosnier Gassion, of Montpellier, was sent out annually to the eastern Mediterranean, to Egypt and Tunisia, to find animals. Huge numbers of animals arrived in Versailles. Hamy records a single consignment of 194 creatures from the Levant (1898: 511). Of all the animals in the menagerie it was the elephant, given by the King of Portugal, which was generally the most popular.

Not only did Louis and the court enjoy themselves in the menagerie, but important foreigners also visited the collection. The bourgeoisie *and* the poor were likewise able to visit and admire the king's animals but they could not get into the park without a ticket, and these were issued only when the king himself was not present. Later, around 1690, it would seem that at certain times the park and the house were open to all. The first guide for foreigners was written in 1674 and this does not refer to any restrictions. In the eighteenth century in England the public was admitted to another royal collection, that of the royal menagerie in the Tower of London. For this privilege the visitors paid a small admission fee or alternatively they brought with them a dog or a cat to feed to the lions.

One of the great menageries of the eighteenth century and one which is often referred to in the history of zoos, was that of the imperial menagerie at

Schönbrunn, near Vienna. It was built for Franz Stephan I in 1752 at the instigation of his doctor Gérard van Swieten. The menagerie was designed by a Dutchman, Adrien van Steckhoven, who took part of his inspiration from two other menageries, that of Prince Eugene of Savoy at Castle Belvedere, south of Vienna, and that of Louis XIV at Versailles. The menagerie, which consisted of thirteen enclosures, was conceived as a total entity. It was about fifteen acres in extent and was totally enclosed by a wall. Within this space, apart from the enclosures for the animals, there were pathways, a pond, ornate pavilions, an English garden, pools with fountains, and for the animal accommodation a small stone house with doors and windows done in the style of Louis IXV.

Animals were brought from other menageries in Franz's empire as well as from collections in Germany, England and the Netherlands. The emperor ordered Nicolas Jacquin, the botanist, to go to South America in the company of two Italian ornithologists to obtain plants, mammals and rare birds. In the end the collection consisted of some 600 to 700 specimens. In 1759 a small octagonal rococo-style pavilion where visitors could rest was added. From this they could climb a set of stairs to a terrace and so see all thirteen enclosures and the animals they contained. We have commented on the sociological and pyschological implications of this style of layout in chapter 3, for it is highly significant that there was one central viewing point and that the walls between the enclosures were so high that one had to be in this central position in order to survey the entire collection with one sweeping glance. The design of this menagerie is clearly similar to that of Louis XIV and has similar implications in terms of relationships of visibility, power and control.

Franz died in 1765 and during the time of the next emperor, Joseph II, the menagerie was open to the public, although it does not seem to be recorded who 'the public' would have been at this time. Joseph wanted to increase the collection, so he sent another botanist, Mathias Léopold Stupicz, to North America along with Franz Boos to collect specimens. They were away from 1783 to 1785 and on his return Boos went to Africa where he collected twelve species of mammals and some 250 birds.

BEYOND EUROPE

It must not be thought that menagerie-keeping was an exclusively European phenomenon. It is difficult to find information about menageries in other parts of the world but there are examples none the less. We have already referred briefly to the menagerie of Montezuma in Tenochtitlan (now Mexico) which was seen by a European in 1519. Cortés, the Spanish conquistador, reported that there was an enormous collection of animals held in a menagerie constructed near the imperial palace and separated from it by gardens. It consisted of a huge aviary, known as the Palace of Birds, containing a collection of birds from all parts of the empire. Cortés was immediately impressed by the sight of so many birds with such splendid and colourful plumage. So large was the collection that it needed a staff of 300 to look after it. They made themselves 'acquainted with the appropriate food of its inmates, often-times procured at great cost, and in the moulting season were careful to collect the beautiful plumage, which, with its many coloured tints, furnished the materials for the Aztec painter' (Prescott, 1847: 319). In a separate building was an aviary for the large birds of prey in which 'no less than five hundred turkeys, the cheapest meat in Mexico, were allowed for the daily consumption of these tyrants of the feathered race' (Prescott, 1847: 319).

According to Cortés, the cages of mammalian carnivores were clean, airy and light, with plenty of space for the animals to have freedom of movement, and were made of skilfully worked wooden planks which were pinned together. They held lions, tigers and leopards (although it is difficult to know where these might have come from), as well as other wild cats, some kinds of martens and foxes. There were two further sections of the menagerie, one for domestic animals and the other for 'a great number of reptiles and serpents remarkable for their size and venomous qualities, among which the Spaniards beheld the fiery little animal "with castanets in his tail", the terror of the American wilderness. The serpents were confined in long cages lined with down or feathers, or in troughs of mud and water' (Prescott, 1847: 319). Cortés and his followers did not seem interested in studying the peculiarities of these new species but 'gazed on the spectacle with a vague curiosity not unmixed with awe; and, as they listened to the wild cries of the ferocious animals and the hissing of the serpents, they almost fancied themselves in the infernal regions' (Prescott, 1847: 320)

A most important aspect of this menagerie was the collection of human freaks – dwarves, albinos, various sorts of deformed people, slaves and others that Montezuma had obtained from all over his empire. Similarly he was able to obtain the animals he needed from various parts of his empire. The animals of the menagerie were principally kept for luxury, adornment and curiosity but they also served other purposes – for hunting, for sacrifices or for their fur and feathers.

French travellers who visited the Arab and Turkish worlds in the sixteenth century found flourishing menageries. Pierre Belon, for example, gives a detailed description of a menagerie in Constantinople at this time:

One sees the ruins of a muchly ancient palace, named by the commoners the palace of Constantine. There the Turk feeds his elephants and other gentle creatures. There is a place in Constantinople where the Grand Turk keeps wild animals which is an ancient church; and there is attached to each pillar of the church a Lion, a thing that one cannot but marvel at on seeing it, given that they untie them and handle them, and tie them up again when they wish, and even lead them sometimes about the town ... thus each nation of the lands wherein the Turk has dominion that has taken any wild animal sends it to Constantinople and there the Emperor has it fed and carefully looked after.

(Loisel, 1912: vol. 1, 187)

Loisel comments that during the European Renaissance, the east continued through the Arabs and Turks to be the greatest purveyor of menagerie animals, as it had been in the time of the Romans (1912: vol. 1, 190).

Exotic wild animals were also regarded as suitably high-status gifts among non-European rulers. For example, Hasan Ibn Muhammad, better known as Leo Africanus, who was born in Granada at the end of the fifteenth century, became ambassador for the King of Fez, and in this capacity made journeys along caravan routes into the interior of Africa. He records:

Myselfe (I remember) once was a most magnificent gift presented to the saide king in the name of theis prince, to wit, fiftie men slaves and fiftie women slaves brought out of the land of the Negroes, tenne eunuchs, twelve camels, one Giraffa, sixteene civet-cats, one pound of civet, a pound of amber, and almost six hundered skins of a certain beast called the Elant (probably some kind of antelope), whereof they make their shields, everie skin being worth at Fez, eoght ducates; twentie of the men slaves cost twentie ducats a peece and so did fifteene of the women slaves; every eunuch was valued at fortie, every camell at fiftie and every civet-cat at two hunderth ducats; and a pound of civet and amber is solde at Fez for three score ducates.

(Lloyd, 1971: 54)

THE GROWTH OF CURIOSITY AND SCIENTIFIC INTEREST

As we argued in chapter 2, many modern zoos aspire to a cultural status equivalent to that of institutions such as art galleries and museums. But the collecting of wild animals for purposes other than display or aesthetic pleasure is not new. Some of the earliest references to collections of wild animals suggest that at least one of the purposes behind the activity of collectors was that of scientific curiosity. For example, the previously mentioned collection of the Chinese emperor Wen Wang was kept in the park Ling-yu ('the Park of Intelligence'), so called because there one saw the divine work of nature. This has led some commentators to suggest that this was the first zoological garden established not simply for amusement but also for scientific purposes. It is also reported that the menagerie at Alexandria owned by Ptolemy II (283–246 BC), which was the largest of its kind in the Hellenic world, was established because Ptolemy had a particular interest in natural science. Despite this very early reference perhaps the first definite case of a menagerie being put to a scientific purpose was the collection of animals assembled during his campaigns by Alexander the Great for his tutor Aristotle, who obtained information from this collection for his works of natural history.

In terms of an early European interest in animals from a scientific rather than a display point of view, it is interesting to note that in the ninth century AD at the monastery of Saint Gall in Switzerland, one of the principal scientific and intellectual centres of the time, there was a menagerie. What is particularly significant about this establishment was its layout:

A plan of this monastery, drawn up in the IXth century, shows a farm with 'a curious divisional system, being of a cellular nature so to speak, more like that of our zoological gardens than the arrangements for more recent farms: there each stable has its special courtyard and is accompanied by a keeper's accommodation. The birds are enclosed in circular parks. The garden, methodically divided up as it is, reminds one, for its part, of a botanical garden and it did, in fact, provision the pharmacy as well as the monks' table.'

(Loisel, 1912: vol. 1, 164; see also Thompson and Goldin, 1975: 9–12)

Despite these early references it is not really until the end of the seventeenth century and the beginning of the eighteenth that one finds an example of the scientific potential of a menagerie being exploited. Although not established for scientific purposes the menagerie of Louis XIV became an institution where much scientific work, especially in comparative anatomy, was carried out by men such as Claude Perrault. Indeed in its days of greatest glory it was able to offer the best collection of living creatures ever to be assembled in one place and it is recorded that there were some 222 different species housed there. Louis XV, the next monarch, had little interest in the menagerie and it subsequently went into decline. By the time of Louis XVI in 1774 the menagerie was in a dilapidated condition and the buildings were in need of repair, yet there was little money for it because the court viewed the place with almost complete indifference. Ironically it was a public attack on this dilapidated menagerie at the time of the French Revolution which set in motion a series of actions which was to lead to the establishment of one of the world's foremost menageries organized for scientific purposes.

In some circles there seems to have been indignation that animals in the menagerie were living a life of luxury, and Loisel quotes one of the encyclopaedists who argued that 'menageries must be destroyed when people have no bread; for it is shameful to feed animals at great cost when one has round about one men dying of hunger' (Loisel, 1912: vol. 2, 159). In October 1789 a group marched out to the menagerie where they were confronted by the inspector in charge. The spokesman of the group: 'In the name of the people and in the name of nature summoned him to set free beings that had freely come out of the hands of the Creator and been improperly detained by the pride and the pomp of tyrants' (Loisel, 1912: vol.2, 160). This, incidentally, is probably the only mass attempt to free animals from menageries or zoos. The director, Laimant, pointed out that the first thing many of the animals would do if released would be to devour their liberators, and therefore, rather than freeing the animals himself, he would prefer to hand over the keys to the mob. The dangerous animals were thus left in their cages, some others were freed, and others were sent to the slaughterhouse.

There was still the problem of what to do with the remaining animals, and the estate manager at Versailles made an application to have them sent to the Jardin du Roi, a garden which had originally been established in 1626 by Louis XIII for the study of plants and which later had broadened its interest to other aspects of natural history. The naturalist Georges Louis Leclerc, better known as Buffon, had tried in 1782 to move the last animals from the run-down Versailles menagerie to the Jardin du Roi but had been unsuccessful. It was the October events in 1789 which prompted change, for the registrar at Versailles wrote to Bernadine de Saint Pierre, the superintendent of the Jardin des Plantes (formerly du Roi), saying that he was authorized to send him animals from the old royal collection. De Saint Pierre decided that it would be a worthwhile thing to 'transport what he calls a "public show" into "a place set aside for the study of nature in the interests of science and the liberal arts, for scientists and for artists"' (Hamy, 1898: 513).

The menagerie of the Muséum National in Paris, founded in 1793, was the first national menagerie in the world. As part of the reorganization of the royal gardens it was decided to establish a menagerie for the study of zoology. There were, however, few animals available for such an institution so in Paris the municipal police were ordered at the end of 1793 to seize animals of travelling showmen and take them to the museum. The professors at the museum under the directorship of Étienne Geoffroy-Sainte-Hilaire were not quite ready for this influx of wild animals, but they quickly prepared accommodation for them. The secretary at the museum at the time wrote:

There is, under the galleries, a place where these animals can be provisionally lodged while we are preparing suitable quarters for them, and this place is even large enough to hold a greater number, if others are brought, and if the committee of public instruction should think it proper to keep them. There is no doubt but that a collection of living animals would be an advantage for the instruction of the public and for the progress of natural history, and that it would be means of acquiring and multiplying, within the territory of the Republic, any useful species that now exist only in foreign countries.

(Hamy, 1898: 514)

They continued to receive animals during the early part of the year. There were animals from the Duke of Orléans' estate, some that had been at a great menagerie at Chantilly; and in 1794 they also received the last animals from the Versailles menagerie. The menagerie at the Jardin des Plantes certainly lived up to its scientific and educational aims for, using its resources, Frédéric Cuvier was able to produce his studies on instinct and intelligence in animals, as well as his work on comparative anatomy. Other celebrated scientists who made use of the specimens in the menagerie include Geoffroy-Sainte-Hilaire, Duvernoy, Milne-Edwards, Gervais, Gratiolet, Lamarck and Latrille.

In other parts of Europe there are also references to important scientific work which made use of menagerie animals. In Belém, for example, in 1726, King Juan established a truly zoological garden. The king was particularly interested in animals and had a good ornithological collection. Some of the first natural-history studies in Portugal by the zoologists Felix de Avellar and Brotero and Domingos Vandelli were helped by this collection. In England, Harvey's work on the circulation of the blood was carried out in part on animals in the royal collection at Windsor Park.

After the establishment of the scientific status of the menagerie in Paris, the next most important creation was that of the Zoological Society of London and the associated Zoological Gardens in the nineteenth century. It was the foundation of this institution which provided a model and an impetus for the development of zoos in many parts of Europe. Sir Stamford Raffles, a colonial administrator and founder of the colony of Singapore, suggested to Sir Joseph Banks as early as 1817 that there was a need for a collection of animals for scientific purposes as well as general interest. It was Sir Humphrey Davy, the new president of the Royal Society, who drew up the 1825 prospectus for the Zoological Society of London. The wording of this is highly significant for the ideas contained within it were to be repeated many times in the nineteenth and twentieth centuries as more and more zoological gardens were created.

It has long been a matter of deep regret to the cultivators of Natural History that we possess no great scientific establishments either for teaching or elucidating zoology, and no public menageries or collections of living animals where their nature, properties, and habits may be studied.... Should the Society flourish and succeed, it will not only be useful in common life, but likewise promote the best and most extensive objects of the Scientific History of Animated Nature, and offer a collection of living animals such as never yet existed in ancient or modern times... animals to be brought from every part of the globe to be applied either to some useful purpose, or as objects of scientific research, not of vulgar admiration.

(Quoted in Olney, 1980: 40)

The Zoological Gardens in Regent's Park in London were opened to fellows of the Society in 1827. In the next few years the Zoological Gardens were stocked with animals, not all of which were bought, for many came as gifts from princes, lords, consuls and foreign rulers. From an inventory of the early stock we find a brown bear presented to the Society by the Marquess of Hertford who brought it from Russia, a squirrel petaurus acquired for the Society by Lady Glengall, and American bison, red fox and a silver fox given by the Hudson's Bay Company, a beaver sent from Canada by Lord Dalhousie, an Italian wolf dog from the Campagna di Roma, a white-cheeked marten brought from India by the Hon. Captain Shore, a white llama from the Duke of Bedford, a pine marten sent from Russia to the Marchioness of Londonderry, and a black ape (*Macacus niger*) 'that in the gardens is understood to have arrived in a vessel from the South Seas, but from what locality it was obtained has not been ascertained' (Bennett, 1830: 190).

The animals from the royal menagerie in Windsor Park were sent to London, and animals from the menagerie at the Tower of London were also transferred to the Regent's Park site. London did not receive all the animals from these two collections but rather shared them with Dublin, where the Royal Zoological Society of Ireland had been formed in 1830 and zoological gardens opened in 1831. It should be noted that London's Zoological Gardens were not established in order to provide a recreational facility for the general public, for when they opened on 27 April 1826 only members and their guests were admitted. This restriction lasted until 1940, when it was changed to Sunday mornings only; it was finally withdrawn in 1957. It was as a result of the opening of the Zoological Gardens to the public in London that the word 'zoo' came into international vocabulary, for it was the music-hall artist 'The

Great Vance' who, in 1867, sang 'Walking in the zoo is the o.k. thing to do'.

CIVIC PRIDE AND THE DEVELOPMENT OF
PUBLIC COLLECTIONS

In the nineteenth century there was a period of rapid expansion of zoological-garden construction, and many of these gardens were municipal institutions established in connection with public parks. In fact the oldest European municipal menagerie is that of Madrid, the old menagerie of Charles III. Of other European countries it was only really Hungary, Germany and France which had municipal zoological gardens, although there were probably only ten major zoological gardens in the world, all of which were in Europe. By about the mid-nineteenth century many of the major European cities had zoological gardens, and from Europe the movement spread to other parts of the world. Many were founded by groups of prominent citizens who felt that their city ought to have a zoological garden, and thus the whole matter became entangled with questions of civic pride. In England a good example was that of Bristol, where in 1835 the Bristol, Clifton and West of England Zoological Society was founded. If one looks at the first balance sheet, dated 7 May 1836, one finds that most of the shares were in the hands of prominent Bristolians such as the Frys, Pountneys, Sturges, and W.D. and H.O. Wills; even Isambard Kingdom Brunel features; it was a list 'which ensured that the new society would have prestige and the business ability to back it' (Green-Armytage, 1964: 7 and 108–12).

A similar question of civic pride can perhaps be seen in the first zoological garden established in the United States, in Philadelphia. A small group of enthusiasts led by Dr William Camac, who was active in city affairs, visited Europe and were impressed by the zoos. They felt that America needed a proper zoological garden rather than the menageries associated with museums, and thus a zoological society was founded in 1859 (although nothing could be done until 1874 because of the Civil War). It had two important features. The first was its *raison d'être*, which was to collect animals 'for the instruction and recreation of people' (Toovey, 1980: 84), and the second that many of the early buildings were copies of contemporary ornate European buildings. The National Zoological Park in Washington DC was established at the end of the nineteenth century under the auspices of the Smithsonian Museum. At the time Dr Casey Wood of the Smithsonian accepted the importance of London as a model when he said that 'although we can never hope to equal your unrivalled gardens, mainly because we do not have contributory agents in the shape of world-flung people who, truly devoted to the outdoor study of nature, bring or send all the treasures of animal life on this earth to your very doors' (quoted in Zuckerman, 1980: 15).

In fact exotic animals *were* sent to the United States as gifts. In 1899, Langley, the secretary of the Smithsonian, requested that all Secretaries of State for War and naval officers should bring back animals following tours of duty. In addition many United States consuls sent gifts – in 1904 Theodore Roosevelt received a lion from King Menelik of Abyssinia, and Ras Makonneu, the governor of Harrar Province in Abyssinia, also sent a lion as well as two zebra and an oryx.

The Royal Society of Zoology in Amsterdam, founded in 1838, was the first to be established in continental Europe, and was followed by Rotterdam in 1857, and The Hague in 1862. Many zoological societies were established in Germany in the second half of the nineteenth century but they had a somewhat different spirit from those already established. Their aim was not simply that of fomenting scientific progress in the field of natural history in tandem with the provision of recreation for the public; an additional purpose was to operate the zoological gardens so as to bring benefits to the society members who were shareholders. The gardens had picturesque and monumental animal houses to attract people, but there were also restaurants, bars, concert halls, rooms for parties and games – a novel combination in the context of zoological gardens. 'However, despite this commercial interest, several of the German menageries have very fine animal collections and it is fair to add that natural history has considerably profited both from the exhibition and the study of these collections' (Loisel, 1912: vol. 3, 223).

Elsewhere in Europe there were other zoological gardens formed by shareholders, namely in Antwerp, Lisbon, Rome and the Bois de Boulogne in Paris. As hardly a year went by from the mid-nineteenth century onwards without a new zoo opening in a major European city or town, trade was extremely good for animal suppliers and in particular for Carl Hagenbeck, the German animal dealer who, as we noted earlier, was of great importance in the development of the modern zoological garden. His trading indicates the considerable market in wild animals which had developed as a result of the growth of zoos, for no longer was it possible to have a collection merely put together out of gifts from fellow rulers and loyal subjects. The following is a list of some of the animals which Hagenbeck imported in the twenty-year period from 1866 to 1886 (and it must be remembered that he was just one of the many suppliers to zoos):

1,000 lions

400 tigers

700 + leopards

1,000 + bears

800 hyenas

300 elephants

17 Indian rhinos

Tens of thousands of monkeys

Thousands of crocodiles, boas and pythons

100,000 + birds

17 Javan rhinos

17 Sumatran rhinos

9 African rhinos

300 camels

150 giraffes

600 antelope

(Reported in Reichenbach, 1980: 574)

Hagenbeck also introduced at least twelve large mammal species to Europe for the first time. He traded with America, Africa, Asia and Australia, and he supplied animals for zoos and circuses in America and Europe, and even supplied exotic game animals to private estates in Europe.

It is somewhat difficult to discover the dates of the foundation of zoos outside Europe, North America and Australia and New Zealand. It is certain that the European model of the zoological garden was exported by various colonial powers to the countries they governed. Writing in 1911, Loisel lists several places where the British had replaced old menageries by zoological gardens – Bombay, Calcutta, Colombo, Karachi, Lahore, Madras, Rangoon, Singapore and Trivandram. The Dutch built a zoo in the centre of what is now Jakarta. In South and Central America, the European influence did not lead to the construction of zoological gardens at this time (with the notable exception of Rosario, Buenos Aires and La Plata in Argentina), probably because in the nineteenth and early twentieth centuries Spain and Portugal, the early colonizers who still exerted some cultural influence on that continent, evinced little interest in such institutions.

The zoological garden, as opposed to the menagerie, was entirely a European invention, but with European colonization the idea was developed in other parts of the world. Although we have seen that kings, princes, nobles and other people of importance in many countries outside Europe kept wild animals privately, it is with European colonialism that the zoological garden develops in these countries. In 1894 the Shah of Persia had an English-style zoological garden built for him in his palace at Teheran. In 1868 the Maharajah of Jaipur had a menagerie built within the municipal park for the poor of the town. In the nineteenth century large menageries were established in Bombay, Calcutta and Rangoon. In Egypt, in the second part of the nineteenth century, there were many menageries, including an acclimatization garden inspired by the

Jardin des Plantes in Paris, which was built at the palace Kasr-el-Nouza, near Cairo. There was an enormous menagerie in Gezeria, and in Giza there was a zoological garden which was actually built by the English. The influence was not simply a one-way process, however, for some of the first English governors in India, wishing to imitate the luxurious style of the rajahs, built up animal collections. At the beginning of the nineteenth century Lord Wellesley, for example, had a park stocked with wild animals, including elephant and rhinoceros.

Once we reach the early twentieth century, there is nothing of special significance occurring except that many more zoos are being built. Many zoos professed to being more than merely entertainment, or saw their role as that of 'rational entertainment', but apart from their links with professional zoologists, they do not seem to have been perceived as cultural institutions on a par with art galleries or museums, where one entered to be edified, educated or aesthetically uplifted.

It is perhaps a crude generalization, but in the main the late-nineteenth- and early-twentieth-century zoos consisted of 'postage stamp' type collections with as many creatures as possible represented, so that they were essentially museums of living creatures. There are two key features here. First we must consider the trends in the scientific zoological climate at the time of the formation of such collections, which can be seen as a representation of contemporary taxonomic interests in zoology and biology. Given the popular nature of the visit to the zoological garden this cannot be the whole story, and so we must also consider the general public which wanted to see a wide range of unusual and interesting animals. We must note, too, the increasing popularity of zoos during the twentieth century, for zoos have multiplied rapidly – up to 1920 there were about 120 zoos, by 1959 the *International Zoo Yearbook* lists 309, and, by 1978 883.

In the latter part of the twentieth century there were changes of emphasis in zoology; animal behaviour was something which began to engage the attention of scientists, and this, combined with an interest in ecology and conservation, began to alter the nature of many major zoos. The visiting public, particularly those in north-west Europe, North America and Australia and New Zealand, were less interested in seeing the animals caged in the old menagerie-style buildings. This was combined with a general philosophical and emotional change in attitudes towards animals in these western industrial nations. In a nutshell, there developed what can best be called an anthropomorphic concern with animal welfare. Perhaps the key element in the modern progressive zoo is that nature is seen as an ideal to be copied and the animals, instead of being mere taxonomic specimens, are resituated in a replica of their environment. Instead of the animals having to adjust themselves to the zoo there is some attempt to have the zoo adjust itself to the animals. The complex interrelation of these themes brought about changes in exhibition philosophy in the zoos in many countries of the world.

Apart from the way in which animals are exhibited in zoological gardens, and the number and species actually exhibited, there have been few changes to the essential form of the zoological garden. Perhaps the only break with the mainstream zoological-garden tradition came in the late 1960s in Europe and particularly in England with the development of safari parks, a concept which is now found in many parts of the world. In these parks a range of animals are kept, but particularly prominent are those with big cats and other large African game animals. They are kept in open paddocks and are popular because the animals can be seen in spacious surroundings, and the public are thrilled at being able to drive close to them. In the early days many of these parks were associated with the stately homes of the aristocracy, and although the safari park was in some ways a novel development it is perhaps possible to see a precedent in the collections of wild animals which many members of the royal families, nobility and landed gentry have kept on their own estates. Examples abound in France, Germany, Hungary and other parts of eastern Europe, Scandinavia and Britain of parks where the owners attempted to acclimatize exotic species to a new environment. Often their motive was simply the aesthetic pleasure of having attractive creatures in their parks, but in many cases they hoped to produce a new creature for hunting or for some commercial purpose. For example, between 1892 and 1911, the Duke of Bedford in his park at Woburn had a collection of 2,000 mammals of some fifty-three species. The significant difference between these collections and the safari parks was that, in the latter, exotic species were introduced in order to bring paying visitors on to the land. The novelty of the safari park was, and is, that people could apparently enter the animals' territory. It was like being in the wild without discomfort, and with the additional guarantee that visitors *would* see the animals. Such a development could of course only come about with increasing affluence, because safari-park visits are dependent on car ownership.

As we have said, there have obviously been changes in the nature of zoological gardens and there have been radical revisions of their exhibition philosophy, a result of the concern for what the zoological garden should be attempting to achieve. From about the mid-twentieth century in the major zoos of North America, north-west Europe, Australia and New Zealand those who were managing zoos became concerned about the nature of the zoo itself. It was no longer enough to have animals solely for exhibition; one had to think about why one had them and what to do with them. But fundamentally whatever the changes prompted by such thinking, zoos still consist of animals kept in enclosures of greater or lesser complexity which the public can walk past to view the animals.

6
The Cultural Status of the Zoo

Museum: A Repository of Learned Curiosities.

(Samuel Johnson's *Dictionary*, 1755)

I'll tell you what's fun – watching other people. I saw one guy whistling at a snake, trying to get its attention. Can you imagine? Whistling at a snake to get its attention? That's like trying to teach my dog calculus.

(Wolf and Tymitz, 1979: 17)

Every museum is in itself a set of inverted commas and every museum exhibit is a quotation. To remove it from the original habitat is to substitute one meaning for another.

(Kenneth Hudson, 1986: 2)

The trouble with the zoo, he said, is that it must always be a compromise between keeping animals in the best possible conditions and the need to exhibit them. A zoo should not be just a show. It should be an education as well. True, the visitor must be given his money's worth. That's one reason why we put our penguins in huge glass-sided tanks with real ice floes. It's a hit with the public but the more important reason is that the penguins are happier on ice and it protects them from airborne diseases. Zoos should not have to pander to the public and should not have to worry about paying their way. Someone, the State or the Municipality, should underwrite the bills. It must be realized that a zoo that communicates the wonder and diversity of wildlife is doing an important job in making people care.

(Dr Scherner, Frankfurt, quoted in Gordon Woodroffe, 1981: 84)

We have shown in our historical analysis how living creatures from different parts of the world were collected not primarily for their zoological interest, but because they were unusual, rare, exotic or in some way attractive, and moreover how their possession indicated wealth, status, power and international connections. Such collections were in the hands of private individuals who kept them for their own personal enjoyment, and it was not until the end of the eighteenth century in the case of the Jardin des Plantes, and, as a general trend in the nineteenth century in Europe, North America and other parts of the world, that one finds the establishment of collections primarily for public display. In that zoological gardens comprise collections of zoological specimens they are similar to natural-history museums (although of course in the former the specimens are alive), and it is illuminating to compare the status of the modern zoological garden with other institutions such as museums and art galleries, which also collect items in order to exhibit them to the public. Such a comparison is particularly interesting in terms of the cultural factors influencing the nature of the collection and its presentation and interpretation, for in almost all societies which have them art galleries and museums are treated as belonging to the realm of high culture, whereas zoos suffer an inferior status and are usually regarded as places of mere recreation and amusement.

Hughes de Varine-Bohan, director of the International Council of Museums, in his useful survey of museums suggests six main periods in the history of these institutions: the Middle Ages, 1400–1700 (i.e. from the beginnings of the Renaissance to classicism), the eighteenth century, 1790–1850, 1850–1950, and from 1950 onwards (1985). Here we obviously cannot discuss such a complex piece of cultural history in anything but the most superficial way, but it is worth examining certain key aspects as they shed light on our particular interests.

In the Middle Ages in Europe, collections of works of a scientific or artistic nature were kept in churches, monasteries and universities. They were kept predominantly for religious, economic and scientific interest, but they were not systematic collections nor were they open to general inspection, although it is recorded that various of the relics held in churches and cathedrals would be shown to members of the congregation on special occasions. Holy relics would often be kept in the same collections as secular curiosities; for example the inventory at St Omer in France in 1346 detailed the following objects:

A drop of the Virgin's milk, a pot that figured in the miracles at Cana, a scrap of the martyr's shroud, nails or a fragment of wood from the true cross, a cameo of the Queen of Sheba, a crystal goblet from King Solomon's temple, souvenirs brought back from distant lands by pilgrims and crusaders, 'thunderstones', griffins' eggs, tortoise shells, unicorns' horns, antediluvian giants' bones and teeth.

(Altick 1978: 6)

Collections of such items with intense religious significance would certainly assist in maintaining the status of the institutions which held them. As with the animals in the collections of kings and nobility at this time, these items are perhaps not immediately identified as luxury items but were so in that they were both rare and indicated connections with distant lands.

In the second period identified by Varine-Bohan, one finds as themes of the Renaissance the discovery of the classical world, the fragmentation of Christianity, the gradual secularization of education and the emergence of cultivated aristocratic and bourgeois classes. We have noted that, as with the collections of animals for menageries of the time, material for museum collections was gathered in the course of the explorations of unknown or little-known parts of the world. Those directly involved – captains of vessels, the explorers themselves and the administrators – returned with all sorts of curious objects which formed the basis of many collections. Gifts of interesting items also came from ambassadors and visiting sovereigns, or might be brought back as part of the spoils of foreign conquests. Many of the major collections which developed at the time, for example at Vienna, El Escorial, Versailles, Florence and the Vatican, gave rise to some of the great museums of our time. Emulating such collections of the kings and nobles were those of the bourgeoisie, whose collections became status symbols. These were not systematic collections – whether in the sense of being ordered according to a particular scientific scheme or in the sense of what was actually collected – and the only factor which related the elements was that they were curiosities. As Altick puts it, the 'abnormal, the strange, the rare, the exotic, the tour de force – all appealed to the indiscriminate sense of wonder, and therefore could be mixed together in a mad pot-pourri without any reference to kind' (1978: 9).

There seemed to have been no intention to preserve for posterity nor, at least initially, for study. It was originally a simple luxury to have them and to be able to show them off to members of the same class. By the sixteenth century, certainly by the seventeenth, however, there was a growing interest in science among members of the emerging bourgeoisie and such collections became important because 'the rise of scientific interest with increasing reliance on observation as a means of explaining the world, and its plants and animals gave these collections new value' (Alexander, 1983: 27). Certainly the natural-history items in the collections gave information to those who were making studies of plant and animal classifications.

Perhaps the most complex and wide-ranging of these collections of the period was that of John Tradescant and son, whose curiosities, together with those of Elias Ashmole, formed the basis of the Ashmolean collection established at Oxford in 1683 (often regarded as the first museum). The Tradescants had a Cabinet of Rarities at their house in South Lambeth. In 1618

118

John Tradescant, who was a gardener to Lord Wotton and Buckingham, went to Archangel and returned with the first Russian flora known in Britain. Merchants, sea captains and sailors brought him plants and fruits from all over the world and in 1656 the Tradescants produced a catalogue of their collection which contained preserved animals, birds, fish, insects, minerals, gems, fruits, carvings, turnings, paintings, weapons, costumes, household implements, coins, medals, plants and shrubs (see Alexander, 1983: 27). Such a collection would certainly fit Samuel Johnson's definition.

In the eighteenth century, the third of Varine-Bohan's periods, we can discern an important development, with collections of such curiosities being held by the nation, intended for a wider audience. A good example of this in England was the collection of Sir Hans Sloane, whose private collection was sold to the British government in 1753. Sloane was well known as a doctor and naturalist, and in his youth had travelled to Jamaica as a medical officer, returning with a collection of some 800 or so plants. He added to it by purchasing other entire collections such as that of William Charleston (a collection which dates from 1684). His main interests were in medicine and natural history but he also had 350 'artificial curiosities' of an ethnographic type (see Alexander, 1983: 28). So large was his collection that its catalogue extended to thirty-eight folio and eight quarto volumes. It was so well known, both nationally and internationally, that it attracted visitors from royalty, members of the nobility and the famous. Voltaire and Handel went to see it, as did Linnaeus and Benjamin Franklin. Linnaeus, the great taxonomist, remarked that 'Sloane's collection is in complete disorder' (Alexander, 1983: 32), meaning that it was an unsystematic collection in which the items were not arranged or classified according to the binomial genus–species principles developed by himself. Altick points out that by the middle of the eighteenth century the cabinets of men like Sloane and other members of the highest ranks of society, which were closed to all but a few, were being imitated in England for the entertainment of a wider public. He suggests, for example, that Don Saltero's London coffee-house which was established in 1695 was really London's first public museum, and that for 'every nobleman and savant given a tour of Sloane's famous collection there were thousands of middle-class citizens ... who examined curios over coffee at Don Saltero's' (Altick, 1978: 21).

Sloane's collection is so important in the cultural history of museums because Sloane himself was in favour of making it more accessible to a wider range of people. When it was finally sold to the British government, the trustees insisted on public access to the collection. Sloane's collection formed the basis of the British Museum, which, on 15 January 1759, was opened not only to scholars but also to members of the public – although it must be said that the procedure for getting a ticket was such as to dissuade any but the most determined:

Entry was by ticket only, secured by application in person to the porter well in advance, stating 'names, condition, and place of abode', and called for later when approved by the principal librarian. Not more than ten tickets were issued for each hour, and parties of five were shown round each department by the under librarians or their assistants.

(Alexander, 1983: 36)

As the museum was only open from 9 a.m. until 3 p.m. on week days and was closed on all religious holidays, it is unlikely that many working people were able to view the collection.

In Europe public museums tended to be based on earlier collections of private individuals which were unsystematic assemblages of curiosities for their personal entertainment. In North America, on the other hand, museums were developing at this time through a significantly different process. As Nathaniel Burt observes:

The American museum was and is an idea. The European museum was a fact. Almost without exception the European museum was first a collection. With few exceptions most American museums were first an ideal.... Almost without exception the largest American museums began with a deliberate appeal to the public. Most of the earlier European museums remained semi-exclusive cabinets of curiosities visitable only to a few. The American museum began, and has remained, wide open.

(1977: 14)

A particularly good example of this pursuit of an ideal is the museum of Charles Wilson Peale, which he opened in July 1786 in Philadelphia. His aim was to establish a museum which was not solely for the researches of scholars or for the delight of connoisseurs, but which would provide 'rational entertainment for all'. Through the selection and arrangement of his exhibits he hoped to teach visitors, and specifically his intention was to promote 'morality and happiness':

Establishing the museum fitted Peale's deistic conception of religion, which held that God's laws and natural laws were identical, and human beings, by using their powers of reason to understand nature, could lead lives of peace and happiness. A natural history museum that presented 'a world in miniature' would serve as a 'school of Nature' providing its beholders with both Enlightenment and 'rational amusement'. The museum ought to arrange in scientific order all living animals, from the lowly worm to the reasoning man; since man was an animal a portrait gallery could be justified. Then there was the vegetable tribe, minerals, human petrifications, and aboriginal dress, arms and utensils.

(Alexander, 1983: 53)

Peale was particularly important not only because of his interest in 'rational amusement' in the context of museums, which was something which many were coming to espouse, but also because of his exhibition techniques. It does not seem that the European cabinets and curiosities were concerned with exhibition; although ordered according to various schema, there seems to have been no concern with overall presentation. In Peale's natural-history museum, however, not only were all the specimens labelled and accessioned, and ordered according to the Linnaean system, but more significantly the items were exhibited. Birds were set in naturalistic poses in glass cases which had modelled foregrounds and painted backgrounds. The ethnographic artifacts were shown with wax models of native people, there was a grotto scene with a pond containing frogs, fish, geese and ducks, and there was a mound on which there were other animals and birds. In other words, there was an attempt to create a complete setting.

To return to the conditions prevailing in Europe, and the growth of public collections, Varine-Bohan insists that it is necessary to understand this movement in terms of factors such as the growth of the bourgeoisie, the broadening of public education, the rise of scientific research, the Enlightenment spirit, and a developing taste for the exotic. The taste for the exotic, as we have shown with regard to animals, had been in existence for centuries, but what was important at this time in Europe was that items which constituted the exotic were more easily accessible to ordinary people.

A further element needs to be added to Varine-Bohan's list: the continued explorations overseas together with the associated colonial process, for interest in distant countries and their peoples came about through those channels. Leisure travel, the travel for cultural and educational purposes, particularly the Grand Tour, further stimulated the pursuit of knowledge and the interest in collecting.

One can see all of these elements operating together in Varine-Bohan's next period, from 1790 to 1850. As we have noted, important private collections of the early eighteenth century often formed the basis through either gift or nationalization of public museums. Interestingly there was a very definite case of nationalization in the realm of menageries with the establishment of the state-run collection in the Jardin des Plantes in Paris, which took over animals from former royal and noble collections. The newly nationalized menagerie operated under the auspices of the Muséum National in Paris.

In addition to the trend of transferring some collections from the private to the public realm, there was a move, particularly in Britain and France, towards the creation of provincial museums at the instigation of local societies of intellectuals who wished to serve their communities, and there is a similar process of course with the establishment of zoological gardens. Indeed we have previously mentioned the case of the Zoological Society of London and how this had influenced the development of many others in the mid-nineteenth century. As we saw in that context many of these zoological societies were also established by local civic-minded dignitaries in the name of science, to provide rational entertainment or amusement for the general public.

THE CULTURAL STATUS OF THE ZOO

It is at the point when there are both public museums and art galleries and public zoological gardens in the nineteenth century that we can begin to consider the comparative cultural status of each. Varine-Bohan suggests that museums were largely collections of an artistic, historical, archaeological character, and were able to play an important part in the development of the consciousness of European or western civilization, in the context of the rise of European nationalism and imperialism. In addition, because the growth of museums coincided with the industrial revolution they played an important part in the preservation of the cultural values of the ancient world, which were being eroded by the industrial revolution's technical and economic progress. They also played a part in the developing interest in new aesthetic patterns.

Collections of living animals which had been kept as curiosities did not develop in this way and could not be used to carry a similar range of cultural messages. The items which were on display do not seem to have been treated as valuable in the way that works of art were treated as valuable. We have seen that at certain times wild animals were considered to be suitable high-status gifts, and that collections of such creatures indicated a privileged position. However, once wild-animal collections became accessible to the public the animals seem to have suffered a curious loss of status, a loss which quite significantly attached itself to the institution in which they were held.

Individual items which formed the collections of museums and art galleries were unique and were therefore irreplaceable. But no individual wild animal in a collection was unique and so could never attain this status of irreplaceability. Animals had no intrinsic worth; nor were they imbued with the aura of being part of an historical, cultural process. Ironically, representations of these same animals in the plastic arts — drawings, paintings, sculpture, architecture, engravings – *could* be seen in this light, whereas living creatures could not. In the presence of living creatures humans were confronted with raw animal nature, a quality which was not positively evaluated, whereas in representations the animal had been transformed by human spirit, imagination and skill. Despite the name *zoological* garden, the institution (with rare exceptions such as Paris and London) was not able to develop a scientific image with the corresponding status. It might well be that important scientific work was indeed being carried out within the zoological gardens, but there was no attempt to give a scientific representation of the natural world. For the general public they were (and we would argue still are) merely places for recreation, places where one could walk and amuse oneself looking at strange and interesting animals. In an important sense they were not serious places, as for example a science museum or art gallery was.

It is interesting that a collection of dead creatures in a museum can gain greater prestige than a collection of living ones. As we have previously argued in the context of anthropomorphism, zoo visitors tend to respond to living animals not simply as creatures which have a separate existence and separate identity from human beings but as reflections of themselves (or at least of something human). In the zoo the activity of animals stimulates a response in the viewer which is not that of a desire to understand something about animal behaviour *per se*. Behaviour is certainly interpreted but it is interpreted as though it were motivated by humanlike emotions or needs: 'It is sitting like that because it is sad.' 'It is splashing about in the water because it is happy.' 'It won't move about because it is lazy.' In a natural-history museum animals cannot, it would seem, elicit this response – they are mere objects. The fact that they are dead and arranged in terms of some zoological schema in a glass case is a proclamation of their scientific status. The range of human responses to them is reduced, the human viewers cannot so easily fantasize about them or imagine mental states for them; they are specimens. They are representations of real animals and in their fixity they are in some senses equivalent to any other museum object whether it be an example of a mineral, a piece of pottery, a part of an ancient building or a piece of exotic costume. This shift of context (from the wild or even a zoo enclosure to a glass case) and status (from living creature to stuffed or mounted specimen) seems to allow the animals to be more readily regarded as something to be studied rather than as a source of entertainment.

If zoo animals were to be seen as part of high culture they would be the only living creatures which, simply by their very existence rather than for anything they did, are so regarded. For the living performers of high culture – singers, dancers, artists, musicians – are interpreters or creators, they have had to *do* something to attain the status they enjoy. It is the music or the dance itself which is cultural. Animals in a zoo, although they might respond to those watching them, are not performers in this sense. They merely act out their own animal nature. But it is not the zoo animal's position on the alive–dead continuum that prevents it from attaining high cultural status; rather it is the fact that the animal is not man-made and as such requires no interpretation that is crucial. Animals do not mean anything; they are nothing more than that which the viewer sees; they do not, in themselves, symbolize or signify anything else.

Unlike museums, zoos could not be used as exhibitions designed to promote a sense of the intrinsic value of European civilization, because people wanted to see exotic, non-native species; indigenous animals were certainly of no great importance. Animals, as items of the natural world, were not suitable for demarcating cultures and civilizations. In the societies which had zoos, men did not use animals for making cultural distinctions and divisions. It is significant that in the nineteenth century they, the animals, are marked by human culture, something we have noted when discussing architecture. So whereas cultural items could be used to demarcate the animal world, the opposite was not true.

If we consider the period from the mid-nineteenth century to mid-twentieth century, we see a continuation of many of the factors which Varine-Bohan noted as influencing the development of museums in the first half of the century: the industrial revolution in Europe, accelerated technical progress, fundamental transformations in science, the institution of democratic regimes, the continued extension of European–American colonization to the whole world, the development of communication systems and the democratization of education and culture. As we have mentioned earlier the celebration of such 'progress' as well as the continuation of colonization, often took the form of the great exhibitions which were held regularly throughout this period in major European and North American cities.

The modern concept of the nature and purpose of the museum developed slowly during the nineteenth century, but from the heterogeneous, non-systematic collections at the beginning of the century they gradually became specialized and highly organized, and although the public was admitted to most there was often a division between what was held in a museum for the purposes of research and what was available for viewing by the non-specialist public. In a speech in 1864, J. Edward Gray, the keeper of the British Museum Zoological Department, showed his keen awareness of the two-fold purpose of public museums. He believed that they should be engaged in the diffusion of instruction and rational amusement among the masses, and that they should also afford the student of science every means of examining and studying specimens. In his address to members of the British Academy for the Advancement of Science he asserted:

What the largest class of visitors, the general public, want, is a collection of the more interesting objects so arranged as to afford the greatest possible amount of information, in a moderate space, as to be obtained, as it were, at a glance. On the other hand, the scientific student requires to have under his eyes and in his hands the most complete collection of the specimens that can be brought together, and in such condition as to admit of the most minute examination of their differences, whether of age, sex, or state, or of whatever kind that can throw light upon all the innumerable questions that are continually arising in the progress of thought and opinion.

(Quoted in van Keuran, 1984: 173)

Lieutenant-General Pitt-Rivers, who made a most important contribution to the history of museums in Britain, suggested that one should not attempt to convert institutions like the British Museum, which had essentially been established for scholars, into educational establisments; rather they should remain research museums. What was needed, he argued, were museums which had specific educational aims in mind and where 'the objects in them should be collected and arranged to further the particular purposes for which they are intended' (Pitt-Rivers, 1891: 115). Such museums, Pitt-Rivers further argued, should have a conscious philosophy of education for particular social purposes (his own belief was that one should look to science for material, social and moral progress), and should make sure that they were designed to achieve this end. It would seem that there was no equivalent attempt to make zoological gardens places of education, although this was spoken about, and was indeed incorporated into their founding charters. What was actually to constitute education in this context was something quite basic, the labelling of cages and enclosures to identify the animals accompanied by a simple comment about their geographical distribution and feeding habits. In this sense zoos were somewhat equivalent to natural-history museums with living specimens. It does not seem, however, that they were responded to in this way by visitors, who were not prompted to visit the zoo in search of zoological information.

We come back to the essential point that although art galleries, museums and zoological gardens shared many elements in their development, the two former institutions entered the realm of high culture whereas zoological gardens became essentially popular. Museums became associated with learning, they were places established by learned people, and this aura naturally conditioned responses to them.

Visitors to museums or art galleries are reverential because they consider that they are in the presence of culture, though often the items on exhibition are difficult to understand and need interpretation. The items on exhibit in the zoo, on the other hand, do not have this quality – they do not need to be interpreted. Moreover, the bulk of the visitors do not want to understand the animals in any scientific way. Such an institution therefore can be popular because it is not intimidating. For the visitor to have an enjoyable experience, he does not need a high level of knowledge. The important thing for him is that he simply sees the animals. Whereas museums and art galleries became involved with connoisseurship, zoos did not. It seems that animals (except when dead and featured in cuisine or as skins or furs) are not suitable material for connoisseurship.

Varine-Bohan characterizes the post-1950 period as one of post-war reconstruction, the expansion of the museum, the development of both specialist and new forms of museum, and lastly the professionalization of the work undertaken in museums with the associated development of related national and international associations. In the zoo world we see similar trends, which coalesce around the issue of whether or not the zoo is or should be an institution devoted mainly to educational purposes. The central problem for those zoos which see themselves as offering something more than mere entertainment is that, unlike museums and art galleries, they do not command respect as elite institutions. Modern zoo philosophy has it that just as other institutions exist to preserve and present a cultural heritage so zoos exist to preserve a fast-disappearing natural heritage.

ZOOS AND EDUCATION

We have argued that unlike museums and art galleries, zoos contain collections which are easy to understand because the items on display need no interpretation. For centuries and in all cultures this display was unproblematic (indeed in many modern zoos it is still unproblematic); the animals were strange and unusual and simply excited the interest and curiosity of those who came to see them – they wanted to know where they came from and whether there was anything special about them. Those who put them on display had to do little more than make them visible.

Although different publics go to zoos with different perceptions and interests, zoos are traditionally places of popular entertainment, and yet we found no director who suggested that the aim of his zoo was primarily to provide entertainment. It would seem that because of international co-operation among zoos, the ideology of conservation and education has spread. All directors claimed that education was a fundamental concern and more particularly they argued that the intention was to give people an understanding of the natural world in order to preserve that world. However poor the zoo, however restricted the resources and however close they were to having basic, bare cages, all directors paid at least lip-service to the ideals of education, to the aim of converting the zoo experience into more than the simple viewing of a caged animal. Some directors explained that, in positing education as their primary aim, they were not looking beyond the zoo and merely wished to persuade their public to respect and not mistreat the animals in the zoo. The problem which all of them face, however great their resources, is that because zoos are not traditionally places of education it is difficult to make them so. Most zoo visitors around the world see the zoo as a cheap place for a day of fun (in most parts of the world apart from North America, Europe and Australasia the price of entrance to the zoo is well below the cost of any other entertainment, and in most cases the ticket price is purely nominal), and do not come predisposed to learn about the animals.

Zoos with considerable financial resources are able to offer formal educational services to certain members of the public. Many have paid teaching staff, classrooms and structured programmes for school groups. Here the zoo becomes an extension of the school. Not surprisingly the zoos of western industrial nations offer the more sophisticated programmes in biology, zoology and ecology, but even the less affluent zoos in other nations attempt to provide some teaching for school groups. Indeed with the international contact between members of the zoo world it seems that zoos must assume some sort of educational character in order to maintain credibility when making a claim for status above that of mere entertainers. The majority of the public, however, do not participate in the main programmes and the majority of directors realize that people do not come to the zoo for an educational experience. They accept that offering obtrusive formal instruction is unlikely either to attract or to hold attention. The requirements of the public on the whole are minimal – they want to know the name of the animal, where it comes from and perhaps some basic information about behaviour. Beyond this they are not much interested.

The sorts of information and programmes one finds in zoos do not vary in essence (although they certainly do in quality) from culture to culture. The essential message is always a similar amalgam of scientific zoology, ecology and conservation. Despite the enormous variety in responses to and attitudes towards animals in different cultures this does not seem to be reflected in zoo philosophies throughout the world. One does not even find the equivalent of the museums which are established to glorify a particular period of history or to give a sense of national pride. The story which zoos implicitly attempt to tell about the relationship between man and the natural world is an acultural one. The idea of developing zoos which are culturally specific seems alien to the modern zoo world. Perhaps the only significant exception to this is the Biblical Zoo in Jerusalem where the enclosures carry notices quoting biblical references to particular animals.

Wild animals are insignificant in the lives of most people who visit zoos, yet the aim of many directors is to make them significant. The thrust of educational programmes seems to be an attempt to neutralize particular cultural perceptions of animals and to take the visitor beyond the primary idiosyncratic experience of the individual animal in the cage in order to explain that the animal is a representative of a particular species with particular zoological and behavioural characteristics which are normally revealed in a particular ecological setting. In an important sense the individual animals on display are of little account in that the story of their lives in that particular setting and of their relations with others in the zoo is not the one the directors wish to tell. Information provided about animals does not focus on the lives of those in captivity but on how they would or should live in the wild. Indeed, in all but the best zoos it cannot be otherwise, for as Batten has argued:

Should one learn that the chimpanzee, for example, is a neurotic humanoid that cadges food from humans, and throws tantrums and excreta should this not materialize? Or that the orang-utan, which by nature seldom descends to the soft forest floor, is a pathetic bundle of matted red fur in the corner of a tiled cell?

(Batten, 1976: 22)

To be fully successful this process of reorientation has to cause a shift of focus beyond the confines of the zoo and to prompt people to place the animal imaginatively in a completely different context: that of a natural habitat of which it might have no experience. For the majority of visitors, though, that is not the purpose of their visit; it is *that* particular animal in the cage in front of them which is important, it is *that* particular animal which provides interest, entertainment or excitement and not some abstract quality or set of relations associated with it. Most do not seek to understand the animal or to think beyond it. In many societies it is especially difficult to achieve this level of interest for it involves establishing a concern for an animal and a habitat of another country which the visitors are unlikely to see. It is difficult enough to persuade people in affluent western nations to take notice of the plight of fellow human beings in other nations, so to expect zoo visitors around the world to interest themselves in the plight of animals seems over-optimistic. 'Jungle World' in the Bronx, New York, was established to foster concern for the fate of the tropical rainforests of the world, but one wonders how many of those who pass through it and express admiration for it will continue to take an active part in what happens to the rainforest in Brazil for example. It is even more difficult to believe that the millions who visit Beijing or Bombay zoos can be persuaded that they ought to be concerned about Chinese or Indian habitats, let alone Brazilian rainforests.

Pegi Harvey, of the education department at San Diego Zoo, said that her objective was to get visitors to 'experience a sense of wildlife'. It would seem that if zoos are going to have any success in reshaping the public's view of animals then a naturalistic setting is essential. To achieve this of course requires vast financial resources to which few have access. There is, however, another element which directors are able to work with – the fact that most people seem to treat the zoo as though it were a variety show. People like to see animals acting and, as we have described, what many directors have done is to restructure the nature of the animal show to carry a message. Most of the shows are quite simple in that they demonstrate how certain animals can leap, climb or manipulate objects, and the presenter then explains why they are able to act in such a way. Perhaps the most 'pure' educational show is that in San Diego Zoo which features only North American wildlife. Here, for example, the trainers demonstrate how far a cougar can jump, and they then bring out a red-tailed hawk and emphasize its powerful sight by pointing to a wooden replica of a San Diego newspaper nailed to a distant tree and explaining that the hawk would be able to make out the words if it could read. A coatimundi is made to find hidden sweets and so demonstrate its powers of smell. And in order to show how an owl pinpoints sound and attacks its prey, the trainers explain the anatomy of the owl on display and allow it to pounce on a model skunk.

In the cage or enclosure an animal is framed by a statement of what it is – its body itself is enough to identify it – whereas in the shows the message is that an animal *is* what an animal *does* – it is identified in terms of behaviour. Unlike traditional circus acts these shows of 'natural behaviour' do not aim to train animals so that they may be humanized; rather they are trained to be natural. As we have argued, an animal in a cage is an actor in terms of the visitors' perception of it – they wish to be entertained by its activity. In the shows, however, the idea of animal as actor is somewhat more complex. The animal is trained to perform on cue actions which are part of the normal lives of members of its species in their natural habitat. On stage in the zoo, however, these actions performed by these individuals are inauthentic, they have no object, they are directed to no end except the performance of the acts themselves and perhaps a food reward from the keeper, for in the zoo the owl does not need to (indeed it cannot) hunt skunks. The actions refer to a way of life outside the zoo which is denied to them. An owl is trained to play the part of being an owl, but it is only a role – it cannot be the expression of an authentic life. The zoo is a theatre of inauthenticity attempting to tell a story of authenticity.

THE HUMAN ANIMAL ROAMING FREE IN THE ZOO

As we have seen, collections of wild animals have been made for many purposes, but the majority in zoological gardens are open to the public, and this is a key factor, for what we are interested in is not simply the nature of the collection, but how that collection is presented to the public and perceived by them. In many cases the directors and their staff have attitudes to the animals in their charge which are very different from those of the public and, although they know that the animals must be exhibited (for that is the *raison d'être* of all but a handful of private collections), they are often ambivalent about this. Privately they would argue that zoos could be run much more efficiently, and the majority of the animals would have a more tranquil life, if they did not have to be continually on show. Jack Throp, director of Taronga Park, Sydney, was employed in 1962 to stock the new zoo in Phoenix, Arizona; for the whole of that year the staff had the place to themselves while the construction work, preparation of the exhibits, and stocking took place, and it was all rather a shock when the public were finally admitted. In a similar way he noted that in the early days of San Diego Zoo there was a sense that 'people were allowed to come in and look at *our* animals' – the visitors were rather looked upon as 'intruders'. Throp adds that this attitude has changed over the years, and now San Diego regards itself as a 'people park', with the animals seen as 'mediums of communication'.

As we have seen, it is rare for the public to be asked what they would like to see in the zoo. As with museum collections, it is the staff who decide the nature of the collection and exhibition policy, although they might well take notice of the comments of the public as revealed in the surveys that some of them make. But it would seem that the zoos of only a few countries are concerned to find out about the public which visits them. We found that most directors and their staff knew roughly how many visitors they had a year, and most of them had some impressionistic idea of the nature of the public, what they wanted to see in the zoo, and how they reacted to what they saw. As might be expected, the most comprehensive studies are to be found in the North American zoos, although even these have only been carried out in recent years. Perhaps the most detailed survey is that of Sea World, San Diego, where they apparently know not only how many visitors they have every year and which states or foreign countries they are from, but also their levels of educational attainment, employment and income levels, and detailed likes and dislikes. This concern is hardly surprising in the light of the fact that Sea World is a thoroughly commercial enterprise which depends for its existence on the money taken at the gate and the revenue from facilities within the park. It needs to know how to market itself, where to advertise and how to produce an environment that delights and satisfies its visitors, who are then likely to recommend it to their friends and relatives. Another institution in the USA which is particularly concerned to understand its visitors, but for very different reasons, is the National Zoological Park in Washington DC. Here the concern is not financial, as the zoo is supported by a federal grant and admission is free; rather the desire here is to develop the best exhibition facilities and educational programmes, and then to evaluate them.

DO GIRAFFES EVER SIT?

Visiting the zoo has been a popular pastime in many cultures, a popularity which is attested by the following sample of attendance figures.

Annual Attendance for Selected Zoos

Zoologisk Have, Copenhagen, Denmark	907, 139
Parc Zoologique de Paris	1,023,457
Tierpark, Berlin (GDR)	2,470,000
Zoologischer Garten und Aquarium, Berlin (WG)	2,455,650
Zoological Society of London	1,338,000
Veermata Jijabai Bhosale Udyan, Bombay	3,875,000
Kebun Binatung Ragunun, Zoological and Botanical Gardens, Jakarta	1,653,731
Ueno Zoological Gardens, Tokyo	7,217,350
Johannesburg Zoological Gardens, South Africa	481,903
Zoological Department, Skansen, Stockholm	1,847,223
Moskovskii Zoological Park, USSR	2,167,930
San Diego Zoological Garden	3,100,000
Chapultepec Zoological Park, Mexico City	12,540,000
Honolulu Zoo	1,500,000
Chicago Zoological Park (Brookfield Zoo)	1,696,836
National Zoological Park, Smithsonian Institute, Washington DC	3,000,000
Beijing Zoological Garden, PRC	8,000,000

(Olney, 1982: vol. 22)

It has long been held that, in the main, people visit zoos in family or social groups, rather than alone. The studies carried out in a number of North American zoos (together with our own experience) suggests that this is indeed true. For example, Fiedler and Wheeler's study of Woodland Park Zoo, Seattle, shows that almost 40 per cent of their sample visited the zoo as 'an outing for the kids', while in response to the question 'Do you usually come here by yourself?', 92 per cent replied 'No' (1985: 4, see also Cheek, 1973: 13, who puts the figure at 96 per cent). This again points to a difference between museums, galleries and zoos. Individuals often go to museums and galleries to browse through the collections or to sit and contemplate the items which particularly attract them. Such a visit often involves aesthetic and emotional responses which do not need to be shared or spoken about. The zoo experience seems to be something which is shared, the animals are spoken about, marvelled at or laughed at with others. Museums and galleries are quiet, reverential places while zoos certainly are not. In many societies, looking at animals smacks of childish behaviour and many people, when questioned, justify their presence in the zoo by saying that they have brought children. Museums and galleries are adult institutions; zoos are not.

Bernard Harrison, the director of Singapore Zoo, found in a survey of some seventy zoos that the annual attendance figure tends to be about 20 per cent of the population of the city in which the zoo is located. At Singapore Zoo itself the pattern of attendance reflects the ethnic composition of Singapore, with approximately 80 per cent Chinese, 10 per cent Malay, 7 per cent Indian and 3 per cent other. The director of Taronga Park, Sydney, also suggested that in his zoo the various ethnic groups were represented in roughly the proportions of the ethnic groups in Sydney. However, an interesting racial–ethnic attitude to zoos is revealed by the limited black attendance registered in North American zoos. In the visitor study of the Woodland Park Zoo, Seattle, in response to the question 'Do you consider yourself to be a member of an ethnic minority?', 89 per cent replied 'No' (Fiedler and Wheeler, 1985: 5). Michael Robinson, the director of the National Zoological Park in Washington DC, commented that the city had approximately an 80 per cent black population and yet there was only a 10 per cent black attendance at the zoo. He has attempted all manner of things to increase this number but without success. The only day when more blacks attend is Easter Monday; then the figures reverse and there is approximately a 90 per cent black attendance in order to participate in a traditional picnic.

Other American zoos describe a similar situation; the assistant director at Baltimore Zoo reports city-population and zoo-attendance figures for blacks in almost identical proportions to those of Washington, while in Philadelphia there is an inner-city zoo but the blacks do not visit it. There are few black curators or veterinary surgeons and we were certainly unable to find a black director. Sandy Friedmann of Brookfield Zoo, Chicago, suggested that it was part of a much wider pattern and that very few people who are members of ethnic minorities are professionally associated with biology, and that anything that is nature-related is held in 'low esteem'.

So zoos in the United States are white-centred but it is difficult to be certain why this is so. Some of the zoo personnel we interviewed suggested that many blacks might view the zoo as a prison and would not want to associate with an institution which persecuted animals. In other words they empathize with the plight of captive animals. There was also a general sense that they were not keen to establish relations with animals, that they were essentially urban-orientated and had little interest in the countryside or in discovering the world of nature. Many American zoo professionals suggest that those living in inner-city areas do not have what might be called an affinity to animals and that most of them register negative attitudes towards them. This, some argue, is hardly surprising when their most immediate experience of animals is probably that of guard dogs, stray dogs and rats.

It is difficult enough for American zoos in inner-city areas to attract a black visitor but if a zoo is outside these areas it is doubly difficult. Brookfield Zoo, Chicago, for example, is surrounded by middle-class white suburbs and suffers from inadequate public transportation from the downtown area. This, combined with the fact that Chicago seems to be a particularly segregated community, means that blacks would have to make a physical and symbolic shift from one community of meaning to another if they decided to travel out to the zoo.

The majority of people obviously go to the zoo to look at animals (although as we noted earlier the total setting diffuses attention), such watching in fact is not intensive or of a long duration. The Woodland Park study surprisingly revealed that the zoo visit was a comparatively short one. Given that for most people there is considerable time and effort involved in getting out to Woodland Park, which is located in Seattle's suburbs, and given the extent of the zoo itself, it is revealing that for 50 per cent of the visitors visit lasts only two hours (Fiedler and Wheeler, 1985: 17). Unless there is some particular activity in a cage or enclosure, or unless the animal is a special favourite, it seems that, for the majority of people, watching consists of merely registering that they have seen something as they move quickly past it. For example, in a recent study of visitors to the Reptile House in the National Zoo, Washington DC, the average time recorded for people in the entire house was 9.7 minutes, with an average of only 0.44 minutes spent in front of each enclosure.

People's attention will be held longer if there is interaction among the animals or if the animals interact with the public. As some of the Washington studies show, most people came for entertainment and 'where there is no movement there is no fun'. This is something that we found from our experience to be a universal factor in zoos. Even animals with great exhibition value such as the giant panda do not hold the visitors' attention for long if they do not move, although in this case people will spend a long time in front of the pandas just in the hope of seeing *some* movement. Animals which have less exhibition value have to produce activity of a more entertaining sort to hold the visitors' attention.

Looked at from the perspective of the other side of the enclosure, if the animals' environment itself does not provide enough stimulation for the animals then they will look to the public for it. This produces the well-known begging syndrome of certain animals, something which the public often responds to positively because it allows them to interact with the animals. We found no zoo in the world that actively encouraged feeding (except in controlled circumstances) and most cages and enclosures carried signs informing the public that the animals had a special diet and that indiscriminate feeding was likely to cause harm. Despite this, so concerned are most zoo visitors to influence what goes on in an enclosure and to cause activity among the animals, that in all but a few zoos, we found a variety of animals are fed. This feeding is not indiscriminate, in so far as certain animals are more likely to be fed than others. For example, throughout the world bears, monkeys and apes are often fed, largely it would seem because of the anthropomorphic response to begging – this is particularly so with monkeys and apes where food can be handed to them. Elephants, seals and some ungulates also tend to be fed. Even within one enclosure, feeding is not indiscriminate. Smaller (apparently ill-fed) animals are more likely to be fed than the larger ones, and younger ones are fed more often than older ones. Certain animals do not elicit this response – birds, fish and reptiles are rarely fed. It would seem that there needs to be a clear anthropomorphic response before humans are interested in interacting with animals in this way. Not only does this promote activity but it focuses attention on the individuals doing the feeding. So once again we see a case of benefit accruing to the human: rather than the animals needing to be fed, it is humans wanting to feed them. Zoos are ostensibly about going to view animals, an activity in which the people are not important except as passive viewers. But this is not how it works in practice. In the zoo the humans *demand* to be noticed by the animals.

Enclosures where animals are actively interacting with the public will hold the attention of visitors. Certain animals undoubtedly use the visitors for their own benefit, because the visitors provide stimulation, and many directors and keepers told us how certain animals apparently enjoy the presence of people with whom they can interact. Not all forms of interaction are positively evaluated by the public, however – llamas may spit, monkeys may grab at clothing, and emus and ostriches may peck. In Zoo Negara, near Kuala Lumpur, members of the public often throw things at the chimpanzees and enjoy seeing the animals play with them. A Coca-Cola can thrown into the cage made a magnificent instrument for one of them to attract a crowd. It raced around the enclosure scraping the can on the concrete surface, an action which produced a fearful noise which soon attracted an interested crowd delighted to see this intense activity. When the chimp looked up and saw that there was a large crowd he grabbed a handful of excrement, scampered up a tree and flung the handful at the horrified and now not quite so appreciative audience.

On rare occasions the desire to see animals move or engage in activity can, if such activity is not aroused, lead to bouts of vandalism. Apart from the sadistic desire to cause injury to animals, vandalism is probably simply the end point of being intrusive, or demanding attention or interaction. In Bombay Zoo crocodiles have been stoned to death in futile attempts to stir them. This is an extreme case of vandalism, but all the zoos we have seen do have management problems concerning those creatures who, unlike the caged animals, roam freely around the zoo. Peter Batten in his discussion of American zoos observes that it is 'doubtful whether any American zoo has escaped vandalism in some form by sadistic, ignorant, or dimwitted humans... zoo animals are maimed, mutilated and killed quite frequently' (1976: 122). Batten talks of alligators with eyes gouged out and birds with broken legs, as well as numerous cases of theft.

It would seem that in North America at least those controlling the organization of zoos have been successful in communicating a message of what the zoo should be about. Visitors are able, when questioned, to reproduce the arguments that zoos are important educational establishments where one goes to learn about animals. But the pattern of their activities during the course of a zoo visit leads us to conclude that they are acting with a different model in mind – a case of cognitive dissonance. Indeed it would see that many visitors can hold two distinctly opposed views at the same time. Of those questioned in the Woodland Park, Seattle, study, 68 per cent claimed that they considered the purpose of the zoo to be primarily educational, but nearly three-quarters of the same group responded positively to the question of whether the zoo was mainly about entertainment. At the behavioural level it is quite clear with which model the majority of the visitors operate. Many studies in the United States show that visitors rarely read detailed information panels, nor do they generally read exhibit-related brochures. In the National Zoological Park,

Washington DC, nearly all visitors said that they read signs but when actually observed they were found not to do so (see King, 1985: i).

Stephen Kellert's studies of American attitudes and knowledge of animals shows that zoo visitors score no higher than non-zoo visitors in their knowledge of animal and wildlife questions (see Kellert, 1979 and 1984). Both Kellert and Wolf and Tymitz (1979) observe that visitors are concerned more on an emotional than an intellectual level – with 'the care of the animals' – so for them captivity must be seen to be comfortable. This interest in the design of habitats is matched by a concern for their cleanliness, and this, argue Wolf and Tymitz, is tied to an overall concern about animals in captivity. In their study no visitor indicated that any animal appeared uncared for; instead attention was focused on how animals could receive better or the best care. As Wolf and Tymitz note, visitors have different ideas of what constitutes best animal care.

> *'The floor in the gorilla cage is concrete. That's too hard on the gorillas' feet, I think.'*
>
> *'Do giraffes ever sit? There's no soft place for them to sit. Is that why?'*
>
> *'Why is the elephant chained up? Doesn't that hurt him?'*
>
> *'I thought polar bears were white – real white, I mean. These don't seem as white. Could there be something in the water to make them white?'*
>
> *'We saw some zebras fighting with each other. Shouldn't someone be supervising them so they won't hurt each other?'*
>
> *'The female giraffe is all by herself. Can't she be in the yard with the others?'*
>
> *'Do snakes need more room? Can they stretch out all the way in there?'*

(Wolf and Tymitz, 1979: 24)

Compared with the zoos found in the affluent western industrialized nations, zoos in other parts of the world might be said to have inferior living standards for their animals. It would seem that visitors from these affluent nations when in the zoo project their own expectations of habitat and living standards on to the animals. Just as the prison image of zoos disturbs people because of the apparent lack of freedom of 'fellow creatures', so substandard 'housing' disturbs. Not surprisingly, given the conditions in which the majority in poorer countries live, in those countries there is not the same concern.

It is simply because the affluent zoo visitors can actually see the animal living in full view of them that they express concern over the conditions. Ironically this concern does not extend to questions about how the animals came to be in these circumstances, or indeed in the zoo as an institution, in the first place.

7
The Animal as Commodity

A mercant of lundon wrote to a factor of his beyoand sea, desired him by the next shipp to send 2 or 3 Apes; he forgot the r, and then it was 203 Apes. His factor has sent him fower scoare, and says hee shall have the rest by the next shipp, conceiving the merchant has sent for two hundred and three apes; if yarself or frends will buy any to breede on, you could never have had such a chance as now.

(Sir Edmund Verney, a royalist soldier and MP, writing to his son in 1636 – quoted in Altick, 1978: 37)

The trade in zoo animals possesses characteristics similar to those in the animal trade generally. Therefore it is essential to understand the general patterns of trading before examining zoo animal trading.

Until the rapid expansion of zoological gardens in the second part of the nineteenth century and the corresponding need to find animals to fill them, there was nothing which could be seen as a specific trade in live wild animals. One can perhaps see exceptions to this in the supply of animals for Roman amphitheatres or the infinitesimal number which were acquired for travelling shows. The animals which made up the collections which we have earlier examined were not usually bought or sold. Rather they came through diplomatic channels or were passed along commercial trade routes. As we have shown, animals came into Europe in the sixteenth century as a result of the trading activities of the Dutch East India and the Dutch West India Companies. Although it is impossible to document the precise numbers of wild animals which passed through such channels, it can safely be suggested that they would have been comparatively few, destined for only a few individuals.

There obviously were animal suppliers prior to the nineteenth century, but it is only at that time that we find specialists of the stature and importance of Hagenbeck, who became the leading animal dealer in Germany, and the prominent London-based dealers Charles and William Jamrach. Given the apparently unlimited supplies of wild animals together with the lack of any serious conservation ethic, the supply of animals to zoos was more or less unproblematic. It consisted merely of the location, capture and subsequent transportation of wild animals. The only difficulties that could arise would be the individual zoo's willingness to pay the price, and the possibility that many of the animals in question would die before reaching their destination, so great were the distances travelled and so slow and uncertain the transport. An important factor to be borne in mind here is that until comparatively recently there was little or no concern to breed animals in captivity. Animals were seen quite simply as an easily renewable commodity, so that when one died it was replaced. The effect of this pattern was that zoos constantly and continually relied on suppliers; moreover there was little inter-zoo trade, which only developed with the advent of successful captive-breeding programmes.

Through the twentieth century, but more particularly after the Second World War, there was a concern and indeed a growing consciousness that wildlife itself was under threat and that many species were vulnerable to extinction. But the trade in wildlife was only 'controlled' by the ecological concerns of individual zoos which attempted to develop breeding programmes, and by the individual and unco-ordinated export laws of the supplying nations, and more particularly the import regulations of the consuming nations. In fact individual zoos operated their own selective ban on trade:

As early as 1962, the members of the American Association of Zoological Parks and Aquariums (AAZPA) established a boycott of the illegal trade in Monkey-eating eagles Pithecophaga jefferyi, *Orang-utans* Pongo pygmaeus *and gorillas* Gorilla gorilla. *In time the boycott was extended to Galapagos tortoises* Geochelone elephantopus, *Komodo monitors* Veranus komodoensis, *Golden lion marmosets* Leontopithicus rosalia, *Zanzibar red colobus* Colobus badius kirkii, *Javan rhinoceros* Rhinoceros sondaicus, *Sumatran rhinoceros* Didermocerus sumatrensis, *and the Mountain zebra* Equus zebra. *The International Union of Directors of Zoological Gardens and the Federation of Zoological Gardens of Great Britain and Ireland also adopted a boycott of illegally exported apes.*

(King, 1974b: 5)

But in fact it is only with the discussions which led up to the signing of the Convention of International Trade in Endangered Species of Wild Fauna and Flora (CITES) that a co-ordinated international attempt to control the trade of wild animals becomes apparent. It should be mentioned however that individual zoos themselves did develop controlled breeding programmes in which they co-operated with other zoos, the aim being to avoid creating a drain on the population of wild animals.

138

CITES

On 2 March 1973, following negotiations between eighty nations, CITES was signed in Washington DC. The Convention had its origins in 1961 when the conference on Conservation of Nature and Natural Resources in Modern African States, held in Arusha, Tanzania, proposed a treaty to curtail poaching and to control international marketing of wildlife (King, 1974b: 2). Two years later in its Nairobi General Assembly, the International Union for the Conservation of Nature and Natural Resources (IUCN) assumed the task of drafting a preliminary agreement. With the passage of its Endangered Species Conservation Act of 1969, the US government was required by law to convene an international conference to discuss the control of trade in endangered species. The March 1973 conference in Washington was the outcome.

CITES regulates trade in both live and dead animals, and in their 'easily recognized parts and derivatives: hides, feathers and fur coats' (King, 1974b: 3). Under CITES provisions a species (including subspecies or geographically separate populations) can be listed in any one of three appendices.

Appendix I consists of species threatened with extinction which are or may be affected by trade. This provision is incorporated to allow for potential trade switching from species to species. Trade in Appendix I species is subject to strict regulation and can be authorized only in exceptional circumstances. Both export and import permits are required before the species can be traded internationally, and these permits are issued only after government-approved experts determine that the trade will not be detrimental to the survival of the wild species, and that the specimen itself was not obtained in contravention of the law. In order to protect live animals further, the authorities must be assured that the shipment meets humane requirements and that the recipient is equipped to house and husband the specimen on arrival. To ensure that no unnecessary delays occur during shipment, the import permit must be issued before an export permit can be given.

Appendix II includes all species which may become threatened with extinction if trade is not regulated. This appendix also includes those species with which other Appendix II species might be confused. Export permits are required from their country of origin before import into another country is allowed. The issue of the export permit depends on decisions by similar experts to those referred to in Appendix I, that the specimen was obtained legally and that the trade will not be detrimental to the survival of the species. These experts must also monitor the exports and issue permits in order to avoid the over-exploitation by trade that might make a species a candidate for Appendix

I or that would so severely deplete its numbers in the wild that it would be unable to fulfil its role in the ecosystem (King, 1974b: 3)

Appendix III includes species submitted by a member country seeking international co-operation in order to enforce adequately particular regulations within its own jurisdiction. Trade in these species merely requires a legal export permit; import permits are not necessary.

Animals found on the high seas outside national jurisdictions require a certificate from government authorities of a signatory state before they can be transported from the sea to the state. The issue of the certificate is prohibited where traffic to the state would seriously threaten the survival of the species. All subsequent international trade is subject to the previously mentioned regulations.

In addition CITES covers the re-export of specimens previously imported. This will of course directly affect zoos, since all subsequent international movement of zoo specimens obtained under the provisions of the Convention will require a re-export certificate from the government of the re-exporting country. Proof that the original importation satisfied the Convention regulations is required before the certificate can be issued. However, CITES does allow for the legitimate trade in animals which, although endangered, have been produced in captive-breeding programmes. A most significant factor in relation to Appendix I animals is that they must not be traded for commercial purposes only. Neither can they be imported to a country simply to enable a resale. The main reason for their import should be for them to form part of a captive-breeding programme the aim of which is to avoid the threat of extinction of the particular species. The provision dealing with resale ensures that animal dealers cannot trade in endangered species by bringing them into the country and simply selling them. It was hoped that such a provision would ensure that the only importers would be those who are directly operating the breeding programmes.

Animals of Appendix I species born in captivity are treated as though they are Appendix II. Before these animals can be traded it is necessary to obtain a certificate to prove that they have been born in such circumstances. This provision indicates that those who drew up the provisions of CITES together with those who administer it create a clear distinction between wild populations, which are in danger, and zoo populations, which are not. In other words there is an implicit argument that it is only the former populations that are the real representatives of the species, an argument we will return to.

In terms of numbers of animals and species, it is pertinent to note that at approximately the same time as the signing of the Convention, the trade in specimens for zoos and aquaria was less than 1 per cent in the total world traffic in traded live wild animals (King, 1974b: 5). It must not be forgotten that CITES forbids the trading of derivatives of endangered animals, and it would appear that the central thrust of the policy is to restrict that sort of trade, because, as we have just noted, provisions were included which allowed the movement of endangered species around the world under the auspices of what were obviously regarded as legitimate zoological gardens.

TRADING REALITIES

As with the purchase and exchange of other commodities, the fact of the existence of CITES does not guarantee the control of the trade in endangered species. Put quite simply, certain species are so valuable for collectors of various kinds that dealers will attempt to circumvent the regulations. They are able to do this for a number of reasons. For example, it is possible to obtain fake certificates: young specimens of Appendix I animals are imported into certain countries where they are issued a certificate to say that they are captive-bred and may therefore enter channels of international trade. Another opportunity arises out of the difficulty in identifying which animals are in fact being traded. We have indicated that people visiting the zoo are unable to identify any but a handful of animals, and therefore it is not surprising that customs officials, who must monitor the movement of wild animals across international borders, are often likewise unable to make identification decisions. It is therefore quite possible for an animal to be issued an export certificate declaring it to be one species or subspecies when in fact it is a similar-looking but actually quite different species. Clearly the giant panda, an Appendix I species, is unmistakable in appearance and even the young panda would not be confused with any other species. However, it seems from our research that quite often the young of various species can indeed be successfully misidentified. In an attempt to minimize this sizeable and serious problem, CITES issues 'identification manuals' for animals which are subject to its regulations, manuals which should be held at ports, airports and land border crossings.

It is not, however, solely a question of illegitimate certification or misidentification which allows the illegal trade to exist and indeed flourish; some authorities are simply not rigorous in their efforts to enforce the regulations. An animal in respect of which there is a combination of rarity, desire to possess the creature, high value, ability to disguise its true identity and ease of contravening the haphazard application of CITES regulations is the Asian bonytongue (*Scleropages formosus*), a species of the primitive group of fishes, the family *Osteoglossidae* (bonytongues), found in the tropical regions of South

Identification Aid – Bear Claws

Measurements refer to length in mm of attached claws taken in a straight line. Size range shown represents the range for adult bears only.

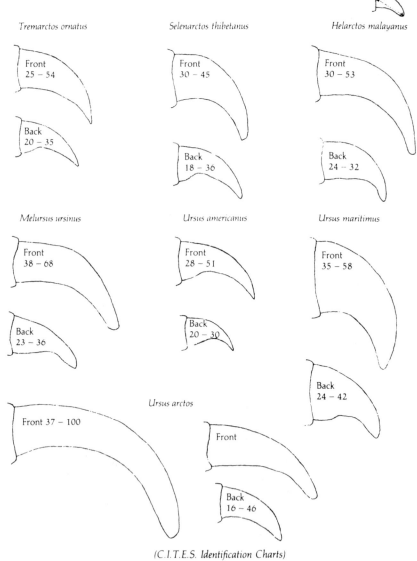

Tremarctos ornatus

Front
25 – 54

Back
20 – 35

Selenarctos thibetanus

Front
30 – 45

Back
18 – 36

Helarctos malayanus

Front
30 – 53

Back
24 – 32

Melursus ursinus

Front
38 – 68

Back
23 – 36

Ursus americanus

Front
28 – 51

Back
20 – 30

Ursus maritimus

Front
35 – 58

Back
24 – 42

Ursus arctos

Front 37 – 100

Front

Back
16 – 46

(C.I.T.E.S. Identification Charts)

Identification Aid – Bear Feet

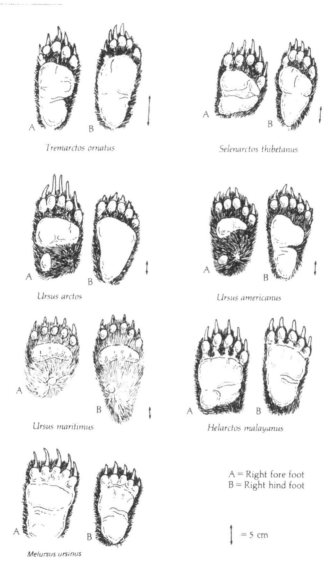

Tremarctos ornatus

Selenarctos thibetanus

Ursus arctos

Ursus americanus

Ursus maritimus

Helarctos malayanus

Melursus ursinus

A = Right fore foot
B = Right hind foot

$\updownarrow$ = 5 cm

(C.I.T.E.S. Identification Charts)

America, Africa, South-east Asia and Australia. Our entire understanding of this fishy issue comes from Joseph, Evans and Broad (1986).

Asian bonytongue (Scleropages formosus) (Joseph, Evans and Broad, 1986: 74)

SCLEROPAGES FORMOSUS

The Asian bonytongue is in much demand as an aquarium fish and has been listed in CITES Appendix I since the Convention came into force in 1973. Despite this, trade had continued almost unabated and the demand for it in recent years seems, if anything, to have grown. There are two other members of the genus, *Scleropages jardini* (northern barramundi) and *Scleropages leichardti* (spotted barramundi) which inhabit parts of Australia and New Guinea, while *S. formosus* is itself distributed widely, but discontinuously, through South-east Asia. It is found in freshwater rivers, lakes and swamps in Malaysia, Thailand, Kampuchea, Indonesia, Vietnam and possibly Burma.

The primitive and striking appearance of *S. formosus* is largely responsible for its popularity in the aquarium trade, and it is this trade which threatens its status in the wild. The fish has an elongated, laterally compressed body with a keeled belly. There are large, bony scales, big eyes, and a bony covering over the head. A fully-grown *S. formosus* may reach a maximum weight of some 16 pounds and a length of 40 inches, although 12 inches is more usual.

Two factors are of crucial importance in the illegal trade in this fish. The first is that within the species there is a great deal of colour variation, the back ranging from olive-brown to lighter reddish-brown, the sides and scales from dull silver to green. Fins vary from light olive-brown to lighter reddish-brown. Although these differences are marked in adult specimens, young fish of up to 4 inches long have more subtle colour differences and may be more difficult to differentiate to species level. The two main colour types distinguished in the trade are the green and the red varieties, but other colours can be identified. The second factor is that the range of names of *S. formosus* is potentially a hindrance to identification: red arowana, green arowana, kelesa, Asian arowana, gold arowana, Malayan bonytongue, golden dragon fish, red dragon fish and emperor fish, as well as numerous local names.

The typical habitat of *S. formosus* is a swamp or flooded forest. In Tasek

Bera, Malaysia, it occurs in an area of flooded swamp forest interspersed with waterways. The water in the main body of the swamp is almost still, peat-stained and slightly acidic. During the night, the fish swim at the surface of open water channels but, during the day, return to hide in vegetation. *S. formosus* has a varied diet, including terrestrial insects, arachnids, non-woody roots and tubers, fish, frogs and snakes. A territorial species, *S. formosus* has an unusual reproductive strategy, notable for late sexual maturity, low fecundity and high survival of young. Spawning takes place between August and October. In Malaysia, the fish may move towards shallow swamp edges to spawn when water levels are high. Twenty or thirty eggs are produced from the single ovary with the maximum known being thirty-seven; after spawning, the male incubates the eggs in his mouth until they hatch. The fry remain near the parent until they are around 3 inches long.

The fish is classified by the International Union for the Conservation of Nature and Natural Resources as 'vulnerable', and is reported as having a population of 2,000. However, other commentators argue that the figure of 2,000 applied only to the population of Thailand and consider that the *S. formosus* is in fact more widespread and numerous than indicated by the earlier reports; they therefore dispute its status as vulnerable. Certainly the fish is poorly known throughout its range, partly owing to the nature of its preferred habitat in swampy and heavily wooded areas, which often prevents access for research and for population estimates.

Although one of the chief threats to *S. formosus* is its attraction as an aquarium item, it is also thought to be under pressure from a loss of habitat, caused partly by swamp clearance in Malaysia and dredging for rubies in Thailand, and from its use as an important source of food. These factors, combined with its natural low fecundity, make it particularly vulnerable. However, despite its Appendix I listing, international trade continues, mainly through Hong Kong, Indonesia, Japan, Malaysia, the USA and Singapore. Most of these are wild-collected in Malaysia and Indonesia, and the majority of the trade is routed through Singapore, an international clearing house and transit port for animals, legally or illegally traded.

Joseph, Evans and Broad point to two of the major problems which we have referred to in our general introduction, which seem to 'inhibit the effective control of this trade; first, species identification and secondly the proof, or otherwise, of captive breeding' (1986: 73). Because a large proportion of trade involves juvenile fish which have not yet developed the distinctive shape and coloration of the adult, they can therefore be 'mixed' in shipments of other species in an attempt to avoid detection. In Japan this problem, combined with the fact that the Washington Treaty Identification Manual produced by the

Japanese CITES Management Authority describes only the adult fish, certainly inhibits accurate species identification. The official CITES Identification Manual sheet for *S. formosus* says of juveniles simply that 'young specimens (up to 10 cm) are normally pale olive-brown with no markings on the fins'. Control of the trade is further complicated by the wide variety of names under which the *S. formosus* is traded. Some of the names are used to describe other species as well, thus confusion can arise when the fish reach customs. In the USA, *S. formosus* has been imported under the name arowana, which is the common name for *Osteoglossum bicirrhosum*, a related fish found in South America. This problem is also exploited in Japan where the young fish are imported under synonyms which are not detailed in the Japanese Identification Manual.

One method of importing *S. formosus* is to claim that the specimens are captive-bred, thus avoiding the restrictions on trade in Appendix I species. In the 1982 Japanese CITES annual report, it was stated that permits had been issued for the import of 2,202 *S. formosus* (20 from Hong Kong, 182 from Taiwan and 2,000 from Indonesia), all of which were declared to be captive-bred. Indonesian government officials have stated that any such trade with Japan was illegal, since the specimens had no official documentation issued by their CITES Management Authority. The validity of the other figures describing imports of captive-bred specimens into Japan must also be doubted in view of the low fecundity of the fish and the difficulties experienced by public aquaria and research laboratories in the captive-breeding of the species. Indeed it is most unlikely that this fish has in fact been bred in captivity in the numbers claimed within the trade. In Singapore various commercial tropical fish breeders have claimed to be breeding *S. formosus*, but it is likely that imported juvenile fish have been used to create this illusion.

Japan has a large number of ornamental-fish enthusiasts and, with an ever increasing number of young collectors, must be regarded as the single largest market for *S. formosus*. This trade continues despite CITES controls, which in fact have simply had the effect of increasing the price for individual specimens. Indeed so high is the demand for the fish that there is a freelance illegal trade, for the potential profits involved greatly outweigh the risk of consignments being seized in customs. As recently as 19 June 1985, fifty juvenile specimens of *S. formosus* were confiscated at Haneda Airport, Tokyo, where they were being smuggled in a vinyl bag placed inside a brandy bottle, one of a consignment of 2,000 bottles on a flight from Singapore. Three of the fish were dead on arrival. It is the general state of the implementation of CITES in Japan that seems to have allowed the illegal trade in this species to flourish. Some of the main problems involved include the large number of points of entry into the country (at one time 123), the lack of accurate export verification, and the inadequacy of domestic legislation to help enforce CITES controls.

At the time of writing Singapore was not a party to CITES, and in 1981 was reported to be the international centre for breeding and exporting tropical fish. As regards *S. formosus* it has been suggested that Singapore was the centre of most of the trade. But this may have changed somewhat since 1983 when the relevant department in the Singapore government advised dealers against trade and informed stockists that it would refuse to issue the necessary import and export certificates. Joseph, Evans and Broad, in their analysis of the trade (1986), report that the only trade involving Singapore which had been the subject of an official CITES report was the import of eight *S. formosus* of unknown origin into Denmark in 1984 ostensibly for zoological purposes.

As we noted earlier Singapore has long been known as a clearing house and transit port for animals traded legally or otherwise. To cite one example: an analysis of the list of birds imported into the USA from Singapore in 1970 shows that forty species or genera of birds were imported. Of these, eleven could have originated only in Indonesia, and an additional twenty-one may have originated in Indonesia but also occur elsewhere in the wild. The number of birds that could have originated only in the wild was at least 247. Two species listed that could have originated only in Indonesia and nine others that may have originated in Indonesia are all protected there. The statistics kept by the Primary Production Department of the Ministry of National Development of Singapore indicated that no birds were imported to Singapore from Indonesia in 1970. Yet Indonesian government figures show 12,341 bird exports to Singapore in 1970. Singapore export statistics for 1970 indicate that 15,979 birds were exported from Singapore to the USA. American statistics for 1970 show that 4,083 birds were received from Singapore. Mortality *en route* accounted for only a portion of this discrepancy. As King bluntly notes, it is 'evident from the comparison of the trade statistics of Indonesia, Singapore, and the USA that we have a very murky picture of the nature and size of the animal trade originating in Indonesia' (1974a: 60).

THE ZOO TRADE

Whether they like it or not zoos are also in the business of trading animals. As we will show there are differences in the patterns and processes of zoo animal trading compared to general trading, but none the less the same universe is shared.

The existence of CITES and the growing concern for the preservation of wildlife have, as we have shown, made the trade in wild animals an extremely contentious issue. From our personal researches we gained the impression that within the zoo world trading in animals was a somewhat distasteful notion. Although many zoos must directly purchase animals from specialist dealers (it is notoriously difficult, however, for outsiders to obtain detailed information about how exactly that trade operates and what monies are involved), it would seem that many of the bigger and more prestigious ones attempt to absent themselves from this trade.

The development of successful captive-breeding programmes has meant that zoos are able to become their own suppliers. In an important sense they have, wherever possible, attempted to distance themselves from direct contact with the wild (or from that contact as mediated by dealers). If anything the contact they wish to maintain with the wild will be as suppliers of endangered animals which they have successfully bred in captivity. In other words they wish to return zoo-bred wild animals to the actual wild.

Zoos which are successfully breeding animals produce surplus stock; animals which they cannot maintain within their establishment − because of lack of space − are traded with other zoos on an uncomplicated cash-nexus basis, although occasionally zoos will in addition swap surplus stock animals. This seems to constitute a mundane trade within the zoos. It reflects successful breeding programmes combined with the need to exercise animal husbandry techniques. One important issue which zoos have to deal with in this context, an issue which quite often causes concern among members of the public, is that the zoos must decide whether to allow animals to continue to breed and at times cull the offspring or whether to make use of contraceptive devices. It appears that individual zoos and particular zoo directors decide on the issue as they see fit. Whatever decision they make, it reinforces the fact that we are not dealing with ordinary wild animals.

There is, however, a rather special exchange of animals within the zoo world, namely the rare animals in danger of extinction which form part of selective breeding programmes. Because zoos cannot or do not want to receive Appendix I animals from the wild, they must endeavour to breed them. But because of the rarity of these animals and the restricted numbers of them held in captivity, no zoo can breed them easily on its own, unless of course it is prepared to produce somewhat hybrid versions of the animals in question − not so much a distortion of the gene pool, rather a cross-breeding, a process which defeats the initial purpose of breeding rare (and pure) animals.

Zoos which have such animals are therefore almost certainly drawn into co-operative breeding ventures. Ironically animals which are in an important sense valuable are moved out of the commercial world since they are simply too valuable to be purchased. The offspring of animals which are subject to international breeding programmes are disposed of not simply at the whim of the curator or director, but in consultation with the relevant stud book keeper who may be located anywhere in the world. They will be placed in a zoo where they are most needed – a need which is defined not solely in terms of exhibition, but also in relation to that zoo's international standing as regards serious breeding intentions.

Endangered animals clearly constitute an elite within the zoo. As we have shown in the case of the kiwis, rare animals do not necessarily possess significant exhibition value – they will not necessarily attract the crowds. But such rare animals are crucially important in the professional world of the zoological garden. They give the institution a certain prestige and this prestige is further increased if the animals are successfully bred.

In addition to the elite of zoo animals, there are other animals in the zoo which constitute a super-elite, the possession of which brings great kudos to the concerned professional zoo. Two of these enter the public (as well as the professional) realm of consciousness because they possess great exhibition value. The most obvious of course is the giant panda, which is rare both in its natural habitat and in terms of zoo population. So valuable is the giant panda that it cannot be purchased. Some directors suggested to us that although even exceptionally rare animals could be obtained through various illegitimate means, it would be absolutely impossible to obtain a living example of the giant panda. In fact the CITES Identification Manual concerned with the giant panda emphasizes this special status: in the 'trade' section it notes that 'legal international trade is restricted to live specimens which are donated to *foreign states* by the Chinese government' (CITES, 1984, our emphasis). This, of course, is reminiscent of the process whereby diplomatic gifts to emperors, kings and nobility have been made throughout time.

We suggest that the koala is the other animal which represents the super-elite and which has a similar quality of value. Although not especially rare in its native habitat, the koala is even more unlikely to be found in the zoological garden than the giant panda. To the best of our knowledge such an animal can only be seen, outside Australia, in Tama Zoological Park, Toyko, San Diego and Los Angeles. The arrival of the koalas in Japan from Australia signified the successful completion of diplomatic negotiations between the two countries, a process exactly parallel to that governing exchanges of giant pandas.

Of course, for the zoo which has only a commercial purpose in mind – the numbers passing through the turnstile – and for the zoo which through the actions of its staff and director deservedly earns a reputation of ill-repute, the processes of careful zoo trading are irrelevant. Such zoos are not interested in the long-term benefit to a species which may accrue from sensitive and planned breeding. Instead they desire the animals which stereotypically possess exhibition value. With these institutions there are closer similarities between general animal trading and specific zoo animal trading, embracing illegal means and the 'profit over nature' ethic. But, as we have argued, the modern zoo attempts to trade somewhat differently.

Originally the menagerie and the early zoo were concerned and motivated to obtain individual specimens for display in their collections, and accordingly the trade in animals was designed to ensure the continuity of specimens in the particular institution. In the modern professional zoo at least one indicator of successful management in the 1980s is the reproduction of animals, and it is through this reproduction of the animals themselves that the zoo is able to reproduce itself. Two questions are raised, however: why is it that we need wild animals to reproduce themselves in captivity? And why is it that we need zoos to reproduce themselves anyway?

8
The Zoo in Evolution

And then there were two. The world's rarest bird declined in numbers by one-third
a few weeks ago when a 14-year-old Crested Ibis died of complications from arthritis
in its caged sanctuary on the island of Sado in the Sea of Japan. The other female
is too old to lay eggs, while the solitary male, though younger and more vigorous,
showed little inclination, despite the frantic encouragement of conservationists, to do
his duty to save his kind. There's a glimmer of hope, however. About 20 birds of
another race of the same species are believed to survive in China. A successful mating
would produce fertile hybrids. One of 24 in the ibis sub-family, the 'toki' Nipponia
nippon is a stately swamp-wader nearly a metre tall and of a most majestic stature –
a brilliant red face, long black beak and dazzling white body. Only half a century
ago it was common in Japan, Korea and Manchuria. The cause of the toki's demise
is chiefly due to the universal use of pesticides, which wreak havoc with the food
chain and introduce toxins that make eggs fragile.

(Asiaweek, 1986)

It is hard to believe or indeed even to understand but it is none the less a
fact that almost 90 per cent of all species that have existed up until now
have disappeared. Norman Myers elaborates this basic point to give an
approximate historical sense of the rate at which animal species have become
extinct. Quite simply, from 1600 to 1900 man eliminated some seventy-five
known species, mostly mammals and birds; since 1900 to the present day he
has eliminated another seventy-five. Between 1600 and 1900 the rate of
disappearance was approximately one species per four years; in the present
century the rate has been approximately one species per year (Myers, 1979:
14). Man cannot be held totally responsible, however, for many of these
species disappeared well before *Homo sapiens* appeared on the planet.

Although Myers concluded his analysis in 1979, the process that he describes
is undoubtedly continuing for, as he himself says, there are currently over a
thousand animal forms threatened with extinction. In many parts of the world
concern is certainly expressed about this, but just as few animals can be
recognized by the public, perhaps even fewer of these thousand forms could
be named and identified. The giant panda, symbol of the World Wildlife
Fund, is recognized internationally as an endangered animal, and many *might*
recognize that the white rhino and the Sumatran rhino are vulnerable, but the
plight of the crested ibis, is likely to attract the attention of few but the
specialist.

Concern for conservation is a cultural factor and must be understood as such, but within cultures the focus of concern is highly selective. A question we could well ask is: if it is important to conserve species why is it that many individuals who might well support the ideals of conservation also support the attempt to destroy certain species such as the Norway rat, the tsetse fly or the malaria-carrying mosquito? Quite simply, why don't these particular living creatures also have the right to exist? Part of the explanation, of course, lies in the fact that such creatures do not elicit sympathetic emotional reactions in people, and in these particular cases they are seen as causing harm to human beings. But the question remains: why is it that conservationists choose to preserve only part of an ecosystem?

Undoubtedly scientific environmentalists operate with a sophisticated model of the organization and functioning of ecosystems, but it is not this knowledge which moves most members of the general public to whom conservationists make appeal. Rather there is a complex of social, cultural and psychological factors involved in the construction of their desire to conserve. This complex of interests and motivations is clearly illustrated in the history of tiger conservation.

INDIA, COLONIALISM AND PROJECT TIGER

To the 'sportsman' of yore, the tiger stood for India's wilderness. The awe and the beastly mystery that go with this 'phantom of the forest' provided the adventure, the thrill and, of course, plenty of raw material for juicy shikar stories.

To the ecologist of today, equally and justifiably, the tiger again is a symbol of the country's wilderness. The flow of nutrients through the complex web of nature in the forest ecosystems, culminates in the tiger. . . .

From the cold Himalayan high-altitude forests to the steaming coastal mangroves of the Sunderbans, from the scorched arid shrublands of Rajasthan to the lush evergreens of the south and the north-east, and from the flat terai swamps to the rolling hard grounds of the peninsula, the tiger is very much at home. The well-being of the tiger is thus synonymous with the health of the Indian wilderness.

(*Project Tiger 1973–83, 1984*)

Before 1970 those working in this area of conservation were under the impression that there were too many tigers in India, so hunting was permitted – Indian VIPs and tourists (especially from the USA) were able to engage in fantasies of adventure. But the results of a 1969 census by the Indian wildlife biologist Kailash Shankla caused a sensation on publication: there were in fact only 2,000 tigers left in India, not the 40,000 believed to be there. The figure of 40,000 incidentally had been produced by the hunter–naturalist E.P. Gee, who had written the first (and standard) book on Indian wildlife a number of years before.

In 1970 the hunting of tigers was banned, a decision which received a certain amount of opposition, particularly from cigar companies who used tiger hunting as tourism and who subsequently appealed unsuccessfully against the decision in the Supreme Court. In 1972 the Wildlife (Protection) Act, India, was passed which provided protection for the tiger and other threatened species together with their habitats. In 1972 the All India Tiger Census counted 1,827 tigers, a result which produced international concern, especially from the World Wildlife Fund.

In 1972 at the Stockholm Conference on Human Settlements, the then Indian Prime Minister, Indira Gandhi, recognized that this was indeed a grave problem and supported the formation of Project Tiger, the architects of which were a special task force of the Indian Board of Wildlife. The Prime Minister observed that: 'The tiger cannot be preserved in isolation. It is at the apex of a large and complex biotope. Its habitat, threatened by human intrusion, commercial forestry and cattle grazing, must first be made inviolate' (*Project Tiger 1973–1983, 1984*).

So in 1973 Project Tiger was launched. Nine reserves were established, a number subsequently increased to fifteen, and currently covering an area of 15,600 square miles. The policy has not been simply to favour the tiger at the cost of other wildlife, because artificial population growth was not desired. Indeed other endangered species like swamp deer, elephant, rhino and wild buffalo have benefited substantially from the environmentally oriented policy. As R.L. Singh, the director of the Project put it, the Project attempts to remove all adverse man-man influences, but none the less the 'tiger has to struggle for his rights ... the tiger is not a VIP in the tiger reserve'. In 1984 the Tiger Census produced a total count of 4,005.

The relationship of Project Tiger with human communities has been a complex and at times contentious one. Many communities were forced to surrender their traditional rights to graze cattle, pick firewood and fell trees in order to make Project Tiger work. Relocation plans had to be made. The need for a genuine working relationship was essential as villagers could have poisoned the whole tiger population in a year if they had felt driven to do so. One strategy taken by Project Tiger therefore was that it would pay full compensation if a tiger killed cattle even if the cattle were grazed in the reserves allocated to the conservation project.

Project Tiger makes no provision for the capture of tigers for the purpose of zoo collections, and it is therefore somewhat ironic that R.L. Singh argues that *no* zoo is providing a line of genetically pure Indian tigers. One of the reasons for the reluctance to assist zoos in this matter is that a number of years ago a British zoo released an 'Indian tiger cub' (which turned out to be a rare case of a man-eater), which in fact was not really Indian, and it subsequently polluted the genetically pure Indian tiger. A policy was then firmly made that no hand-reared animal would ever be allowed to be introduced into the wild.

Currently there is a debate about the breeding rate in the reserves. The growth from 1,827 to 4,005 could have been due more to protection than to breeding – there were fewer fires so the cubs had a better chance of survival. In other words mortality has gone down. This is a plausible theory, particularly if the 1972 census had been low (that is, if it had failed to take account of stray tigers). Certainly breeding is slowing down, with such factors as population control by nature (limitations of space) and cannibalism in tigers being partly responsible. It has also been reported that a 'killer weed' is threatening almost all the reserves. The multi-coloured flowering shrub *Lantana camara*, introduced from South Africa in the early twentieth century as an ornamental plant for gardens, escaped into forests and spread through India. By restricting the regeneration of Indian trees and encroaching over grassland, the shrub has reduced the fodder for wild animals, thus disturbing their food cycle. Indeed in some areas it is estimated that 40 per cent of ground cover is encroached by the shrub. Tigers could therefore face severe problems because the herbivores which are their prey are disappearing. A possible remedy is the Indian plant Narkul (*Arundo djnax*), which grows faster than *Lantana camara* and surpasses the weed and finally kills it in its own ground. Narkul is also enjoyed by deer, elephants and other grazing animals of the Indian forest. In addition it provides good shade to attract tigers for afternoon naps.

On the question of breeding, R.L. Singh argues that Indian zoos themselves should breed more, and that an effective group breeding programme must be devised. He also notes that zoos on occasion encourage the illegal poaching of tigers by private trappers – as he puts it, 'There is money in it so someone must be doing it.'

In conclusion Singh argues that the internationalization of consumer desires and the rise of market values have resulted in the destruction of natural resources. Furthermore he maintains that the issue should not be seen as a problem merely for developing or poor countries; rather the reverse – which is of course quite true.

INDIA AND COLONIALISM

India offers a particularly powerful illustration of key themes in the complex interrelation between naturally occurring wildlife, indigenous cultural perceptions of that wildlife, the exploitation of that wildlife for overseas populations and finally a colonial experience. Indian wildlife was raided to supply animals for European menageries and later for zoological gardens. But as a result of European intrusion into India as part of the colonial process, an intrusion which brought with it Anglo-Saxon cultural forms, the zoological garden was imposed on India. The result of this was that an alien cultural artifact was used to frame animals within their country of origin in a way which was artificial for the indigenous observers. Thus the colonizers had attempted to reshape Indian views of their own wildlife.

With the development of western concern for conservation, interested western bodies have asked Indians to look at their wildlife in yet another way. It is perhaps understandable that people in the west are concerned about the plight of the tiger, but they would probably have had no cause for concern if the west had not depleted the population in the first place. It seems clear that the colonial exploitation of wildlife together with the subsequent depletion of stocks is a significant factor in the current crisis to which western-based conservation agencies are attempting to respond.

However, India does highlight the fact that human–animal relations are complex and often contain ambivalent features. Moreover, the interpretations of such relations can both lead to and be based on mystification. Currently some 3 per cent of the geographical area of India is devoted to conservation, there being 15 tiger reserves, 54 national parks and 241 wildlife sanctuaries. Clearly British rule, American tourists and Indian princes had a great deal of impact on Indian wildlife, but what of the Indian population in general? R.L. Singh argues that the traditional Indian respect for animals is religious in nature. The problem is that the people who can now be seen occasionally stoning the animals in zoos are immune from traditional values – they possess a different world-view: 'Seeing an animal is just entertainment. It has not gone deeper. Family life has been dissolved. They want every animal to dance for them. They want a return – a cost-benefit analysis.' A cursory glance at the relationship between the Indian human and animal worlds reveals that it is not particularly easy to stereotype a nation's culture; and in a country like India where there are 16 major languages, 4,000 dialects and 500 million non-literate people such stereotyping is especially misguided.

It is certainly true that the symbolic relationship of man – through his religion – and the animal world is an immensely visible and powerful one. If we consider the characteristics of a number of Hindu deities we see that there are important animal associations: Śiva is frequently adorned by a tiger skin; Kāli wears snakes; while Gaṇésa, the elephant-headed god of wisdom, rides on a rayt, his vāhana or carrier; Viṣṇu is carried on the gleaming golden back of Garuda, a huge bird with the head and wings of an eagle and the limbs of a man. Popular belief also credits Garuda with the power to cure those suffering from snake-bites. The interpenetration of men and animals in these symbolic relationships is taken further through the role of the vāhana. Brahmā has a goose, haṃsa, and, as we have seen, Viṣṇu has the Garuda bird. Similarly there are the relationships of Śiva with a bull, Gaṇésa with a rat, Kāma with a parrot, and so on.

Despite this profound symbolism there is not a parallel knowledge of actual animals. In other words Hindus – who make up the majority of the population – know less about animal behaviour than one might imagine in a country in which 80 per cent of the population live in villages. Two further elements are worth adding here. First, at this social level there has not been a strong tradition of hunting for sport, something which demands good practical knowledge of animal behaviour. Secondly, there has not been a tradition of natural history as there has been since early modern times in Europe; it was the incoming British colonialists who brought such traditions with them.

The religious attitude towards animals in general is still alive and of great significance in modern India. Hindus theoretically see all animals as sacred, but the Jains are even stricter; they do not take any life, because all life is seen as valuable and sacred. Hence they would not even swat a fly. Almost 300 years ago the Jains established *panjanapols,* or cages in neighbourhoods, where they kept destitute and stray animals. Towards the establishment of these *panjanapols* they would put a percentage of their income. Moreover, Hindu gurus have in the past also kept cheetahs, deer and elephants predominantly as pets.

However, there are other traditions of man–animal relations in India which do not lead to the treatment of animals that one might expect given this religious tradition. For example, in circuses or street shows we can observe performing (and chained) bears, snakes, rhesus monkeys, mongooses, parakeets and finches. Similarly the traditional use of animals in sport is still in evidence – hawks, falcons, sparrowhawks, eagles, hunting cheetahs and, for Muslims, pigeons. Another extant tradition, one which treats animals more circumspectly, is the keeping of animals for medicinal purposes, such as the use of the fat of the spinytailed lizard for the 'cure' of rheumatism. Incidentally, in a number of zoos in India the keepers receive numerous requests for animal products: rhinoceros urine as a treatment for asthma, or mud from lions' and elephants' feet for holy purposes.

India did have princely menageries, which were particularly associated with the Moghuls, and some of the menageries were transformed into zoos, as in Baroda, but the majority merely withered away. During the period of British rule, zoological gardens based on predominantly European models were developed. A more important transformation came about after 1947, in the post-independence period, when there was a decline in the interest in and development of zoos, mainly because the British traditions had not become indigenous. As Kartikya Sarabhai, Project Director at the Centre for Environment Education, Ahmedabad puts it, 'The princes had lost power, the British had lost power, few commoners were interested in zoos.' It is true of course that the British killed tigers and birds, but there were also instances of positive British conservation, with the setting up, for example, of the Botany Survey and the Zoological Survey. But one serious impediment to post-independence development was that the British simply did not link zoos with the common man.

In the late 1960s, as in the rest of the world, popular movements like ornithology grew, and then came Indira Gandhi's 1972 speech. All of this has offered prospects of a more enlightened and indigenous zoo culture. But it remains an open question what direction Indian zoos will take.

THE 'ZOO ANIMAL'

A fundamental question is this: why preserve wildlife at all? One might well respond that the world would be impoverished if the animals under threat of extinction were allowed to die out. But who precisely would be impoverished?

Our answer is that the human world would be impoverished, for animals are preserved solely for human benefit, because human beings have decided they want them to exist for human pleasure. The notion that they are preserved for *their* sakes is a peculiar one, for it implies that animals might wish a certain condition to endure. It is, however, nonsensical for humans to imagine that animals might want to continue the existence of their species. Although, in one sense, the biological drive or reason for existence of any animal is to perpetuate the species, we are not referring here to that level of biological or evolutionary process. Animals other than man cannot have a sense of species identity; they cannot reflect on the nature of their collective identity, nor can they have a sense that it would be a good thing for them to continue in existence. A Siberian tiger or a giant panda cannot know that they are threatened with extinction; all they can do is respond to a biological imperative and continue to reproduce. The *desire* for a species' continuity is merely a

157

projection on the part of human beings. The few giant pandas or Siberian tigers in captivity cannot have any sense of what they represent or the potential fate which threatens their species, for they do not know of the existence of other animals. Other members of the animal world will not, of course, mourn the passing of the last Sumatran rhino or the last Siberian tiger – only humans will mourn.

The preservation of the natural world is only a preservation for our benefit even though this might well be expressed in terms of an altruistic concern with animal welfare. If the ideals of preservation were based simply on a concern for animals, would it not be best to establish reserves where humans were excluded even from viewing the animals?

Jonathan Barzdo, in discussing captive-bred populations held in zoos, argues that: 'Purists may even say these animals have been altered by captive breeding and are no good for the wild; but they are good enough for me' (1982: 23). But is it good enough for the animals? Of course the animal cannot reflect on its condition as a selectively bred captive animal, but the breeding in question has been arranged so that the humans, not the animals, enjoy the continuance of the species.

Many zoos have established highly successful breeding programmes of both endangered and non-endangered species, often with the aim of ensuring the continuance of the species by establishing a secure population within the zoo, with the hope that these animals might form the basis for a 'reintroduction into the wild' programme. But the directors of zoos with such programmes tend to recognize that there may well be no wild left to reintroduce the animals into. After all, each year approximately 30 million acres of forest (an area almost the size of England) are being eliminated, mostly in the moist forests and open woodlands of the tropics. In addition, there is the degradation of at least a further 24 million acres of forest a year, again mainly in the tropics. Furthermore, as Project Tiger shows, the animals successfully bred in zoos might not be suitable for reintroduction anyway. We cannot help but conclude that given the zoos' success in reproducing their populations there will in time be a repository of permanent populations of 'zoo animals' which are structurally equivalent to wild populations even though they are in an important sense thoroughly culturized.

THE 'ARCHITECTURE OF GUILT'

Such populations are presented in many zoos with the intention of conveying to the viewing public an impression of what individual members of that population would do were they in their natural habitat. The problem with this is that the animals in the zoo tend not to act in ways the public are told they do. The very structure of the zoo itself, as we have seen earlier, mitigates against such behaviour. Despite the number of carefully crafted graphics and informative texts which the zoo staff might provide alongside say the lion enclosure in order to explain the animals' behaviour, there is none the less usually a sense of disappointment in the visitor when the sleepy and lethargic beasts visible in front of him are not easily imagined as the accomplished hunters of the African plain. The zoo cannot but fail in its attempt to give a full understanding or appreciation of natural behaviour and natural relationships for these cannot be displayed in an environment which consists of artificial segments of the whole, all within yards of each other. This is an artificiality that fools nobody. Indeed the most complex and sophisticated attempts at the representation and recreation of the natural world in the context of the zoo, could be interpreted as examples of an 'architecture of guilt', albeit a somewhat unconscious one. It is within cultures where there are people concerned about the morality of putting animals on permanent display, that a pressure exists to provide them with a better stage and with more complex scenery and props to make the illusion more satisfactory and more morally acceptable.

HUMAN DESIRES

Zoos are institutions established for human pleasure, but it is pleasure that can quite clearly be problematic. For zoos represent the power of human beings to command the presence of living creatures which would normally absent themselves from human gaze. Confined in the zoo in an alien environment, they are 'displaced' creatures, and the human visitor must at some level recognize this for there is clearly a disjunction between the animal's environment in the zoo and that in which it would live if allowed. In a subtle way anthropomorphism disguises this fact by humanizing the animal, thus suggesting that it is in its appropriate environment. The danger is that the anthropomorphized animal will be equated with a human prisoner, so that the pleasure of seeing it in this environment will be ambivalent.

Whether animals in the zoo are seen simply as creatures having little in common with the human viewers and towards whom the humans owe only the minimum for physical survival, or whether the distance is reduced and the animals become creatures with needs like ours, varies from culture to culture. We suggest that it is the oscillation between 'like us' and 'not like us' which accounts for much of the fascination of watching the varied activities of animals in the zoo. Animals are able to behave without the restraints of cultural considerations. The open displays of sexuality, uninhibited play, unrestrained aggression – in general, raw animal behaviour unmediated by the rules of civility or morality – perhaps allow members of the public to reflect both on the basic distinction between humans and animals, and the confusion of the two: the human in the animal skin and the animal in the human. Despite the fact that humans and other animals share a common animality in the biological sense, in a significant cultural sense animals present an 'otherness' and it is the very 'otherness' which provides a contrast with our humanness.

Giraffes do not naturally belong in the middle of Tokyo, nor polar bears in Washington and certainly not lions in Copenhagen, but unfortunately for them humans seem to need them there and, furthermore, can command them to be there. In zoos man has been able to go beyond nature and transform it, to alter the natural distribution of animal species such that there are now populations of animals existing completely outside their natural environment. This relationship of the human to the animal world has taken different shades of meanings in different cultures and different eras but, at the most basic level, zoos are institutions of power, in that they reflect the uniquely human ability to hold in captivity and dominate large numbers of diverse wild animals for the purpose of human enjoyment and human benefit. The zoo constitutes a gallery of images constructed by man. The fact that he is able to arrange around him living creatures from all parts of the world, to make decisions with regard to the quality and conditions of their lives and to give shape to the world for them in terms of his imagination and desire is, in the end, an expression of power.

Bibliography

Aflalo, F.G. (1902) 'Some Private Zoos', *Annual Report of the Smithsonian Institution 1901*, Government Printing Office, Washington DC.

Alexander, Edward P. (1983) *Museum Masters: Their Museums and Their Influence*, American Association for State and Local History, Nashville, Tennessee.

Altick, Richard D. (1978) *The Shows of London*, Harvard University Press, London.

Amory, Cleveland (1974) *Mankind? Our Incredible War on Wildlife*, Harper & Row, New York.

Asiaweek (20 July 1986).

Aspinall, John (1976) *The Best of Friends*, Macmillan, London.

Bacon, J. and Hullet, M. (1981) 'Exhibit Systems for Reptiles and Amphibians at the San Diego Zoo: Dioramas and Graphics' in P.J.S. Olney (ed.) *International Zoo Yearbook*, vol. 21, Zoological Society of London, London, pp.14–21.

Barber, Lynn (1980) *The Heyday of Natural History 1820–1870*, Jonathan Cape, London.

Barton, Russell (1959) *Institutional Neurosis*, John Wright, Bristol.

Barzdo, Jonathan (1982) 'The Trouble With Zoos' in Jonathan Barzdo, John Berger, Chris Rawlance, John Roberts, the artists and the ICA (1982) *Zoos*, Institute of Contemporary Arts, London, pp. 19–23.

Bateson, P.P.G. and Hinde, R.A. (eds.) (1976) *Growing Points in Ethology*, Cambridge University Press, Cambridge.

Batten, Peter (1976) *Living Trophies*, Thomas Y. Crowell Company, New York.

Beddard, Frank E. (1905) *Natural History in Zoological Gardens*, Archibald Constable, London.

Belin, P.H. (1985) *Architectures Zoologiques France 1662/1932*, Ministère de l'Urbanisme et du Logement École d'Architecture de Clermont-Ferrand.

Bendiner, Robert (1981) *The Fall of the Wild, the Rise of the Zoo*, Elsevier-Dutton Publishing Co., New York.

Bennett, E.T. (1830) *The Gardens and Menagerie of the Zoological Society Delineated*, John Sharpe, London.

Benson, Thomas (1983) 'The Clouded Mirror: Animal Stereotypes and Human Cruelty' in Harlan B. Miller, (ed.) *Ethics and Animals*, Humana Press, New Jersey.

Berger, John (1980) *About Looking*, Writers and Readers' Publishing Cooperative, London.

Berger, John (1982) 'Why Look at Animals?' in Jonathan Barzdo, John Berger, Chris Rawlence, John Roberts, the artists and the ICA, *Zoos*, ICA, London. *Zoos*.

Bettleheim, B. and Sylvester E. (1948) 'A Therapeutic Milieu', *American Journal of Orthopsychiatry*, vol. 18, pp. 191–206.

Blackwelder, Richard E. (1967) *Taxonomy: A Text and Reference Book*, John Wiley & Sons, London.

Brennan, Tom (1978) 'Visitor Watching: What People Do at the Zoo', *Brookfields Bison*, August–September 1978, pp. i–v.

Burt, Nathaniel (1977) *Palaces for the People: A Social History of the American Art Museum*, Little, Brown & Co., Boston.

Burton, Benedict (1986) Untitled paper read at 'Making Exhibitions of ourselves: the Limits of Objectivity in Representations of Other Cultures', February 1986, Museum Ethnographers Group, The British Museum.

Bynum, William F. (1981) 'Rationales for Therapy in British Psychiatry 1780–1835', in Andrew Scull (ed.), *Madhouses, Mad-Doctors and Madmen: The Social History of Psychiatry in the Victorian Era*, Athlone Press, London, pp. 35–57.

CITES (1984) *Amendments to Appendices I, II and III of the Convention on International Trade in Endangered Species of Wild Fauna and Flora*, HMSO, London.

Chambers, Peggy (1982) *Four Seasons Demographic Study*, Education Department, Philadelphia Zoological Society, Philadelphia.

Cheek, Neil (1973) 'People at the Zoo', *Animal Kingdom*, June 1973, pp. 9–14.

Cherfas, Jeremy (1984), *Zoo 2000*, BBC Publications, London.

Clark, Stephen R.L. (1977) *The Moral Status of Animals*, Oxford University Press, Oxford.

Clarke G.C.S. and Miller R.S. (1980) 'The Natural History Museum and the Public', *Biologist*, vol. 27(2), pp. 14–18.

Conway, William (1984–5) 'Report of the General Director', in *New York Zoological Society Annual Report*, New York, pp. 4–15.

Crandall, Lee S. (1964) *The Management of Wild Animals in Captivity*, University of Chicago Press, Chicago.

Darwin, Charles (1872) *The Expression of the Emotions in Man and Animals*, (1965 reprint), University of Chicago Press, Chicago.

Desmond, Adrian (1979) *The Apes Reflexion*, Blond & Briggs, London.

Duplaix-Hall, Nicole (ed.) (1974) *International Zoo Yearbook*, Zoological Society of London, London, vol. 14.

Edwards, Edward (1870) *Lives of the Founders of the British Museums*, Trübner, London.

Ellenberger, Henri F. (1974) 'The Mental Hospital and the Zoological Garden', in J. Klaits and B. Klaits (eds.), *Animals and Man in Historical Perspective*, Harper & Row, New York, pp. 59–93.

Eltringham S.K. (1984) *Wildlife Resources and Economic Development*, John Wiley & Sons, Chichester.

Evans, E.P. (1906) *The Criminal Prosecution and Capital Punishment of Animals*, William Heinemann, London.

Fiedler, F.E. and Wheeler, W.A. (1985) *A Survey of Visitors to the Woodland Park Zoological Gardens*, The Zoological Foundation of Woodland Park, Seattle.

Flower, Sir William Henry (1870) *Essays on Museums*, Macmillan, London.

Foucault, Michel (1973) *Madness and Civilization*, Vintage Books, New York.

Foucault, Michel (1979) *Discipline and Punish*, Penguin Books, Harmondsworth.

Fowler, Murray E. (1974) 'Veterinary Aspects of Restraint and Transport of Wild Animals', in Nicole Duplaix-Hall (ed.), *International Zoo Yearbook*, Zoological Society of London, London, vol. 14, pp. 28–34.

Garnett, D. (1924) *A Man in the Zoo*, Chatto & Windus, London.

George, Wilma (1969) *Animals and Maps*, Secker & Warburg, London.

George, Wilma (1980) 'Sources and Backgrounds to Discoveries of New Animals in the Sixteenth and Seventeenth Centuries', *History of Science*, vol. XVIII, pp. 79–104.

Girouard, Mark (1981) *Alfred Waterhouse and the Natural History Museum*, Yale University Press, New Haven and London, in association with The British Museum (Natural History).

Gould, Stephen Jay (1979) 'Mickey Mouse Meets Konrad Lorenz', *Natural History*, May 1979.

Green-Armytage, A.H.N. (1964) *Bristol Zoo 1865–1965*, Arrowsmith, Bristol.

Griffin, Donald (1976) *The Question of Animal Awareness*, Rockefeller University Press, New York.

Grove, Noel (1981) 'Wild Cargo: The Business of Smuggling Animals', *National Geographic*, vol. 159(3), pp. 287–315.

Hagenbeck, Carl (1910) *Beasts and Men*, Longmans and Green, London.

Hahn, Emily (1968) *Zoos*, Secker & Warburg, London.

Hamy, E.T. (1898) 'The Royal Menagerie of France and the National Menageries Established on the 14th Brumaire of the Year I (Nov. 4th 1793)', in *Annual Report of the Smithsonian Institution 1897*, Government Printing Office, Washington DC, pp. 507–17.

Hancocks, David (1971) *Animals and Architecture*, Praeger Publishers, New York.

Hancocks, David (1979) *Woodland Park Zoo 75th Anniversary, 1904–1979*, The Zoological Foundation of Woodland Park, Seattle.

Harrison, Barbara (1974) 'Animal Trade, an International Issue', in Nicole Duplaix-Hall (ed.), *International Zoo Yearbook*, Zoological Society of London, London, vol. 14, pp. 13–21.

Hastings, Duke of Bedford (1949) *The Years of Transition*, Andrew Dakers, London.

Hays, H.R. (1973) *Birds, Beasts and Men*, Dent & Sons, London.

Hediger, Heini (1964) *Wild Animals in Captivity*, Dover Publications, New York.

Hediger, Heini (1968) *The Psychology and Behaviour of Animals in Zoos and Circuses*, Dover Publications, New York.

Hediger, Heini (1970) *Man and Animal in the Zoo*, Routledge & Kegan Paul, London.

Hudson, Kenneth (1986) 'Problems in Museum Presentation of the Westernisation of Other Cultures', unpublished manuscript.

Humphrey, N.K. (1976) 'The Social Function of Intellect', in P.P.G Bateson and R.A. Hinde (eds.), *Growing Points in Ethology*, Cambridge University Press, Cambridge, pp. 303–18.

Jennison, George (1937) *Animals for Show and Pleasure in Ancient Rome*, Manchester University Press, Manchester.

Johnston, Norman (1973) *The Human Cage: A Brief History of Prison Architecture*, Walker, New York.

Jones, J. and Fowles, A.J. (1984) *Ideas of Institutions*, Routledge & Kegan Paul, London.

Jones and Jones (1976) *Woodland Park Zoo: Long-Range Plan, Development Guidelines and Exhibit Scenarios*, Jones and Jones, Seattle.

Jones and Jones (1985) *Kansas City Master Plan*, Jones and Jones, Seattle.

Jones and Jones (1985) *Belize Zoo Master Plan*, Jones and Jones, Seattle.

Joseph, J., Evans D. and Broad S. (1986) 'International Trade in Asian Bonytongues', *Traffic Bulletin*, vol. III(5), pp. 73–6.

Kabbani, Rayna (1986) *Europe's Myths of Orient: Devise and Rule*, Macmillan, London.

Keeling, Clinton H. (1985) *Where the Crane Danced*, Clam Publications, Sheldon.

Kellert, Stephen R. (1979) 'Zoological Parks in American Society', *Proceedings of the American Association of Zoological Parks and Aquariums*, pp. 1–39.

Kellert, Stephen R. (1984) 'Urban American Perception of Animals and the Natural Environment', *Urban Ecology*, vol. 8, pp. 209–28.

Kiernan V.G. (1969) *Lords of Human Kind*, Weidenfeld & Nicolson, London.

King, J. (1985) 'Studies and Observations of Zoo Visitors', unpublished manuscript, Office of Education, National Zoological Park, Washington DC.

King, Warren B. (1974a) 'Aspects of International Trade in Indonesian Birds', in Nicole Duplaix-Hall (ed.) *International Zoo Yearbook*, Zoological Society of London, London, vol. 14, pp. 56–61.

King, Wayne F. (1974b) 'International Trade and Endangered Species', in Nicole Duplaix-Hall (ed.), *International Zoo Yearbook*, Zoological Society of London, London, vol. 14, pp. 2–13.

Klaits J. and Klaits B. (eds.) (1974) *Animals and Man in Historical Perspective*, Harper & Row, New York.

Klingender, Francis (1971) *Animals in Art and Thought to the End of the Middle Ages*, Routledge & Kegan Paul, London.

Koppelkam, Stephan (1981) *Glasshouses and Wintergardens of the Nineteenth Century*, Rizzoli International Publications, New York.

La-Croix, Jean Bernard (1978) 'L'Approvisionment de ménageries et les transports d'animaux sauvage par la Compagnie des Indes aux xviiᵉ siècle', in *Société Française D'Histoire D'Outre Mer*, vol. 65(2), pp. 153–79.

Lawrence, Elizabeth A. (1983) 'Neoteny in American Perceptions of Animals', unpublished manuscript.

Lewinsohn, Richard (1954) *Animals, Men, Myths: An Informative and Entertaining History of Man and the Animals Around Him*, Harper & Row, New York.

Livingstone, John (1976) *One Living Instant: Man's Fleeting Supremacy*, Houghton Mifflin Co., Boston.

Lloyd, Joan Barclay (1971) *African Animals in Renaissance Literature and Art*, Clarendon Press, Oxford.

Lockwood, Randall (1983) 'Anthropomorphism Is Not a Four-Letter Word', unpublished manuscript.

Loisel, Gustave (1912) *Histoire des ménageries de l'antiquité à nos jours*, Octave Doin et Fils/Henri Laurens, Paris.

Luoma, Jon (1982) 'Prison or Ark?', *Audubon*, Fall 1982, pp. 102–8.

MacNeice, Louis (1938) *Zoo*, Michael Joseph, London.

Markowitz, Hal (1982) *Behavioral Enrichment in the Zoo*, Van Nostrand Reinhold Company, New York.

Midgley, Mary (1983) *Animals and Why They Matter*, Penguin Books, Harmondsworth.

Morris, R. and Morris D. (1981) *The Giant Panda*, Macmillan, London.

Murphy, Howard (1986) 'Reflections on Representations', *Anthropology Today*, vol. 2(8), pp. 24–5.

Myers, Norman (1979) *The Sinking Ark*, Pergamon Press, Oxford.

Myers, Norman (ed.) (1985) *The GAIA Atlas of Planet Management*, Pan, London.

Myerson, A. (1939) 'The "Total Push" Method in Schizophrenia', *American Journal of Psychiatry*, vol. 95, pp. 1197–204.

Nietschmann, B. (1977) 'The Bambi Factor', *Natural History*, vol. 86(6), pp. 84–6.

O'Donoghue, Edward Geoffrey (1914) *The Story of Bethlehem Hospital*, Fisher & Unwin, London.

Olney, P.J.S. (1980) 'London Zoo', in Solly Zuckerman *Great Zoos of the World: Their Origins and Significance*, Weidenfeld & Nicolson, London, pp. 35–48

Olney, P.J.S. (ed.) (1981/2) *International Zoo Yearbook*, Zoological Society of London, London, vols. 21 and 22.

Parry-Jones, William (1981) 'The Model of the Geel Lunatic Colony and Its Influence on the Nineteenth Century', in Andrew Scull (ed.), *Madhouses, Mad-Doctors and Madmen: The Social History of Psychiatry in the Victorian Era*, Athlone Press, London, pp. 201–17.

Passmore, John (1974) *Man's Responsibility for Nature*, Duckworth, London.

Peel, C.V.A. (1903) *The Zoological Gardens of Europe*, Robinson, London.

Pieters, Florence F.J.M. (1980) 'Notes on the Menagerie and Zoological Cabinet of Stadholder William V of Holland, Directed by Arnold Vosmaer', *Journal of the Society of the Bibliography of Natural History*, vol. 9(4), pp. 539–63.

Pitt-Rivers, Lieutenant-General Augustus (1891) 'Typological Museums, As Exemplified by the Pitt-Rivers Museum at Oxford and his Provincial Museum at Farnham Dorset', *Journal of the Society of Arts*, 18 Dec. 1891, pp. 115–22.

Polo, Marco (1982) *The Travels*, Penguin Books, Harmondsworth.

Popper K.R. and Eccles J.C. (1977) *The Self and Its Brain*, Springer International, Berlin.

Prescott, William H. (1847) *History of the Conquest of Mexico and History of the Conquest of Peru*, Boston.

Project Tiger 1973–1983 (1984), Department of Environment, Government of India.

Reed, Robert Rentoul (1970) *Bedlam on the Jacobean Stage*, Octagon Books, New York.

Reichenbach, Herman (1980) 'Carl Hagenbeck's Tierpark and Modern Zoological Gardens', *Journal of the Society of the Bibliography of Natural History*, vol.
9(4), pp. 573–85.

Said, Edward (1985) *Orientalism*, Peregrine Books, Harmondsworth.

Schomber, Geoffrey (1974) 'The Responsibilities of the Zoos, Shippers and
Dealers', in Nicole Duplaix-Hall (ed.), *International Zoo Yearbook*, Zoological
Society of London, London, vol. 14, pp. 1–2.

Scull, Andrew (ed.) (1981a) *Madhouses, Mad-Doctors and Madmen: The Social
History of Psychiatry in the Victorian Era*, Athlone Press, London.

Scull, Andrew (1981b) 'The Social History of Psychiatry in the Victorian Era',
in Andrew Scull (ed.), *Madhouses, Mad-Doctors and Madmen: The Social
History of Psychiatry in the Victorian Era*, Athlone Press, London, pp. 5–
32.

Scull, Andrew (1981c) 'Moral Treatment Reconsidered: Some Sociological
Comments on an Episode in the History of British Psychiatry', in Andrew
Scull (ed.), *Madhouses, Mad-Doctors and Madmen: The Social History of
Psychiatry in the Victorian Era*, Athlone Press, London, pp. 105–18.

Shepard, Paul (1978) *Thinking Animals*, Viking Press, New York.

Showalter, Elaine (1981) 'Victorian Women and Insanity', in Andrew Scull
(ed.), *Madhouses, Mad-Doctors and Madmen: The Social History of Psychiatry
in the Victorian Era*, Athlone Press, London, pp. 313–36.

Smit, Pieter (ed.) (1986) *Hendrik Engel's Alphabetical List of Dutch Zoological
Cabinets and Menageries*, Nieuwe Nederlandse Bijdragen tot de Gesch-
iendenis der Geneekskunde en der Natuurwetenschappen, no. 19, Amsterdam.

Smith, Anthony (1977) *Animals on View: An Illustrated Guide to Britain's Safari
Parks, Zoos, Aquariums and Bird Gardens*, Weidenfeld & Nicolson, London.

Stanton, Alfred H. and Schwartz, Morris S. (1954) *The Mental Hospital*, Basic
Books, New York.

Storr, Anthony (1970) *Human Aggression*, Penguin Books, Harmondsworth.

Strahan, Ronald (1974) 'Australian Faunal Import and Export Regulations', in
Nicole Duplaix-Hall (ed.), *International Zoo Yearbook*, Zoological Society of
London, London, vol. 14, pp. 21–3.

Thompson, J.D. and Goldin, G. (1975) *The Hospital: A Social and Architectural
History*, Yale University Press, New Haven.

Toovey, J. (1980) 'Philadelphia Zoological Garden', in Solly Zuckerman *Great
Zoos of the World: Their Origins and Significance*, Weidenfeld & Nicolson,
London, pp. 79–90.

Toynbee, J.M.C. (1973) *Animals in Roman Life and Art*, Thames & Hudson,
London.

Tuke, Daniel Hack (1882) *Chapters in the History of the Insane*, Kegan Paul and Trench, London.

Turnbull, Colin (1981) 'East African Safari', *Natural History*, vol. 90(5), pp. 26–34.

van Keuran, David K. (1984) 'Museum Ideology: Augustus Pitt-Rivers, Anthropological Museums and Social Change in Late Victorian Britain', *Victorian Studies*, vol. 28(1), pp. 171–89.

Varine-Bohan, Hughes de (1985) 'Museums', in *Encyclopaedia Britannica*, Helen Hemingway Benton Publishers, Chicago/London.

Walker, Stephen (1983) *Animal Thought*, Routledge & Kegan Paul, London.

Walton, John (1981) 'The Treatment of Pauper Lunatics in Victorian England: The Case of the Lancaster Asylum 1816–1870', in Andrew Scull (ed.), *Madhouses, Mad-Doctors and Madmen: The Social History of Psychiatry in the Victorian Era*, Athlone Press, London, pp. 166–97.

Wolf, Eric (1982) *Europe and the People Without History*, University of California Press, Berkeley.

Wolf, R.L. and Tymitz, B.L. (1979) "Do Giraffes Ever Sit?": A Study of Visitor Perceptions at the National Zoological Park, Smithsonian Institution', unpublished manuscript, Office of Education, National Zoological Park, Washington DC.

Woodroffe, Gordon (1981) *Wildlife Conservation and the Modern Zoo*, Saiga Publishing, Hindhead, Surrey.

Zuckerman, Solly (1980) *Great Zoos of the World: Their Origins and Significance*, Weidenfeld & Nicolson, London.

Loisel, Gustave, 89, *passim*
London Zoological Gardens, 10-11
Lorenz, Konrad, 24-25
Louis xiv, 43, 48, 101-3
Louwman, Jan, 28
MacNiece, Louis, 1
madness and madmen, 35-39
Magic Kingdom, Disney's, 25
Malik, Abdullah, 57
mental hospitals, similarities with the
    zoo, 31-45
Mickey Mouse, 24-26
Midgley, Mary, 7, 14
Morris, Desmond and Morris, Ramona,
    25-28
Murphy, Howard, 70
museums and art galleries, and compar-
    isons with zoos, 116-29
Myers, Norman, 151

Naidu, M. Kamal, 68
naming of animals, 8-12
Naranjo, Eliciaro, 56
National Zoological Park, Washington
    DC, 8, 133-34
neoteny, concept of, 24-28
New Delhi, National Zoological Park of,
    68

Olney, P.J.S., 109, 131

panopticanism, 42-43, 102, 103
Penguin Encounter, Sea World, 19, 55-56
Pepys, Samuel, 32-33
Pereya, Luis, 49-50
Philadelphia Zoological Gardens, 47
princely collections of animals, 96-101
prisons, similarities with zoos, 31-45
Project Tiger, 152-55, 158

Rabb, George, 52
Ragunan Zoo, 57, 75
Reed, Robert, 34, 36

sacred menageries, 89-91

safari parks, 114-15
Samustprakaran Crocodile Farm,
    Bangkok, 17-18
San Diego Wild Animal Park, 66-67
San Diego Zoological Gardens, 18, 129
Sarabhia, Kartikya, 157
Schöbrunn, 48, 101-3
scientific interest and the development
    of zoos, 105-10
Scull, Andrew, 37, 39-40
Sea World, 19-23, 72, 130-31
Shamu shows, 19-23
Showalter, Elaine, 36
Shanghai Zoological Gardens, 25-26, 57
Shepard, Paul, 5, 12
shows, animals in, 16-23
Singapore Zoological Gardens, 18, 29, 47,
    132
Singh, R. L., 153-54
Skansen Zoo, Stockholm, 7, 8, 74
stud books, 9-10

Taronga Zoo, Sydney, 18, 74, 130, 132
Throp, Jack, 72, 130
Towne, David, 66
trade and wild animals, 91, 93, 97, 100-
    101
trade in animals, 137-50
training of animals, 29
Tropical World, Brookfield Zoo, 77
Tuke, Daniel, 35-36

vandalism in the zoo, 135
Varine-Bohan, Hughes de, 117, *passim*
Versailles, 43, 48, 101-3, 107
visitors, zoo, 132-36
    behaviour of, 135-36
    zoological knowledge of, 132-36

Wassenaar Wildlife Breeding Centre,
    25-28
wild animal, concept of, 1-8
wolf, image of, 7-8
Wolf, R.L. and Tymitz, B.L., 116, 136
Woodland Park, Seattle, 59-67, 132

Woodroffe, Gordon, 48-49, 77, 116
World Wildlife Fund, 151

'zoo animal', 157-61
zoo, history of, 89-115

zoological classifications, 1-12
Zoological Society of London, 108-10
Zoo Negara, Kuala Lumpur, 57
zoos, attendance, 131-32
Zuckerman, Solly, 111